For Bob
with be

Pursuit of Meaning

Nirmalya Narayan
Chakraborty

Pursuit of Meaning

New Age

First Published 2004

Published by
NEW AGE PUBLISHERS PRIVATE LIMITED
12 Bankim Chatterji Street, Kolkata 700 073
email: newagepub@vsnl.net

ISBN 81-7819-039-7

Typeset in Times New Roman 10/12 at Annapurna Commercial College, 14/1/1, Dharmadas Kundu Lane, Shibpur, Howrah 711 102 and Printed in India by Giri Print Service, 91A Baithakkhana Road, Kolkata 700 009.

Book Design and Cover: Soumen Paul

For my parents
who sacrificed everything for my education

Contents

PREFACE

Though language has been a constant object of concern in philosophical analysis, emergence of philosophy of language as an area in philosophy is an early twentieth century phenomenon. The anti-metaphysical stance of the Logical Positivists in the 1920s drew philosophers' attention to this apparently innocent but extremely complex and at times mind boggling phenomena of knowing a language and communicating through it. Since language is an ineliminable part of our knowledge of the world, an account of our linguistic behaviour seems to be a prerequisite of our account of our theory of the world. And one of the most important concepts that we invoke to explain our understanding of a language is that of meaning. Hence a quest for a theory of meaning marks the academic pursuit of many philosophers of language of our time.

In the present work I analyze and defend Donald Davidson's (1917-2003) proposal to generate a theory of meaning out of Alfred Tarski (1902-1983) style theory of truth. The criterion of a valid theory of meaning is that it suffices for the speaker's mastery of a language. I argue that Davidson's theory of meaning is a "full-blooded" theory in the sense that it explains the speaker's linguistic knowledge. Sentences for which there is no effective procedure of determining whether or not their truth conditions are fulfilled can be accommodated in a truth conditional semantics, provided by 'knowledge of the truth condition' we mean the ability to state the truth condition and not the ability to observe whether or not the sentence is true.

My defense of truth conditional semantics leads me to support a version of what I call 'non-reductive extensionalism'. Taking clues from w.v.o Quine (1908-2000) and Davidson I explain the reasons for having a theory of meaning on the basis of extensionalism. I show that non-reductive extensionalism does not deny 'creativity' of the speaker's knowledge, nor does it make the speaker's linguistic knowledge extremely limited. Truth conditional semantics does not generate bizarre T-sentences of the form '"Snow is white" is true, if, and only if, grass is green', if we take into consideration the holistic structure of a theory of meaning.

This leads to a discussion of semantic holism. I make a distinction between extreme and moderate versions of holism and I argue for a moderate holism. I try to show that if a theory of meaning is supposed to represent the speaker's linguistic knowledge, then it must possess a holistic structure. Disagreement about the truth value of a sentence makes sense only in the background of a set of shared beliefs and only a holistic theory of meaning can represent the speaker's knowledge of those shared beliefs — the sentences which both hold true. I also argue that the denial of the compositional structure of a theory of meaning leads to absurdities.

Extensionalism along with its holism leads to indeterminacy of meaning. I argue that the notion of 'radical translation' or 'radical interpretation' is a logically coherent notion. Radical interpretation is possible in the sense that we can have a theory of truth for the language L that will act as a theory of interpretation for L. I explain that the indeterminacy thesis does not reject meaning, it only makes room for the possibility of more than one interpretation of the language. I introduce the notion of semantic supervenience and show that both extensionalists and anti-extensionalists accept semantic supervenience, but they disagree about the range of non-semantic facts. I argue that a better understanding of each other's language cannot eliminate indeterminacy. Here

I bring in the 'just more theory' objection to counter the arguments which attempt to restore determinacy.

In the conclusion I explain, very briefly, some ways of extending the truth conditional semantics to different parts of natural language. Various philosophers, including Davidson himself, have worked towards that aim.

The idea of the particular topic, which the present book deals with, first cropped up in the course of many thought provoking discussions I had with Pranab Kumar Sen, Tushar Kanti Sarkar and Arindam Chakraborty. I still remember the summer afternoon in Kolkata when Professor Sen introduced Davidson's works to me by explaining the general philosophical framework within which Davidson is working. My deepest gratitude to all of them for their ungrudging help and advice.

My words fail to express my debt to my teacher James Van Evra for his constant encouragement and suggestions during the research on this project. His friendly criticism has helped me to sharpen my arguments.

I would also like to express my thanks to Angus Kerr-Lawson and William Abbott for the meticulous care with which they read the earlier draft of this book and helped me with numerous suggestions. I deeply appreciate their efforts. Let me take this opportunity to pay my respect to my teachers with whom I have had many fruitful philosophical discussions. I would like to mention especially J. Mayer, D. Sinha, M. Miles, D.Goicoechea, J. Narveson, J. Horne, and R. Holmes. My thanks are also extended to Anne Wagland and Debbie Dietrich for their care and concern to see my successful completion of this book. My debts to my wife Madhucchanda are too many to mention. Finally I want to express my deepest gratitude to my parents for their love and patience during all these years. I must also thank Subas Moitra and Siladitya Sinha Roy for the care they have taken in publishing this book.

INTRODUCTION

0 The semantic canvas

It is interesting to note that though 'philosophy of language' as a branch of philosophy is a twentieth century phenomenon, concern with a proper understanding of language and how it works has been the subject matter of philosophers since the Greek period in the West and even earlier in Indian philosophy[1]. In spite of many differences, all these philosophers have stressed the point that adequate theories of knowledge, logic, etc. require a proper understanding of language, for it is primarily through language that we communicate our knowledge.

In recent times, M. Dummett[2] has tried to convince us about the centrality of philosophy of language. Dummett thinks, quite correctly, that unless we have a proper understanding of language in terms of which we apprehend the world, our knowledge of the world will remain incomplete. Further, since it is only by analyzing language that we can analyze thought, a theory of meaning is a desideratum. Language matters to philosophy in the way it matters to any discipline whatsoever, for we express and communicate our thoughts in and through language. But there is a special connection between the study of language (meaning) and philosophical problems.

Philosophy deals with the very special kind of problems where we do not even know whether we are asking the right questions! Think of the question of a sceptic: Can we have the knowledge of the external world? Many philosophers think that this is not the right question to ask. Is this sceptical question comparable to the question: Can sound walk on the sky? The latter question does not have any answer, because it is not a proper question. Notice that the answer to the sceptical question cannot be given in terms of scientific investigation, for the sceptic might raise the same question about our knowledge of science.

One way of handling the issue is by analyzing the question itself. So we can analyze the terms employed in the question and we can try to find out what exactly the question is asking. We can start analyzing the word 'knowledge'. What do we mean when we say that we know something? What are the conditions fulfilment of which leads one to know? While attempting to answer these questions, we have already entered the domain of philosophy. And here actually what we are doing is that we are clarifying our ways of thinking. Many philosophers have claimed to (dis)solve problems by analyzing the different terms involved and by making fine distinctions. So the reason why language matters to philosophy is that by an analysis of language philosophers hope to clarify the philosophical problems and consequently they can solve those problems.

It is true that concern with meaning is not the monopoly of the philosophers. Physicists talk about the meaning of the Big Bang Theory, sociologists talk about the objective and the subjective meanings of an action, psychologists talk about the meaning of dreams, and so on. But philosophers' concern with meaning is more general in nature. When philosophers talk about 'meaning', they talk about the essentially public features of language, the features that are shared by the speakers of a linguistic community and these shared features are what make communication successful. And by analyzing these public features philosophers hope to show whether we are asking the right questions or whether the differences of opinion among philosophers is due to misleading uses of language, etc. So the philosophical theories of meaning are theories of those features of language which make it possible for the speakers to talk to each other and not just talk past each other.

In the present work I propose to analyze 'meaning' in a natural language. This project owes its source to the writings of W. V. Quine and D. Davidson. Their writings have greatly influenced the contemporary philosophy of language. Some people have defended them, some others have been outraged, but none can ignore them. The present thesis is not meant to be an exegesis of Quine or Davidson. The problem that I am after is conceptual, not historical or chronological.

The primary topic of this thesis is an analysis and defense of Davidson's version of a theory of meaning in the face of protracted criticism. In order to situate Davidson's works in a broader perspective, let me make a brief historical survey of different philosophical approaches to the concept of meaning.[3]

First, I will, very briefly, mention the different attempts made by different philosophers to explain 'meaning'. Then I will say a few words about Kant, Bolzano and Frege whose observations on meaning seem to be particularly related, either by way of defense or by way of critique, to Quine's and Davidson's approach. Meaning has been explained in various ways by different philosophers in different ages. Locke argues that since whatever a person knows is in his mind, and all that are in a person's mind are her ideas, words, in primary signification, stand for nothing but the ideas in the mind of the speaker who uses them. This is a classic example of what sometimes is known as "ideational theory of meaning."

Mill rejects the view that words are names of ideas. He defends the claim that words are names of things themselves. According to Mill, when we use a word, we intend to give information about a belief concerning the thing itself and not concerning the idea of it. In the same vein, Russell advocates a theory of meaning based on reference. Such words like 'and', 'in spite of' do not have meaning in isolation. According to Russell, they modify the meaning of whole sentences where they occur. This conception of meaning can be called 'referential theory of meaning.'

Later, Wittgenstein introduced the doctrine of meaning as use. By defending meaning as use, Wittgenstein emphasizes three points: i) It is a mistake to look for 'the meaning' in some realm of being or other, ii) We should recognize the diversity of uses of language, and we should guard against a narrow view of language where language is only used to convey information, and iii) In order to look for meaning we have to focus on the behaviour of the speaker. This doctrine can be called 'use theory of meaning.'

Since the birth of the rationalist and the empiricist schools in philosophy, meaning is explained in terms of experience. In order to explain the meaning of 'pain' or 'love', we have to analyze the human experience of love, pain, etc. So the meaning of these terms consists in the mental experiences which we express by these words. On this view, 'representation' is an important semantic category, which, as Kant thought, is a modification of the mind and belongs to the inner sense. This is a mental state designed to represent something.

One dominant view of explaining meaning (to be found in Locke, Kant) is in terms of a complex representation which can be broken down into its constituents. By analyzing the complex we can arrive at some simple constituents. And the way the constituents are formed together constitute the complex representation. Even though representation normally represents or refers to the things in the world, we can occasionally take the representation itself as the reference, while we become conscious of the representation itself and analyze it.

The link between analyticity of judgements and analysis of conceptual representation (meaning) is evident in Kant. In a judgement, two concepts are related and, in a categorical judgement, this is a subject-predicate relation. A categorical judgement is analytic, according to Kant, if the predicate concept is contained in the subject concept. So we come to know an analytic judgement by conceptual analysis of the subject concept.

But how are we going to interpret the expression 'contained in'? Which criteria will determine whether a concept is 'contained in' another concept? After examining some prevalent views, Kant discovered that analyticity is stronger than truth and necessity. Analyticity and a priority are different things. There are a priori truths that are grounded on conceptual analysis. In other words, Kant discovered that there are synthetic a priori judgements. And Kant thought that the aim of philosophy was to explain the foundation of these synthetic a priori judgements.

All analytic judgements rest on one principle, which Kant calls "principle of analytic judgements." This is the principle of identity or contradiction, meaning thereby that if we deny an analytic judgement we will be contradicting ourselves.

Similarly, synthetic judgements rest on another principle which Kant refers to as the "highest principle of all synthetic judgements." In synthetic judgements, since the predicate concept is not contained in the subject concept, we must have, besides the subject and the predicate, a third element upon which our understanding of synthetic judgements relies. For even though the predicate is not contained in the subject, it is related to the subject. So, in a synthetic judgement, subject and predicate must be related by a third element. But this third element cannot be a concept, for then we would have a third concept involved in a categorical judgement other than the subject and the predicate. Also, from mere concepts we cannot have synthetic knowledge. Kant discovered that this third element is intuition. So the principle of synthetic judgement is that synthetic judgements are possible under the condition that intuition binds the subject and the predicate.

Thus we can say that there are two principles working behind Kant's treatment of analytic and synthetic judgement. First, since analytic judgements are true by virtue of their concepts or meaning, consideration of semantics is relevant to explain the foundation of analytic judgements. The second principle is that the ground of synthetic judgements lies not in semantics, but in intuition. Thus Kant's, notion of representation plays an important role in his analysis of the knowledge of analytic and synthetic judgements. It is through representation that things present themselves to us. In an intuitive representation we perceive things through our visual sense organs. In conceptual representation we think of the concepts, for example, concepts of virtue, etc. Kant analyzes meaning of the subject concept and the predicate concept in terms of representation. So I take representation to be a primitive semantic category in Kant. Kant's theory of knowledge seems to rest on his theory of representation, which, in the ultimate analysis, is a theory of meaning. No wonder why people who tried to refute Kant's theory of knowledge, especially his theory of a priori, tried to show that Kant's misunderstanding is due to his confused doctrine of meaning or representation. Of course, there is a long tradition even before Kant where representation has been explained in terms of pictures, images, mental ideas, etc. John Locke, Antoine Arnauld of *Port Royal Logic* , Leibniz are some of the venerable members of this tradition.

That Kant is caught up in a psychologistic understanding of meaning can be shown from his equating representation with mental states that represent something. Meaning turns out to be a subjective state that we possess when we analyze concepts. In this sense the intuitive representation and conceptual representation do not differ — for both of them are the subject's mental state. But they differ in their content, for in the former, we have the things in the world and, in the latter, we have the concepts as their contents. Admittedly, here we are using vague terminologies. The reason for this is that Kant himself was not precise in his use of the term 'representation'. This psychologistic understanding of meaning or representation led Kant to believe that there are some judgements where the representation of the predicate concept is contained in the representation of the subject concept (analytic), and there are some other judgements where it is not so (synthetic). It is Bolzano, as we shall see shortly, who for the first time analyzed the term 'representation' in all its facets and uncovered different aspects that were ignored in Kant.

Many of the post-Kantian philosophers had problems with explaining a priori knowledge. They tried to have a theory of the a priori where Kantian intuition would not play any role and which would serve as the basis of a new theory of semantics. Bernard Bolzano is one of the most prominent members of this group. Bolzano's philosophical endeavour is aimed at eliminating intuition from a priori knowledge. According to Bolzano, many of the confusions arise due to Kant's ambiguous use of the term 'representation'. Bolzano distinguishes two uses of the term 'representation'. First, by 'representation' we might mean the mental states or determinations, such as my mental state when I perceive an object. These subjective representations are the subject matters of psychology. Secondly, there are inter-subjective contents of the mental representations that can be called "objective representations." Each semantic unit of a language has many subjective representations corresponding to each speaker, but it has only one objective representation that is shared by all the speakers. This objective representation is different from and independent of the object of representation. While subjective representations are real in the sense that they exist at a certain time in a certain subject, objective representations are not real. They subsist even though no thinking subject may have it. As we shall see a little later, Bolzano's threefold distinction of subjective representation, objective representation and the object of representation reappears in Frege's semantics. According to Bolzano, the main purpose of objective representation is to join together, in a proposition, the objective content and the subjective judgement.

Bolzano's distinction between the objective representation and its psychological accompaniments led him to criticize the Kantian notion of analyticity. For Bolzano, the importance of analytic propositions lies in the fact that their truth/falsity are independent of the individual subjective representations of which they are constituted. Kant conflates subjective representation with objective representation and mistakenly housed the foundation of the concepts in intuition. Bolzano justifies our belief in a priori judgements simply by saying that our understanding has and knows the two concepts involved in an analytic judgement. We are in a position to judge those concepts, just because we have them. The justification of synthetic a priori knowledge is conceptual and not intuitive as Kant thought.

The main problem that the post-Kantian semantic tradition had to deal with is the a priori. All these semanticists tried to develop a conception of the a priori where intuition played no role, and to do this would be to develop a semantics that would be able to explain the meanings of the concepts in a priori judgements without taking refuge in intuition. The root of the problem, according to Bolzano, lies in the ambiguity of the term 'representation'. By a careful dissection of the word 'representation' Bolzano showed that in pre-Kantian days — and in Kant as well — the concept itself is confused sometimes with the thought (a subjective state) and sometimes with the thing that is its object. Consequently, people were led to the idea that analysis of subjective representation will show in it as many parts as there are in the object represented. Bolzano flatly denies this, for there can be a complex representation of a simple object. There is an isomorphism, but it is between a subjective representation and objective representation, not between a representation (subjective or objective) and the object.

However, in Bolzano we saw the first attempt to free semantics of its psychological trappings. By his threefold distinction in representation, Bolzano gave us a clearer picture of what is involved when we talk of the meaning of the concepts. Although Bolzano was not clear about the status of these three elements involved in a representation, his discussion at least helped later generations to see what is important and what is not while explaining meaning in a natural language. For Bolzano, language is a reliable picture of the form of objective representations. Thus the objective representation of 'The triangle is large' consists of the representations 'the', 'triangle', 'is', and 'large'ness. This is a picture of theoretic semantics at its earliest form. These and many other important semantic issues were refined in the hands of Frege. But Bolzano still deserves the credit for giving birth to a semantic tradition that played a decisive role in the days to come. The transition from Kant to Bolzano is the transition from a stage where meaning remains unanalyzed and, consequently, is used without proper understanding, to a stage where meaning is analyzed — and we get to see the different aspects of meaning.

Like Bolzano, Frege emphasized the distinction between the psychological and the logical, between the subjective and the objective representations. Even though an utterance of a word is often accompanied by a subjective representation, it is not what the word means. The word means an objective representation. When we link the objective representations together in an appropriate way, what we get is the content of a possible judgement. According to Frege, objective representation can be divided into concept and object. For Frege, objects are ordinary things like tables and chairs, numbers of mathematics, truth-values of logic, etc.

While dealing with concepts, Frege starts with an analysis of judgements first and then allows the formation of concepts out of these judgements. In pre-Fregean time, the formation of concepts was presupposed in the theory of judgement. Frege reversed the method. Borrowing the notions of argument and function from mathematics, Frege applies these to the meaningful sentences of natural language. Take the sentence 'John is tall'. If we take the word 'John' out of this sentence what we get is 'x is tall' which is a function of a general type. This is what Frege means by the concept 'tall'. So here we derive the concept (function) from its values by removing the name of the object from the latter. We move from values to function, from judgement to the concept. In this analysis the concept is an "unsaturated" or incomplete expression. For the function 'x is tall' is in need of an argument to put in the place of 'x' to have a value.

Here we see the origin of a holistic theory of meaning that we will discuss later in detail. It is not the individual concept, but the whole judgement that is the starting point of our analysis. We can arrive at individual concepts only by analysis of complete judgements. For Frege, singular and general representations, semantically, belong to different sematical kinds. Singular representations are proper names that are given to us independent of judgement.

But we can explain general representations only after a judgement takes place.

In Bolzano we found the recognition of something which lies inbetween subjective representation and the objects we talk about. Bolzano calls this "objective representation". Frege was led to recognise something very similar while analyzing identity statements. We can take, for example, the following two identity statements :

i) The morning star = the morning star

ii) The morning star = the evening star

We can think of the content of the identity statements as containing the identity relation with both gaps saturated by the names of the relevant objects. Since the morning star is the evening star *de re,* the content of (i) would be the same as the content of (ii). Consequently, if knowing that a sentence is true amounts to knowing its content to be true, anyone who knows (i) to be true also knows (ii) to be true. So if we regard identity as a relation between the designates of the names, it seems that there is no difference between (i) and (ii).

But there is a cognitive difference between (i) and (ii) and one person might know the truth of (i) without knowing the truth of (ii). Frege concludes that the contents of (i) and (ii) do not talk about names. What they say is that the two methods of determining a referent results in the same referent. This method of determining a referent is what Frege calls "sense". The source of our puzzle of identity statements is our conflating what we say and what we say it about. In other words, we ignored Bolzano's distinction of objective representation and its object. So the content of an identity statement does not concern only the object, but also the mode of designation or "sense" of the expression. Thus, for Frege, every grammatical unit performs its semantic task in two ways; first by expressing its sense and, second, by signifying its referent. And the totality of these two processes is represented in the syntactic structure of a fully analyzed sentence.

The basic task of a sentence is to say something. What the sentence says is its sense and the sense of each constituent is simply its contribution to this message. Since we are interested in the truth of what we say, we are also concerned with the reference of the sentence. And the truth-value of a sentence is not only determined by its sense, but by its sense and the way things are situated in the world.

It is Frege who took great pains to convince us that a theory of language and how it works must be free from any psychologistic explanation. We cannot rest our theory on subjective ideas, mental images, etc. It is important to note that, for Frege, 'logic' does not mean a system of derivation by some rules of inference. According to Frege, logic is a theory of content, of what we say in a judgement, for example, its nature and structure. Therefore, semantics is an important part of this logic. And it is semantics that separates logical from the psychological.

But how can we develop this kind of semantics that is free from subjective basis? Frege attempts to answer this question in his *Begriffschrift*. Here Frege tries to develop a symbolism which will express not the things we talk about, but our thought itself. It describes the logical structure of what we mean when we use sentences. *Begriffschrift* is a symbolic presentation of a theory of meaning. While working out the details of this project certain important results emerged some of which we have already discussed. From the very beginning Frege was aware of the ambiguity of the term 'representation'. A subjective representation is not the word's meaning. The word means an objective representation. And an objective representation is divided into concept and object.

While talking about the semantic structure of sentences, Frege arrives at semantic dualism where the two basic semantic categories are sense and reference. Both semantic dualists and their opponents (semantic monists) agree that for the sake of semantic analysis we must analyze language into its basic grammatical units and then assign them appropriate semantic correlates. The controversy lies in the number and character of the semantic categories required to perform this kind of semantic analysis. The dualist (Frege) thinks that we must associate two semantic categories with each grammatical unit, i.e., what the sentence says and what the sentence is about. The semantic monists (Quine, Davidson, and my own position) say that for semantic analysis we need to associate one semantic category with each grammatical unit and the source of that semantic category is the world. The way to solve this debate of semantic dualism versus semantic monism is by giving an adequate description of our knowledge of the meaning of the sentences. So the question that we should focus on is: What is it that we know when we know a language? I have tried to give an answer to this question following Davidson and I have defended Davidson against many of his critics.

However, Frege's decisive steps in logic and semantics mark an important development in the contemporary history of semantics. The anti-psychologistic trend that started with Bolzano reached its apex in Frege. The doctrine of semantic holism can be traced back to Frege as well. Fregean semantics helped us to sharpen our questions about a theory of meaning and showed us what is important while developing a theory of meaning. Frege's doctrines have shaped the future course of the semantic tradition.

All along from Kant to Frege, we find the recognition that one part of what we call meaning is directly related to the world of tables and chairs, rivers and mountains, etc. The Vienna School of Logical Positivism takes this aspect of meaning very seriously and claims that, to repeat the famous slogan, 'the meaning of a sentence is its method of verification'. The assumption is that everything that can be said can be said in terms of elementary statements. Elementary statements are statements that correspond to absolutely simple facts. All statements of higher order, even the most abstract scientific hypotheses, are, at the end, descriptions of observable events. All those complex statements rest on a foundation of elementary statements. Rudolf Carnap made an elaborate attempt to reconstruct the whole apparatus of our statements of physical objects in terms of sense-data statements. But this program faced many problems and Carnap himself later gave up this project. This choice of making sense-data statements the basis also raises the problem of solipsism, i.e., the problem of the transition from one's own experiences of sense-data to the experiences of others and of the public world as well.

The more serious problem the verification theorists face is that of explaining the meaning of a universal statement. A universal statement may be confirmed by countless favourable instances, but the possibility that a further instance will refute it must always remain open. So universal statements are not conclusively verifiable, but they are conclusively falsifiable in the sense that a negative instance contradicts them. For this reason, Karl Popper puts forward his falsifiability criterion according to which what we require of a factual statement is that it be capable, in theory, of being falsified.

Because of these and many other difficulties, the logical positivists opted for a weaker criterion of meaning. They held that a statement should be capable of, to some degree, confirmed or disconfirmed by observation. And if the statement is not an elementary one, it should be such that elementary statements could support it; they need not entail it or its negation. But the problem remains as to how to explain the notions like 'support' or 'confirmation'.

There was a growing realization among the positivists that the empirical content of a sentence could not be exhaustively expressed by any class of observation sentences. When we use an empirical hypothesis for the prediction of an observable phenomenon, it involves using subsidiary hypotheses as well. The sentence 'All apples are red' entails the observation sentence 'That fruit is red' only when combined with other observation sentences like 'That thing is a fruit', 'That fruit is an apple', etc. In other words, the meaning of a sentence is reflected in the totality of its relationship to other sentences in that language. This is a direction toward semantic holism.

But one might ask : What is the status of the positivist criterion of meaning itself? This criterion is not an empirical hypothesis, nor is it an analytic sentence. Faced with this question the positivist acknowledged that they were not proposing a new criterion of meaning. They were only trying to give an adequate explanation of the idea of a meaningful sentence. How can we judge whether the positivist criterion of meaning is an adequate explanation? First, there is a large class of sentences which we generally recognize as meaningful and we regard others as lacking meaning. The logical positivist criterion of meaning, in order to be adequate, must conform to this generally agreed usage. Second, explication does not mean mere description of the accepted usage. An adequate explication of meaningful sentences must also show how— in spite of ambiguities and inconsistencies in ordinary usage — we can arrive at a consistent and comprehensive theory of knowledge. This comprehensive theory will include abstract sentences of advanced scientific theories, on whose meaning our ordinary usage can hardly shed any light. So the logical positivist's criterion of meaning is an analysis of our commonly accepted meaningful usage, and it is also a theoretical systematization of the contexts where we use sentences that we claim to be meaningful. I view the project of a theory of meaning in very much the same way and I will discuss it a little later.

This brief recounting of the history of semantics has prepared the way to enter into a detailed discussion of Quine and Davidson. Some of the major topics which I will discuss with regard to Quine and Davidson — extensionalism, holism, etc.— have already appeared and been discussed in one form or another. The journey from Bolzano to Quine and Davidson is the journey toward freeing 'meaning' from its psychologistic trappings. People came to realize that we could not have a theory of meaning on the basis of one's mental ideas or images. A theory of a person's intentions, etc. cannot act as the evidential basis of a theory of interpretation or meaning of that person's utterances.

0.1 Quine on naturalized epistemology

Let me briefly state Quine's version of epistemology and then I will pass on to Davidson's theory and a comparison of the views of these two philosophers.

Epistemology inquires into the possibility and structure of knowledge. This inquiry can proceed in two ways. Quine calls them conceptual and doctrinal sides of epistemology.[4] The conceptual side deals with the concepts employed in explaining the phenomenon of knowledge. Here we define the various concepts, sometimes by defining complex concepts in terms of simpler ones. On the doctrinal side, we formulate and develop laws to prove those concepts. So the conceptual side deals with a theory of meaning of the concepts involved and the doctrinal side deals with the theory of truth for the statements or theorems involved. For example, the conceptual side of epistemology will analyze the meaning of the notion of physical body that we employ in our knowledge of the external world. Now we make several statements expressing our knowledge of the world which, directly or indirectly, involve the notion of physical body. The doctrinal side analyzes the truth of those statements in a systematic manner. It is a theory of justification of our knowledge of truths about nature. It is easy to see that these two aspects are related to each other. If I define one concept with reference to another concept, I am reducing one set of laws to another. The application of every concept is guided by certain laws. Relation between two concepts shows relation between laws governing the use of those concepts. So any change on the conceptual side necessitates change on the doctrinal side too.

Epistemologists down the history have worked on both the conceptual and doctrinal sides, but with little success. Perhaps the most recent and the most detailed attempt to develop an epistemology from immediate sense-experience was made by Rudolf Carnap and others in the Vienna Circle. On its conceptual side Carnap tried to define all the concepts which we employ to systematise our surrounding world in terms of sense-data. While doing this he tried to translate all sentences about the world into sentences about sense-data. Our theory of the world consists of theorems which are sentences describing the world. Carnap tried to reduce those theorems into theorems about immediate sense experience. Here he applied the principles of logic and set theory. But soon the project ran into problems. The fact that a sentence can be couched in physicalistic terms does not mean that the sentence can be proved by immediate observation. For one thing, a sentence of a generalized nature cannot be pinned down to a single sense experience. So, on the basis of a single bit of experience, we cannot claim to prove a sentence that is applicable to countless other cases. Moreover, in his reductionist attempt, Carnap applied the techniques of logic and set theory, which we clearly do not apply when we undergo immediate sense experiences.

In spite of this failure, two doctrines of empiricism hold true, according to Quine.[5] First, the evidence that we need for science is sensory evidence. Second, learning the meanings of sentences ultimately rests on sensory evidence. In spite of the failure of the empiricist attempts at translational reduction, Quine sticks to these two fundamental tenets of empiricism. It is interesting to notice that these two "unassailable" tenets pave the way for empiricist epistemology and empiricist semantics. Quine uses the word 'science' in the sense of our theory of the world, i.e., the way we organize and interpret our surrounding world. Our interpretation of the world consists of a set of sentences. We use sentences to describe the world. And the kind of evidence that serves as a checkpoint for our knowledge of world is sensory evidence.

The fact that epistemology and semantics are closely related to Quine can be shown from his talking about 'semantic ascent'. Quine is interested in exploring the evidence of our knowledge of the external world. And, since this evidence is primarily empirical evidence, evidence relates to the objects in the world. But while talking about objects, Quine often talks about the terms referring to those objects. So there is a shift from talking of objects to talking of words. It is a shift from talking in certain terms to talking about those terms. This shift is called 'semantic ascent' by Quine.

But why do we need 'semantic ascent'? What purpose does it serve? The first reason, according to Quine, is that by performing 'semantic ascent' all the parties in a debate can have a fruitful discussion as to where and why they disagree. Words, unlike points, relations or classes, are better understood and all the parties can agree on their use in a language. Philosophers of divergent views can at least agree on the words and their use, on the basis of which they can communicate at their best. So by 'semantic ascent' we ascend to a level where we all agree. And then we can start talking about our divergent philosophical positions. Otherwise, there is every possibility that we will get bogged down in a debate where we tend to argue past each other. The second area where we need 'semantic ascent', according to Quine, is in logic. Many of the statements in elementary logic contain extra-logical terms, like "If all Greeks are men and all men are mortal ...". It is clear that the truth of these statements depend on the use of a language that contains those terms. And the validity of an argument depends on the truth or falsity of its premises.

However, if empiricist attempts at reconstructing the statements about the world from statements about immediate sense experience — along with the attempt to translate the former statements into statements of observation — fail, then the consequence seems to be that the meanings of such statements turn out to be ineffable. If we cannot show what kind of sensory evidence supports a particular sentence, then it is hardly possible for us to determine the meaning of such a sentence. This is a kind of *reductio ad absurdum* argument. If empiricist attempts at rational reconstruction fail, then the meanings of the statements — which constitute our theory of the world — become inaccessible. But we do know the meanings of those statements. Quine saves empiricism by introducing holism. Earlier empiricist attempts failed because they held that each individual sentence had its own sensory connection. Quine argues that only a substantial chunk of a theory has sensory import. So, when we talk of sensory evidence, we do not talk of individual sentences, but of a group of sentences which constitute a theory, or at least a part of a theory. It is only a set of sentences that can claim to have empirical significance of its own. Similarly, when we make empirical predictions, those predictions hold true — not of an individual sentence, but of a whole group of sentences. If the prediction fails to obtain, we might have to change the truth-value of some sentences in that group. In any case, it is only a set of sentences that can or cannot be empirically verified.

If no sentence can claim to have empirical implication on its own, then no sentence can claim to possess meaning on its own. The unit of meaning is not a single sentence, but a group of sentences. We can talk of the meaning of a sentence only in the background of meanings of other sentences that constitute a simple coherent group. Meaning, truly speaking, is a property of a community of sentences. If we take a close look at our knowledge of the meaning of sentences, this holistic structure becomes apparent.

Thus, we can still aim at 'rational reconstruction.' We can still hope to reconstruct statements of our theory of the world in observational terms. But we must do so taking theories or parts of theories as wholes. If we translate large chunks of theories, then we can understand the meanings of those sentences, for it is only a set of sentences which has empirical significance and our knowledge of meaning rests on that empirical evidence. So meaning does not turn out to be ineffable. At the same time, we do not have to give up the main tenets of empiricism. Carnap's attempt failed, because, according to Quine, Carnap did not pay attention to the holistic structure of a theory. Now, empiricism blended with holism seems to give a satisfactory explanation of evidence and the meaning of sentences that constitute our theory of the world.

So the act of translation still persists, but at a different level. It is to be noted that when we translate a chunk of a theory in observational terms, we not only provide empirical evidence for that theory, we also specify the meanings of sentences of that theory. For meaning is ultimately based on empirical evidence. But, as we shall see later, if we carry on this task of translation, the problem of indeterminacy crops up. We will end up with the possibility of having two translation manuals that are incompatible with each other, but both of them fit the total available evidence. This seems to threaten the very purpose of epistemology. Epistemology is an attempt to provide a foundation of our knowledge system. Now translation seems to lead us to the indeterminacy of that evidence and, consequently, to indeterminacy of meaning as well.

Does this signify the death of epistemology? Quine does not think so. "Epistemology, or something like it, simply falls into place as a chapter of psychology and hence of natural science."[6] Epistemology will study the process that enables a human subject to construe a theory of the world out of empirical input. Epistemology studies the relation between knowledge and its evidence. Our new kind of epistemology is doing the same thing and in a better way. Epistemology in its new setting–with the help of psychology– will trace back the history of the edifice of knowledge that we have built, and it will also study the evidence or data out of which this edifice is built, as well as the nature of the mechanism which produces that edifice.

Cartesian epistemologists thought that we could stand aloof from our epistemic system and then we could provide an evidential basis for that system.

But the new epistemology is contained within that knowledge system. Here also we aim at studying the relation between evidence and outcome, but working within science itself. Traditional epistemologists sought to come up with a solid foundation of knowledge, but they were asking the wrong question when they tried to discover the set of indubitable beliefs on which the rest of the belief system could be founded.

Consequently, those projects ran into problems. The new epistemology, like the old, tries to reconstruct knowledge on the basis of sufficient evidence. It achieves its purpose not by trying to introduce evidence from outside the system, but by working within the system itself, changing bit by bit. This is important since our theory is holistic in nature and there is no external standpoint that would enable us to reconstruct the whole of epistemic system at a time. (I am skipping the debate of foundationalism versus non-foundationalism, since this is not very important for our present purpose.)

If the new epistemology is contained within science, what is the nature of this science, what does it look like? Quine uses the word 'science' rather broadly. He describes science as "a linguistic structure that is keyed to observation at some points."[7] Sentences that are directly hooked on to observation are called 'observation sentences' by Quine.

Observation sentences are those whose truth value depends on the occasion of its utterance, which is inter-subjectively available and which elicits assent from any witness present who is conversant with the language. 'This is red,' 'There is snow' are examples of observation sentences. These observation sentences are starting-points in scientific theory, because earlier we have said that the evidence on which any scientific theory rests is sensory evidence, and observation sentences are reports of that sensory evidence. Observation sentences, being inter-subjectively verifiable to which all relevant witnesses assent, serve as checkpoints for scientific theory, which, in turn, makes scientific discussion and progress possible.

It is not difficult to see the important role observation sentences play in a theory of language, because they possess all these above-mentioned characteristics. Observation sentence is the first step in the history of language learning. Because of their inter-subjective nature, observation sentences enable a child or a linguist (in radical translation) to share the sensory evidence and to assent to the sentence. This is where we can see the close relation between evidence (theory of knowledge) and meaning (theory of language). Theory of knowledge aims at reconstructing the epistemic system on the basis of evidence and theory of language aims at explaining the mastery of one's language. In both cases we have to start with observation sentences, for they give us appropriate evidence and their meaning builds the rest of the linguistic structure.

It is true that at a certain stage in scientific theory— as well as in the theory of language— we have to go beyond observation sentences to make room for theoretical sentences that are not directly related to inter-subjectively observable stimuli. A description of that mechanism is a matter of detail that we need not enter here. We are only interested in conceptual relation between meaning and evidence. Observation sentences manifest this relation to us. Even in cases of theoretical sentences, we can show how these theoretical sentences are connected with observation sentences for their evidence or meaning. One way of showing this relation is by translating theoretical sentences into observational terms, or by showing how the meaning of those theoretical terms is constructed out of the meanings of relevant observation sentences.

The difference between this reconstruction and that attempted by Carnap is that now we are taking a chunk of a theory as a whole as the unit of significance. We are now acting under the constraints of holism. In fact, in this new project, we might use the expression 'evidential support' instead of 'construction'. For what we are in fact doing is to provide evidence for a scientific theory which ends up giving meaning to the sentences of that theory.

0.2 Where Quine and Davidson parted

This is the history of how epistemology becomes related to semantics in the hands of Quine. Davidson starts his journey from Quinean epistemology. He agrees with Quine in rejecting the two dogmas of old empiricism. He also accepts two "unassailable" tenets of empiricism, viz. that we have to explain knowledge on the basis of sensory evidence, and that meaning is to be based on some kind of empirical evidence. From here he goes on to develop his semantic theory based on Tarski's notion of truth. Perhaps it would not be inappropriate to view Quine's epistemology as a logical ancestor of Davidsonian semantics. Nonetheless, in recent years, Davidson has questioned some important aspects of Quine's philosophy. In what follows I will state Davidson's position as opposed to Quine's.

Quine often talks about two types of sentences. Observation sentences are directly related to external stimuli and they are the first step in the history of language acquisition. Theoretical sentences are not so directly related to external stimuli but,, nevertheless, their truth-values can be built of the truth-values of observation sentences. Davidson questions this distinction and thinks that this bipartite division rests on an epistemological confusion. Observation sentences are direct reports of sensation, according to Quine's version. Since observation sentences are direct links to experience on which all our knowledge claims ultimately rest, these sentences occupy a special epistemological status in Quine's theory. For Quine, sensations serve the justificatory ground for beliefs. Davidson precisely denies this. According to Davidson, only beliefs can justify other beliefs. The only evidences we have for a particular belief are other related beliefs. Let us study this in more detail.

Davidson wants to defend a coherence theory of truth and knowledge which "is not in competition with a correspondence theory," but where it is shown "that coherence yields correspondence."[8] A coherence theory of truth says that the claim that a sentence is true means that it coheres with a system of other sentences, that it is a member of a system whose elements are related to each other by ties of logical implication. Correspondence theory, on the other hand, holds that the truth of a sentence consists in some form of correspondence between the sentence and what it describes. Here truth is defined in terms of the relation of agreement or similarity between the two. But how can we combine elements of coherence and correspondence in one theory? Davidson shows that in order to have a satisfactory explanation of our belief system, we must have both coherence and correspondence. Neither of them can work by itself. When we talk of coherence, we mean coherence of beliefs or sentences held true by a subject. Davidson of beliefs is true. Nor, I think, is it possible to say that every single belief in a coherent belief system is true. If by belief we mean a sentence held true by the speaker who understands it (à la Davidson), then a new experience might cause us to change our estimation of its truth-value which was so far regarded as a member of an otherwise coherent system of belief. Alteration of the truth-value of that sentence might necessitate adjustments in other areas of the system.

So mere coherence, however strong it might be, cannot guarantee the status of a true belief. All that a coherence theory can tell us is that the majority of the beliefs of a coherent system are true. But the problem is that we are never in a position to specify which particular belief is true or not if coherence is all that matters. This would generate a massive scepticism. So coherence alone will not work.

Davidson does not mean to define truth in terms of coherence of beliefs. He is rather trying to determine what form a theory of truth should take in order to interpret a language. In other words, he is concerned with the adequacy of a theory of truth. For Davidson, truth is a primitive concept. He starts from the notion of truth and tries to arrive at a satisfactory notion of meaning and knowledge. The truth of an utterance depends on what the sentence means and how the world is arranged. This can be shown from the fact that when two speakers differ on the truth-value of a sentence, either they differ on the meaning of the sentence or they differ on the interpretation of the relevant segment of the world. So we cannot ignore the element of correspondence while explaining the notion of belief. Coherence theory, if we want it to work, must accommodate correspondence too. But why can we not have a theory that rests on correspondence alone? Why do we need coherence? Davidson argues, "A major reason, in fact, for accepting a coherence theory is the unintelligibility of the dualism of a conceptual scheme and a 'world' waiting to be coped with."[9]

Davidson agrees with Quine in rejecting the analytic-synthetic distinction and he goes further by claiming that Quine still retains the scheme-content distinction which should be abandoned as well. The analytic-synthetic distinction was explained in terms of some sentences being true by virtue of their meaning alone, while some others are true in terms of their empirical content. Quine questions the analytic-synthetic distinction by questioning the mentalistic theory of meaning, but retains the notion of empirical content, where empirical content is explained with reference to the relation of the sentence and corresponding state-of-affairs. So here the idea is that there is language (which is often associated with the notion of a conceptual scheme) and it stands in a certain relation with the world. Conceptual scheme stands for the system of categories that systematize or give form to the data of experience. Since it is through language that we express our knowledge of the external world, language quite often comes to be closely associated with conceptual scheme.

When philosophers talk of how language is related to world, this relation can be expressed either in terms of organizing or fitting in with the world. And Davidson argues that we cannot make sense of either of these two kinds of relations or the entities related, the details of which need not concern us here.

Notice that the scheme-content distinction is retained in the Quinean distinction of observation sentence and the rest of the language. Observation sentences are directly related to the world, they are keyed to inter-subjectively observable events. They come first in our language acquisition. Then we carry on these terms learned in observation sentences to non-observational (theoretical) contexts. We learn to know the theoretical sentences of a language by establishing a linkage between them and previously learned observation sentences. This is, roughly speaking, Quine's picture. If this is true, then our belief in observation sentences is justified by sensation or sensory irritation and our belief in theoretical sentences is justified by our belief in other sentences (observation and theoretical as well). So observation sentences provide us with some basic content which we apply to interpret the non-observational part of our experience. Observation sentences provides us with the content, for they are keyed to sensory experience and sensory experience justifies observation sentence. As we shall see shortly, Davidson denies that sensory irritation can justify our belief in observation sentences. And if it cannot, then we are not in a position to build the theoretical part of a language on the basis of observation sentences and also observation sentences cannot provide us with the content we need. Consequently the whole distinction between observation sentences and the rest of the language turns out to be spurious.

As I have stated earlier, if we depend on coherence alone, it will lead to scepticism. We can ascribe truth to a particular belief on its cohering with a set of beliefs only when we are certain of the truth of that set of beliefs. But how can we ascertain the truth of this body of beliefs? If we depend on coherence alone, we have to justify one belief by referring to another belief. Since we are not aware of the truth-value of any particular belief, a sceptic might quite legitimately question: Even if all beliefs cohere with each other, there is no guarantee that all those beliefs are true about the actual world. For it takes little effort to construct a set of coherent beliefs which are, nevertheless, false.

Attempts have been made by philosophers to avoid this imminent sceptical attack. Philosophers have tried to find out something that lies outside the belief system and yet can act as the foundation of those beliefs. An important candidate for such a justificatory purpose is sensation or sensory evidence. It is quite plausible to argue that sensations are what connect our beliefs with the external world and, hence, sensations are the best candidates for justifiers of beliefs.

Davidson thinks that here we are conflating causality with justification. It goes without saying that if one has a sensation, one will be led to entertain a belief. But this relation of sensation to a corresponding belief is causal in nature. At best we can say that a sensation is the basis or ground of a belief. But this hardly serves a justificatory purpose. Part of this confusion arises from the ambiguity of the word 'reason'. 'Reason' is sometimes used in the sense of causal explanation. It is also used to mean justification. 'Reason' seems to contain both descriptive and normative elements. Even if we conflate causation with justification, the sceptic's question persists. A sceptic might ask: Sensation might justify a belief in sensation. But how can it justify the belief in the external world?

According to Davidson, Quine's attempt to justify belief on the basis of sensory evidence is an example of this confusion— confusion of causation and justification. Davidson quotes Quine saying that our source of information about the external world is through the effect of light rays and molecules on our sensory surfaces. Davidson interprets 'source' as cause and 'information' as beliefs held true or knowledge. Quine, along with others, has been trying to justify beliefs by confronting them with the tribunal of sense experience.

Davidson thinks "No such confrontation makes sense...."[10] He puts forward two reasons in support of his scepticism regarding Quine's attempt. Firstly, "we can't get outside our skins to find out what is causing the internal happenings of which we are aware."[11] What I take this to mean is that when I try to justify my belief by comparing it to my sensory experience, I am still caught up within my beliefs about my sensory experiences. For there is no vantage point outside the totality of beliefs from which I can verify my belief with sensory evidence. Even if there were such a vantage point, what I would be comparing my belief with is only my belief about sensory evidence. We can hardly get hold of sensory experience in its pristine purity that is untainted by my belief.

Secondly, according to Davidson, introducing intermediary steps like sensations, etc. does not help. If sensation falls in the causal chain of the external world causing a belief about the external world where sensation is an intermediary step, then this is merely a description of the causal chain. The external world causes a sensation and sensation, in its turn, causes a belief. This does not amount to saying that sensation justifies a corresponding belief. As we have said earlier, causal explanation is not to be confused with justificatory explanation. Just because sensation causes a belief does not necessarily mean that sensation is trustworthy. Once again we are confronted with the old sceptical question. And the moral of all this is, according to Davidson, "we should allow no intermediaries between our beliefs and their objects in the world."[12]

Incidentally, here again we can see the connection between epistemology and a theory of meaning. If knowing the meaning of a sentence involves knowing the condition under which the sentence can be uttered, then epistemology is supposed to tell us the conditions under which we are justified in asserting it or the conditions under which we are justified in entertaining a true belief.

What Davidson is concerned with is that if to explain meaning we have to fall back on sensation or sensory stimulation which lies in between our beliefs and external objects (this is Quine's view), then this would open the floodgate to scepticism. For sensory stimulations are nothing but another set of beliefs and there is no guarantee that those beliefs truly describe the segments of the world. So a sceptic might legitimately propose that many of the sentences we hold to be true may, in fact, be false. Davidson concludes, "I now suggest also giving up the distinction between observation sentences and the rest."[13] Davidson is not denying that meaning must depend on sensory experience, but this dependence is of the nature of causality, not of the nature of justification. Sensory experience gives rise to knowledge (of the world as well as that of the meaning of the sentence expressing that knowledge), but, as we have seen just now, it cannot justify that piece of knowledge. So the onus is on Davidson to show how can we justify most of our beliefs without taking recourse to an evidential explanation. Davidson goes on discussing how this can be achieved. I will deal with this later. Let us rather carry on our explanation of differences between Quine and Davidson.

More recently Davidson has made a distinction between what he calls "proximal" theory and "distal" theory of meaning and evidence.[14] On the proximal theory (which is Quine's official theory) sentences have the same meaning if the same pattern of stimulation prompt assent to or dissent from those sentences. On the distal theory (which Davidson is inclined to accept) sentences have the same meaning when identical objects or events in the external world cause assent to or dissent from those sentences. Though Davidson admits that elements of both theories can be found in Quine's writings, Quine does not attach much importance to distal theory to which Davidson is inclined. The difference between these two theories lies in their respective ways of explaining meaning and placing the evidence in the causal chain of external objects or events giving rise to knowledge.

So Quine puts the burden of meaning and evidence on the pattern of stimulation. We determine meaning by looking at the sensory impacts. But Davidson places meaning and evidence directly on external objects and events. It is an object or an event that provides evidence for a belief or determines the meaning of an observation sentence.

Now we can see why Davidson calls Quine's theory "proximal" and his own theory "distal". We can picture the causal chain involved in any knowledge situation as follows:

External World (objects & events)	→	Patterns of stimulation on sensory surface	→	Knowledge (True Belief couched in a sentence)

According to Quine, meaning and evidence centre

around patterns of stimulation that are situated closer to knowledge than external world in the causal chain. So Quine's theory is a proximal theory, since he ties meaning and evidence to proximal stimulus. Davidson, on the other hand, ties meaning and evidence to external objects and events that are situated further away from knowledge in the causal chain. Hence Davidson's is known as distal theory.

However, Davidson raises two arguments against Quine's proximal theory. Davidson construes a hypothetical example, where someone has the pattern of stimulation, when a warthog trots by, which is identical with mine when a rabbit passes by in front of me. Let us assume, that the one-word sentence which that person is prompted to assent to in the presence of a warthog is 'Gavagai'. Then I will translate his sentence 'Gavagai' to 'Rabbit' in my language, though I see no rabbit but only a warthog. So Quine's proximal theory leads me to translate 'Gavagai' as 'Rabbit' even though I do not see any rabbit, simply because my patterns of stimulation in the presence of rabbit are the same as the patterns of stimulation possessed by another person not in the presence of rabbit but in the presence of a warthog.

According to Davidson, we can generalize this example by simply rearranging sensorium. We can construe very many cases where we seem to have the same patterns of sensory stimulation but we have a totally different interpretation of external world. The causal connection between the external world and sensory stimulation is no guarantee that we have a correct view of the world. Since, on a proximal theory, it is the pattern of stimulation that determines meaning and knowledge and since we can vary meaning and knowledge keeping pattern of stimulation intact, none of us are sure whether we have the true picture of the world. Although each person knows that he got it correct for his patterns of stimulation if they are satisfied by the external world, when he finds that others' world views are mistaken it is no wonder he starts questioning his own world view.

According to Davidson, the only way out of this sceptical outcome is to hold truth as immanence. Immanence theory of truth says that a sentence may be true for any interlocutor even though it turns out false to me if translated in my language. In the example mentioned above, I translate the native's utterance 'Gavagai' as 'Rabbit' in my language, even though 'Gavagai' is held true by the native and 'Rabbit' is held false in my language under that circumstance. It is not relativity of truth that we ordinarily talk about, nor is it a form of indeterminacy of translation conceded by Quine. In immanence of truth, we find that even though the translation is correct, the sentence being translated is true to one speaker and the translated sentence is false to another. And this might happen to two speakers speaking the same language. The problem is: If the translation is correct, meaning is preserved. If meaning is preserved, how can two speakers speak two sentences that fail to agree in truth-values? If they (speakers) differ in ascribing truth-values, they differ in their justifications of those two sentences. Difference in justification presupposes difference in available evidence. But if evidence is tied to patterns of stimulation, the speakers are supposed to be exposed to the same evidence, since they have the same range of stimulation. Clearly we are in trouble here.

Davidson views the opposition of the proximal and distal theories as the opposition of two theories of meaning, one that makes evidence primary (Quine's theory), while the other that makes truth primary.[15] The proximal theory makes evidence rest on sensation that determines meaning. The distal theory, on the other hand, interprets meaning in terms of external objects and events that make sentences true or false. And we saw a little earlier, how, according to Davidson, a theory of truth and knowledge contains elements of coherence and correspondence.

One might ask, if we can have a theory of meaning based on evidence, one in which evidence is not tied to sensory stimulation, but rather to the external world. This is an attempt to combine proximal theory with distal theory. If we base evidence on the external world, then that is a distal theory in disguise, for meaning would be determined by shared external situations and causal intermediaries like sensation would drop out of the picture.

However, that the notion of truth plays an important role as an explicatory concept for Davidson is manifest in his use of the expression 'Radical Interpretation,' whereas Quine talks about 'Radical Translation.' As Davidson himself says, 'Interpretation' implies a greater emphasis on the explicitly semantical.[16] When we hear someone uttering a sentence, we presuppose that the speaker's utterance is intentional and linguistic in nature. Here 'intentional' means nothing subjective or mysterious, but only that the speaker has consciously and wilfully given expression to her belief. We start interpreting the utterance, what she means by her utterance. Since, on the distal theory, meaning is tied to external objects and events and that is where evidence comes from, in order to interpret an utterance we have to fit the utterance in the causal chain of the external world giving rise to a belief. A direct connection between what an utterance means and that utterance being held true is evident in a distal theory. The word 'interpretation' conveys this close relation between truth and meaning.

Davidson claims that if interpretation is our aim, "a method of translation deals with a wrong topic."[17] In interpretation we are dealing with only one language, the language to be interpreted. It is true, of course, that our theory itself is couched in one language, but that itself is not the object of interpretation. In a theory of translation, we are concerned with three languages; object language (the language which is being translated), subject language (the language into which object language is being translated) and meta-language (the language of the theory which says that which expressions of the subject language can be translated as which expressions of the object language). Davidson's main objection here is that the ability to translate the object language into the subject language does not necessarily mean that we know the meaning of object language and subject language. If the translation manual tells me that the German sentence "Schnee ist weiss" is translated in French as "La neige est blanche," this does not tell me the meaning of the German sentence unless I already know French. So success of a translational theory depends on the assumption that the subject language is identical with the language of the theory of the translator. Only then does a translation manual inform the translator about the meaning of object language statements. But this assumption is totally arbitrary. If we want a translation manual to work, it must work between any two languages, irrespective of the fact that the subject language is identical with the language of the theory (meta-language) or not. In Davidson's theory of interpretation, if one understands the theory, one can interpret any language whatsoever, for one applies the theory of interpretation to the object language and there is no room for a subject language separate from meta-language. A theory of interpretation will work for any interpreter and for any language.

According to Davidson, a theory of translation does not provide "any insight into how the meanings of sentences depend on their structure."[18] But a satisfactory theory of meaning must show how meanings of complex expressions systematically depend on meanings of simpler expressions. We need this feature because language, potentially, consists of infinitely many sentences and a theory of meaning for a language must be able to specify meaning of any given sentence of that language. This aim is achieved by a Davidsonian theory of interpretation. If we still stick to a theory of translation, we need to combine it with a theory of interpretation. But then the theory of translation becomes superfluous, for a theory of interpretation is capable of giving interpretation of an object language along with revealing the semantic structure of how complex sentences depend on simpler sentences for their meanings. And reference to a subject language is redundant. We have the object language and then the meta-language by which we are interpreting the object language.

Like Quine, Davidson acknowledges that it is likely that we will end up having possibly more than one interpretation of the object language. This is similar to Quine's indeterminacy of translation. But Davidson claims that the degree of indeterminacy will be less in his theory of interpretation than in Quine's theory. And the reason is that Davidson adopts the principle of charity "on an across-the-board basis" and "the uniqueness of quantificational structure is apparently assured"[19] in a theory of interpretation à la Davidson.

Let us clarify these two points. Earlier, with regard to describing how radical translation works, I talked about assuming minimal rationality in our interlocutor. In other words, if my translation ascribes obvious falsehoods— such as that the interlocutor assents to a sentence and its negation at the same time in the same situation— it is more likely that my translation is not the correct one than that the interlocutor subscribes to such different notion of logical laws. So the Principle of Charity rules out those possible candidates for translation which ascribe too much silliness to my interlocutor.

So, according to Quine, if a certain translation goes against our present logical sense, we are better not to rely on that translation. Davidson applies it in a more general way. We should not only look at logical contradictions, we should also assume that both interpreter and interpretee believe in the same set of non-logical truths that constitute the framework of our belief system. Even in the case of disagreement with regard to any particular belief, we should not ignore a massive area of shared beliefs. This means that in a radical interpretation we must assume that the subjects of our interpretation, by and large, share our beliefs.

Earlier we have seen that Davidson rejects Quine's proximal theory and upholds his distal theory. According to the distal theory, meaning and evidence are tied directly to external objects and events, which leave no room for sensation as an intermediary in the causal chain. Since Davidson rejects the Quinean distinction of observation sentence and rest of the language, he denies that "there is only a sub-basement of content which can be separated from the linguistic framework."[20] Language and what language is about are inextricably related. Justification of a belief (sentence held true) comes from another belief and beliefs are directly related to external world. This is why Davidson claims that the quantificational structure of a sentence in his theory of interpretation is assured. For Quine, revision of a translation manual is needed when an observation sentence is translated by another observation sentence which is keyed to a different set of sensory stimulation. Davidson denies any status to sensory stimulation. For him, revision is required only if we can find out another scheme of interpretation that makes room for greater agreement among interpreter and interpretee.[21]

0.3 On the viability of the project of a theory of meaning

Now let me state my position with reference to Quine and Davidson. In the next chapter entitled 'Truth Conditional Semantics' I will support Davidson's distal theory of meaning, which makes meaning explicable in terms of truth. The reason for my defending Davidson's move is as follows. I want to explain (even though my explanation is Davidsonian in spirit, I have included new elements in order to strengthen Davidson's theory) what it is that one knows when one knows that a sentence S in language L means P. Since a language potentially consists of an infinite number of sentences, a theory of meaning for a language L must explain how meaning of a finite stock of words can generate meanings of endlessly many sentences in L. Assume that we have a theory of meaning that is sensitive to this compositional structure of language. Now such a theory will state, for any sentence S of language L, 'S means P'.

But it does not help us. We wanted to explain

meaning. Our theory seems to involve the very notion that it is supposed to explain. So what we need is a device to substitute 'means' in 'S means P' by something which we understand better than 'means' and, most importantly, which does the same job as 'means' does in 'S means P'.

I support Davidson's attempt, in the face of many criticisms, to use truth in place of 'means'. I will argue that 'S means P' can be treated as 'S is true if and only if P' (T-sentence) where we explain meaning in terms of truth. So what we need is a theory of truth for a language L that generates a sentence of the form 'S is true if and only if P' for any sentence S of L. Such a theory will also show how the truth condition of a sentence (we can extend it to the whole language) is built of truth conditions of smaller parts.

While arguing against Davidson's critics, I will explain the aim of a theory of meaning. A theory of meaning is not a device to determine whether a particular sentence is meaningful, nor does it stipulate meaning of the expressions in a language. It rather clarifies our knowledge of what one knows when one knows what a sentence means. If this is our aim, then M. Dummett's direct ascription theory of meaning won't serve our purpose. Direct ascription theory generates sentences of the form 'The sentence X means ...' (Dummett calls this M sentence). But then our original question remains unanswered, viz. What is it for a sentence to mean something? So M sentences do not help. Here Davidson's T-sentences give us an answer in a non-circular way.

Following Dummett's distinction between modest and full-blooded theories of meaning, I argue that Davidson's theory is a full-blooded one. A full-blooded theory is one that explains what it is to possess the knowledge of the concepts expressible in the object language. I will show that Davidson's version of a theory of meaning is a full-blooded theory since it has a holistic structure and it is empirically verifiable. Dummett conflated his M sentence and Davidson's T-sentence and then concluded that since a theory of M sentences is a modest theory, Davidson's theory is a modest theory as well.

Dummett thinks that a theory of meaning (Davidson's) which rests on a theory of truth will not work, for there are large numbers of sentences in natural language for which there is no effective procedure to determine whether or not their truth conditions are fulfilled. Here I will distinguish (following Dummett) two ways of explaining the knowledge of the truth condition of a sentence. One is the ability to state the truth condition and the other is the ability to observe whether or not a sentence is true. I argue that we should take the former model and, if we do so, then Dummett's undecidable statements can be accommodated within a truth conditional semantics.

Along the same line, I will argue against J. Foster and B. Loar. I will show that since Davidson's theory acts under certain formal and empirical constraints, Davidson's theory is interpretative in nature. The existence of predicates that are coextensive but possess different senses does not pose any threat, for all we need is to give a philosophical description of one's knowledge of a language. This we can do provided we have a theory which possesses a holistic structure and which we can verify with the behaviour of the native speakers. If two predicates have different meanings, we will have different T-sentences for them which form a part of a coherent network. The fact that a speaker's knowledge of a predicate differs from her knowledge of another predicate will be manifest in two different T-sentences.

Davidson's theory is a theory of linguistic meaning. It gives us the apparatus to develop a theory of meaning of a natural language. Once we have an adequate theory, they by applying that theory to particular speakers of particular languages, we can give a description of the speaker's knowledge of language. And, since one's knowledge of a language involves one's knowledge of the meaning of the expressions of that language, by giving a description of one's linguistic knowledge we can shed some light on what meaning in a natural language is.

Attempts to explain meaning in terms of truth condition result in what is known as extensional semantics. In the second chapter on extensionalism I defend extensional semantics not because I espouse classical behaviourist theory of mind, but because intensional notions like Frege's conception of sense do not help us in developing a theory of meaning in a non-circular manner. I do not deny meaning; rather I explain meaning in terms of a theory of truth condition, following Davidson. Since meaning is a significant part of what one knows when one knows a language, a theory of meaning explains part of one's knowledge of the language. And, in this sense, even Quine will not be opposed to a theory of meaning, i.e., a theory of one's knowledge of a language.

Extensional semantics is not as narrow as critics like Noam Chomsky and Jerrold Katz try to make it look. I acknowledge what Chomsky calls 'creativity' in human language. Following Quine, I show that extensional semantics does justice to this feature. By briefly explaining the main two methods of language acquisition, firstly, by direct conditioning of an utterance with a non-verbal stimuli and, secondly, by 'analogic synthesis', I will show that we can speak and interpret new sentences.

I argue that there are two ways we can interpret the expression 'innate ideas'. Extensional semantics does not deny 'innate ideas' in the sense of an innate ability or predilection to learn a language. But I do deny the explicatory power of 'innate ideas' if by 'innate ideas' we mean some mental ideas we are born with and then carry on stamping those ideas on the expressions throughout the language learning procedure. I explain the three sets of evidence put forward by Chomsky to support his innateness hypothesis. I argue that extensionalism does not reject those features of a language mentioned by Chomsky, but solely on the basis of that evidence we cannot justify innateness hypothesis.

Chomsky claims that Quinean extensionalism rests on the assumption that learning by direct conditioning is "simpler" than learning by analogic synthesis and Chomsky doubts this assumption. I argue that Chomsky's claim is wrong. Moreover, Chomsky's use of the notion of a 'physical object' to show how complex this notion is results in conflating the tasks of semantics and ontology. I will also show that Chomsky's allegation that Quine II has abandoned Quine I's position stems from Chomsky's misunderstanding of Quine. Quine does not advocate three methods of language learning as alleged by Chomsky.

Contrary to what J. Katz thinks, by embracing extensionalism one is not engaging in a reductionist thesis. I am opposing intensionalism because I do not think that we can have a theory of meaning (which will illuminate our knowledge of meaning) on the basis of intensional notions. In fact, this whole issue of reductionism can be bypassed if we focus our attention on how to develop a theory of meaning which will give us a description of a speaker's knowledge of a language. By defending Davidsonian theory of meaning against these attacks I am working within a theory of reference as opposed to a theory of sense, but this theory of reference gives whatever we want from a theory of meaning and that too without resting itself on intensional notions.

The apprehension (expressed by Katz) that a truth conditional semantics would generate bizarre T-sentences of the form '"Snow is white" is true if and only if grass is green' is ill founded. Since our theory works under formal and empirical constraints, it cannot generate such T-sentences given the fact that the theory works perfectly well with the other parts of the language.

In the present work, while arguing for extensional semantics, I have primarily focused on the meaning of indicative sentences. But this does not imply that we are ignoring the meaning of the statements expressing emotions, aspirations, etc., which Charles Taylor calls "invocative use" of language. I argue that if we start developing a theory of meaning on the basis of extensionalism, we will be able to interpret sentences expressing the speaker's aspirations, goals, etc.

Earlier I said that a theory of meaning must explain the meaning of given sentences of a language. Since language potentially consists of infinitely many sentences, our theory must specify the device for generating the meaning of each sentence out of a finite stock of words. In order to do this we have to make our theory recursive in structure. A theory of meaning must show how the meanings of a group of sentences are related to each other by exhibiting their logical form. This is a suggestion toward holism, which I will discuss in the third chapter. After distinguishing moderate holism from extreme holism, I will argue for a moderate holism.

I argue that interpreting a language is not just random ascription of meaning, rather, it is a systematic imposition of a complex semantic structure on the speaker's utterances. Our theory of interpretation must show how the speaker is able to utter meaningful sentences of an infinitely large number out of a finite stock with the help of combinatorial rules. In other words, our theory should exhibit a holistic structure.

Allaying Michael Dummett's misapprehensions I show that the inclusion of a new sentence in our linguistic system does not pose any threat to holism. Rather, I think, it is only the theory that possesses a holistic structure can make sense of the inclusion of a new sentence. We must interpret this new sentence in such a way that its components play the same semantic role in many other sentences. Contrary to Dummett, I think that it is only a holistic model of language that successfully explains our linguistic communication and how we acquire mastery of a language.

Acknowledging Hilary Putnam's three-fold requirements of a theory of meaning, I argue that the theory of meaning I am defending satisfies all those requirements. I show that extensional-holist theory of meaning conforms to a native speaker's linguistic usage.

Contrary to what Jerry Fodor thinks, semantic holism does not imply that no two people can be in the same intentional state, i.e., entertain the same belief. First, in any disagreement there is a vast area of beliefs, that are agreed upon by both the disagreeing parties. And, with respect to these shared beliefs, both the disagreeing parties are in the same intentional state. Second, if the disagreement is a radical one, i.e., if the disagreement occurs at the level of observation sentences, then, in fact, the disagreeing parties are using two different languages. But even at this stage of radical disagreement, if we want to interpret what each one is talking about, we have to impose a holistic structure on their utterances. By opposing Fodor and E. Lepores' attempt to show the lack of any arguments to back up the holism thesis, I will give a transcendental argument for the possibility of the compositional structure of a natural language. I will also argue that a theory of truth can be interpretative in nature, if we take into consideration the nomological nature of the T-sentences.

If we accept extensional semantics along with its holism, we will be led to indeterminacy of meaning. In the fourth chapter I will argue that semantic indeterminacy is not a *reductio ad absurdum* of extensionalism.

I accept that indeterminacy crops up only if we start from 'radical translation' as opposed to 'actual translation'. But I argue that the philosophical point raised by radical translation can hardly be denied. Radical translation is not a logically incoherent notion. Contrary to Fodor and Lepore, I argue that Davidsonian radical interpretation is possible, i.e., we can have a theory of truth for a language L that will act as a theory of interpretation for L. I explain Fodor and Lepores' 'Nothing is hidden' principle and I argue that neither the metaphysical nor the epistemological interpretation of this principle lead to the problems which Fodor and Lepore claim that it would.

I will discuss one historical example of radical interpretation as mentioned by John Wallace, viz., interpretation of Minoan Linear B. I argue that Wallace conflates decipherment with interpretation. I will also argue that the Quine-Davidson project can give convincing replies to the three questions Wallace asks about the radical interpretation of Linear B.

With reference to the 'first person' perspective advocated by William Alston and John Searle, I will argue that indeterminacy is not counterintuitive if we critically examine a speaker's linguistic knowledge. Indeterminacy thesis does not reject meaning, it only makes room for more than one possible interpretation of the language. Searle talks about the necessity of introducing speaker's intentions to explain meaning. I argue that Davidson's theory is not opposed to intention as such. He only denies their foundational role in a theory of meaning. I give reasons for why we cannot have a theory of meaning based on intention etc. Here I introduce the notion of semantic supervenïence, i.e., that non-semantic facts determine semantic facts. I argue that both extensionalists (Quine-Davidson) and anti-extensionalists (Alston, Searle) can accept semantic supervenience. But they will differ as to the range of non-semantic facts.

Indeterminacy of meaning is not to be equated with the common phenomenon that occurs when two speakers of a language disagree about the truth of a sentence. Disagreement among two speakers about the truth of a sentence is an accidental feature. Indeterminacy of meaning is more radical in the sense that it is always possible, in principle, to construct rival theories of truth condition for the same object language. This is why, contrary to Dummett, I argue that indeterminacy cannot be eliminated simply by a better understanding of each other's utterances. This is where I bring in the 'just more theory' objection to Dummett. This is the argument originally used by Putnam against metaphysical realism. I will argue that Dummett's comment that better understanding of each other's utterances helps eliminate indeterminacy faces 'just more theory' objection. I explain James Van Cleve's attempt to rescue meaning (reference) from indeterminacy where he compares epistemic principles with those of semantics. Then I show that Van Cleve pushes this analogy too far and thus confuses the task of semantics with that of epistemology. Acknowledging Dummett's distinction between dynamic and static accounts of language, I argue that indeterminacy of meaning is not antithetical to dynamic account of language that Dummett seems to be inclined to accept.

Even though I accept distal theory as opposed to proximal theory, I am still working in the neighbourhood of Quine. My support for distal theory leads me to argue for extensionalism, holism and indeterminacy, all of which have been supported by Quine. Since I have given considerable importance and spent much time in discussing and criticising the opponents of all these three doctrines, I have drawn heavily on Quine while answering those critics.

Quine's interest in natural language is "incidental" in his own words.[22] His main interest is in exploring the flow of information on our sensory surface that gives rise to our knowledge of the external world. Davidson's main interest (and mine as well) is in exploring the working of natural languages. And one aspect of that project is to develop a theory of meaning for a natural language. Davidson is not trying to define meaning as such. Nor is he trying to formulate a theory of meaning for any particular language like English, German, etc., Davidsonian project aims at construing what form a theory of meaning should take if it is to interpret the sentences of a language. Davidson aims at developing a theory of meaning that is adequate for a natural language.

The difference in the approaches of Quine and Davidson can be shown from their different reasons for getting involved in the analysis of language. When Quine talks of 'semantic ascent', i.e., the necessity of explaining the meaning of the expressions in a language, it is only a means to gain clarity about the different notions that we employ in our epistemology and ontology. For Davidson, the study of a natural language is an end in itself. As a semanticist, he wants to explain meaning in a natural language. Since meaning starts to play its primary role in an inter-subjective communicative process, Davidson puts the whole problem of meaning in the perspective of a speaker-hearer situation (be it a child learning from its elder or a linguist learning a foreign language). Since a theory of meaning interprets the meaning of a language and, since a speaker becomes a speaker by virtue of being able to interpret her language, a theory of meaning represents the speaker's knowledge of her language. So by 'theory of meaning' I mean a theory which, if a person knows, she can claim to know the language for which that theory of meaning is designed. So when Davidson talks about language, he means natural language— with all its vagaries. Thus the differences that have cropped up between Quine and Davidson are due to their different emphasis or stress.

Nevertheless, there is a large area of agreement between Quine and Davidson. I view Davidson's theory as an extension of Quine's, insofar as a theory of meaning for a natural language is concerned. It is not an exaggeration when Davidson refers to Quine as "without whom not". Davidson shares Quine's idea of language as an inter-subjective, social phenomenon. So whatever sense we make of a language and its meaning, it must be amenable to inter-subjective observation and understanding. Davidson accepts Quine's rejection of any mentalistic notion of meaning (along with the analytic-synthetic distinction) not because there is no such thing as 'meaning', but because the mentalistic notion of meaning is philosophically barren. It does not give us what we want from a theory of meaning. Davidson denies being a behaviourist, but accepts that natural language can be best approached in an extensional manner. Since Quine is a behaviourist, he puts the burden of proof on the sensory surfaces (Proximal theory), for it is there that the world impinges on a knowing subject. Davidson puts the evidence further away in the external world (Distal theory). For Davidson, we should not employ meaning to explain meaning, since to do so would get us involved in a circularity. And, according to Davidson, truth will aptly do the job of explaining meaning. Since truth consists in the agreement of the sentence with what it describes, Davidson puts the evidence of meaning on the external world of objects and events.

Davidson accepts Quine's rejection of the second dogma of empiricism, viz., that each sentence has its own independent meaning. He ascribes a holistic structure to a theory of meaning. He accepts indeterminacy of meaning and comments that indeterminacy should not be regarded as something startling or abnormal. Thus Davidson's agreements with Quine run very deep. Their differences can be traced back to their differences in emphasis and not in some fundamental principles. Davidson is a kind of field linguist who is trying to apply Quinean principles to explain semantics of a natural language. While doing this, Davidson makes amendments to Quine's doctrines but remains faithful to overall Quinean approach.

People might express their scepticism about the whole project of a theory of meaning. They might go on arguing like this. Language is an infinitely complex phenomenon. It is simplistic to think that words refer to certain things. There is much more involved here. Language expresses one's personality, one's view (in a broad sense) of the world (mental, physical, spiritual), one's hopes and frustrations, in other words, one's very being. The very attempt to reconstruct language and its meaning in a systematic rigorous pattern (in the way I am defending) is wrong-headed. So any attempt to develop such a theory will be incomplete.

Now I agree with the premises here. It would be too naive to suggest that language does not express one's personality. I admit that the theory of meaning that I am defending is incomplete in the above-mentioned sense. But does this show that this theory has no value at all? I do not think so. What is accomplished in the incomplete system can be shown to have great value when incorporated within a fuller system. It is only when by positive efforts and restricted means we construct a theory that we are in a position to know the limitation of the basis, and also realize the supplementation needed. So incompleteness, by itself, is no decisive objection to building a theory of meaning in the form in which I am defending.

One might argue that constructing a theory of meaning is epistemologically false. It misrepresents our actual cognitive process of language. A theory of meaning employs notions that are results of highly sophisticated analysis and so it gives a distorted picture of the actual linguistic knowledge.

This charge against a theory of meaning does not hit the target, for a theory of meaning is not a portrayal of the actual language learning procedure. It is a "rational reconstruction" of the meanings of the expressions of a language. It demonstrates how a speaker's knowledge of the meanings of the expressions of her language could have been arrived at, and this too for the purpose of showing the logical connection between the elements involved. The theory of meaning is not a study of the genesis of language and its learning.

Others might oppose building any theory of language whatsoever. They would complain that any attempt to theorize involves definitions and analysis which puts language in a Procrustean bed and thereby constructs a bloodless caricature of the rich and varied experiences of using a language. Conceptualization and abstraction are instruments of extirpation and ruthless conformity with a certain given doctrine.

This sounds like an objection to philosophy in general, if by philosophy we mean analysis and argumentation. However, a theory of meaning does not aim at recreating the experience of one's knowledge of linguistic meaning. It rather explains meaning. Explanation differs from re-creation in the sense in which an atlas differs from the country of which it is an atlas. An atlas is sketchy, selective, condensed, has its own method of measurements, has its own vocabulary to state the difference between a plateau and a mountain, between a state highway and a rural highway, between sea-route and air-flight route, etc. And these are not vices, but the virtues of an atlas. So too with a theory of meaning. It is selective and condensed only because it gives us a systematic and comprehensive picture of linguistic meaning. As an atlas can show us new paths and facts about a certain area, a theory of meaning also can show us new directions, it can also throw new light on old vexed problems.

Notes

[1] I have done some research on a related topic of the relation between perceptual knowledge and the language we use to express that knowledge as developed in Indian philosophy which is entitled "Knowledge and Language in Classical Indian Philosophy", *Language and Meaning*, Ed.by Raghunath Ghosh, Allied Publishers, Kolkata, 2003.

[2] Dummett, M., "The Justification of Deduction" in his *Truth and Other Enigmas*, Cambridge, Mass., Harvard University Press, 1978, p. 311.

[3] While doing this brief historical study I have drawn heavily on J. Alberto Coffa's *The Semantic Tradition from Kant to Carnap*, Cambridge, Cambridge University Press, 1991.

[4] Quine, W. V., "Epistemology Naturalized" in his *Ontological Relativity and Other Essays*, New York, Columbia University Press, 1969, p. 69.

[5] Ibid., p. 75.

[6] Ibid., p. 82.

[7] Quine, W. V., "The Nature of Natural Knowledge" in *Mind and Language*, Ed. by Samuel Guttenplan, Oxford, Clarendon Press, 1975, p. 72.

[8] Davidson, D., "A Coherence Theory of Truth and Knowledge" in *Truth and Interpretation,* Ed. by Ernest Lepore, Oxford, Basil Blackwell, 1989, p. 307.

[9] Ibid., p. 309.

[10] Ibid., p. 312.

[11] Ibid.

[12] Ibid.

[13] Ibid., p. 313.

[14] Davidson, D., "Meaning, Truth and Evidence," in *Perspectives on Quine*, Ed. by Robert B. Barrett and Roger F. Gibson, Oxford, Basil Blackwell, 1990, p. 73.
[15] Ibid., p. 75.
[16] Davidson, D. *Inquires into Truth and Interpretation*, Oxford: Clarendon Press, 1986, p. 126 (footnote).
[17] Ibid., p. 129.
[18] Ibid., p. 130.
[19] Ibid., p. 153.
[20] Wheeler, Samuel C., "Indeterminacy of French Interpretation: Derrida and Davidson" in *Truth and Interpretation*, Ed. by Ernest Lepore, p. 489.
[21] Wallace, John. "Translation Theories and the Decipherment of Linear B" in *Truth and Interpretation,* Ed. by Ernest Lepore, p. 219
[22] Quine, W. V. "Three Indeterminacies" in *Perspectives on Quine*, Ed. by Robert B. Barrett and Roger F. Gibson, p. 3.

CHAPTER 1
TRUTH CONDITIONAL SEMANTICS

This chapter starts with a brief description of what a theory of meaning is supposed to achieve and how it can attain its goal. Then I will describe D.Davidson's attempt to develop a theory of meaning with a brief reference to A.Tarski's theory of truth. After the positive thesis is laid down, I will take on the critics. I will argue that M. Dummett's "direct ascription of meaning" which generates M sentences does not do the job a theory of meaning is supposed to do. Appropriating Dummett's distinction of "modest" and "full-blooded" theory of meaning, I will argue that Davidsonian theory is a full-blooded theory of meaning. I will explain Dummett's examples of undecidable sentences, i.e., sentences where we do not have the effective procedure of determining their truth conditions. I will mention two models for explaining the knowledge of the truth condition of a sentence; one is the ability to state the condition, and the other is the ability to observe whether or not the sentence is true. I will argue that we should take the former model and, if we do this, then Dummett's so-called "undecidable sentences" can be incorporated in a truth conditional semantics.

Contrary to J. Foster, I will argue that a theory of meaning à la Davidson is a theory of interpretation, i.e., possession of a Davidsonian theory of meaning enables one to interpret the sentences of the language for which the theory is given. In Davidson's theory, we do not have to be armed with a notion of translation to begin with. The right hand side of a T-sentence is a translation of the left hand side, but this is a happy coincidence. We do not start with translation and then arrive at meaning.

Even though when I am talking of a theory of meaning, my emphasis is on the *form* a theory of meaning should take in order to be an interpretative theory, this does not go against the Tarskian vision of semantics as the study of the relation between language and something extra-linguistic.

Acknowledging K. A. Taylor's requirement that a theory of meaning must be "modally projectible", i.e., a theory of meaning must be put in a finite form and yet it must be able to give the meanings of potentially infinite number of sentences, I will argue that Davidson's theory fulfils this requirement. As opposed to Taylor, I argue that the indeterminacy of interpretation is not to be conflated with the failure of modal projectibility.

I.I What is a theory of meaning?

The question I am faced with is: What is meaning? Meaning is one of the important categories we use in order to explain how language works. An explanation of what meaning is amounts to a theory of meaning in the sense that it will present to us an analysis of meaning, what are its components, how it works, etc. It is important to remember that long before philosophers talk about a theory of meaning, native speakers know what the sentences in their languages mean. So our theory of meaning must adequately explain the speaker's knowledge of the meaning of the sentences of her language. In other words, a theory of meaning must correspond to the speaker's knowledge. Thus the criterion of a successful theory of meaning is that it must reflect the speaker's knowledge of the meaning of the sentences. To put it otherwise, if someone knows a theory of meaning, she should be able to know the meanings of the expressions of the language for which the theory of meaning is being given. Notice that when we are talking of a theory of meaning, we are taking the theory in its generality and we are not dealing with the practical project of having a theory of meaning for particular languages like English, German, etc. Rather, we are aiming at specifying certain principles on the basis of which we can have a theory of meaning for any particular language. And an exposition of those principles will help us to formulate a theory of meaning, which, in its turn, will give us some insight into what meaning is. So, when I talk of a theory of meaning, I am talking of certain general principles which, when applied to specific languages, will generate a theory of meaning for those languages. And this will further our understanding of what meaning is. My theory of meaning is not a theory of communication in the sense that speakers do not engage in linguistic communication after they acquire the knowledge of this theory. Nor is my theory of meaning a theory of language, because a theory of language includes many other things like our knowledge of phonology, syntax, etc. My theory of meaning is a "rational reconstruction" of the speaker's knowledge of linguistic meaning. So, when I talk of "mastery of language", I am referring to the mastery of the meanings of the expressions of the language.

An English speaker hears the sound 'Snow is white' and knows that it means that snow is white. This bit of knowledge is part of her competence as an English speaker to interpret sentences of the English language. For one who is interested in the philosophy of language, the question of great significance is: What is it that an English speaker knows when she has mastered English. Since the speaker's competence spans over an indefinitely large number of sentences, we cannot list her interpretation of each sentence one by one. So we have to ascribe to the speaker some finite body of knowledge (a theory) from which the speaker's interpretation of any given sentence of English can be extracted. Such a theory must show how the infinitely many expressions of English are constructed out of a finite stock, and the theory does this by identifying the general principles of combination of the finite elements that generate different interpretations. Now we can see that, if we try to give a theory of the general competence of a speaker of English, we end up giving a theory that gives the meaning of each English sentence on the basis of a structure. And this is not surprising, for meaning is what is needed in order to explain one's mastery of a language. An ordinary speaker of English is not aware of a theory of meaning which philosophers of language are envisaging. A speaker of English can interpret any given sentence of English, but she cannot state the general principles to which her interpretation conforms. Given this, one might ask: Is it not unnatural to ascribe a theory to a speaker which the speaker is not aware of at all? So, instead of talking of ascribing a theory to a speaker, let us talk of a theory whose knowledge would suffice for one's mastery of language. We are no longer saying that a speaker should possess the knowledge of a theory of meaning. What we require of a theory of meaning is that it should state those facts the explicit recognition of which gives one the mastery of a language. So a speaker does not need to be (and, in fact, is not) actually aware of a theory of meaning. The theory of meaning, by being a sufficient condition (not necessary) for one's linguistic competence, gives some important semantic information about the language.

But why do we require of a theory of meaning that it should suffice for one's mastery of a language? Remember that a theory of meaning does not aim at providing a language manual for students. Our aim is to gain philosophical insight into the nature of language and meaning. We want to put the semantic character of language in its proper philosophical perspective. This perspective is not provided by a theory that only gives the meaning of the expressions of some particular language. If we can put the right constraints on what giving-meaning involves, and if we can construct the form a theory of meaning should take which will satisfy all those constraints, then we can shed some light on what meaning-in-language amounts to. By uncovering the conditions of a theory of meaning and its form in which those conditions can be met, we can hope to explain meaning. It is in this perspective that we have to understand why a theory of meaning should suffice for one's mastery of a language. The problem of meaning arises from the properties certain sounds (or words— in the case of written language) are said to possess and by virtue of these properties there is something to be said or understood. This is why when we talk of meaning we cannot discard its link with the speaker's linguistic competence. So, instead of asking ourselves the question 'What is meaning?', we are going to ask : 'How can we develop a theory of meaning for a natural language?' Naturally the focus of our discussion is now shifted to what form a theory of meaning should take.

As expected, different philosophers have suggested different versions of a theory of meaning. But one might argue : Does not the very attempt to develop a theory of meaning presuppose the knowledge of what meaning is and so is not a circularity involved here? The answer is 'No'. A theory of meaning is not an empirical study of the language–learning mechanism. We do not learn a theory of meaning to learn a language. We learn a language by various methods as enunciated by linguists and philosophers.[1] A theory of meaning represents our knowledge of the meanings of the expressions of a language. It answers the question : What is it the knowledge of which enables us to know a language?

Here we can employ the distinction between 'knowing how' and 'knowing what'. An empirical study of the language–learning mechanism is a description of 'knowing how'; it explains various ways by which we come to know how words are used. But a theory of meaning gives us a knowledge of 'knowing what'. It describes the knowledge that we could possess by virtue of being a speaker of a language. It represents the knowledge in a systematic fashion by virtue of which an English speaker could know that 'Snow is white' means snow is white, etc. A theory of meaning does not describe how we come to know the meanings of different expressions. Rather, it explains what is involved in the claim that an English speaker knows that 'Snow is white' means snow is white. It is true, of course, that a theory of meaning must be empirically verifiable, and the only evidence against which this verification can take place is the knowledge of a native speaker of a language. Since the aim of a theory of meaning is to understand the workings of a natural language, it must conform to native speakers' verbal behaviour.

Quine's version of naturalized epistemology, described earlier, has several important consequences. Davidson accepts many of these results but claims that a theory of meaning in the form of a theory of truth will better serve our purpose. Davidson endorses Quinean extensionalism but qualifies his (Davidson's) opposition to reified meaning by saying that he objects to those intensional entities only because they do not explain the problem that a theory of meaning is supposed to explain. Hence Davidson exploits the notion of truth in order to have a theory of meaning where truth is extensional in nature. So the question whether there can be an extensional theory of linguistic meaning is tantamount to the question whether a Davidsonian theory of meaning is successful. First, I will explain Davidson's positive thesis about the form of a theory of meaning— as he envisages it. Then I will mention some problems with his theory as pointed out by some critics and we will see how Davidson can deal with those problems.

I.2 Tarski's semantic conception of truth

Before going into Davidson's theory, let me explain Alfred Tarski's semantic conception of truth on which Davidson draws heavily to generate a theory of meaning. This will also help us to notice the differences between Tarski and Davidson.

Tarski aims at giving a satisfactory definition of truth : "a definition which is *materially adequate* and *formally correct*".[2] A definition is materially adequate when it reflects the actual meaning of the definiendum, the meaning that we attach in our everyday use. A definition is formally correct when the language in which the definition is given is set out explicitly, showing its formal structure. All the words must be well-defined and the rules for forming the language in which the definition is couched must be given beforehand. When we talk of truth, we mean truth of a sentence and, since a sentence is a part of a particular language, we must relate truth to a specific language.

Since our definition of truth has to be materially adequate, Tarski starts with the Aristotelian conception of truth that satisfies our general intuitive use of the word 'truth'. If we paraphrase Aristotle's conception in modern terminology, it would stand as follows:

The truth of a sentence consists in its agreement with reality.

Let us, for example, take the sentence 'Snow is white'. Our pre-philosophical notion of truth will tell us that this sentence is true when snow is white. So, if our definition is to be materially adequate, it must have consequences which will read as :

The sentence 'Snow is white' is true if, and only if, snow is white.

Notice that on the left side we have quoted 'Snow is white', while, on the right side it occurs without quotation. We have used quotation because we are talking about the sentence, we are naming it or mentioning it. On the right hand side we are talking about the condition in the world which, if it obtains, will make the sentence true. Here we are using the sentence to state the situation in the world.

So, if we generalize the above example, our theory should imply equivalences like :

S is true if and only if P.

S is the name of the sentence whose truth we are trying to define and p is the sentence itself. Tarski calls this schema "equivalence of the form (T)".[3] Hence our definition of truth is materially adequate if it implies all the equivalences of the form (T) for a language.

Let us turn to another aspect of the definition of truth, viz., its formal correctness. According to Tarski, a definition of truth can be given with precision only for those "whose language has been exactly specified".[4] By "exactly specified" Tarski means a language where all the primitive terms must be shown, where we must have precise set of rules of introducing the new terms, where we must have a specific criterion for determining certain groups of terms as sentences. We should also indicate axioms or primitive sentences and rules of inference by which we can derive new sentences or theorems.

That natural languages are not "exactly specified" in this sense can be shown from the fact that if we try to define truth for them as they are, it gives rise to various antinomies of which the Liar's Paradox is perhaps the most well known. Let me explain the Liar's Paradox very briefly. Let us take the formulation that Tarski uses. Consider the sentence: 'The first sentence on this page is not true'. We can abbreviate this sentence as 'S'. According to the convention with regard to the usage of the term 'true', we can say: (1) 'S' is true if and only if, the first sentence on this page is not true. By introducing the custom of abbreviation 'S', we assert: (2) 'S' is identical with the first sentence on this page. Now it follows from (2) that we can replace the expression 'the first sentence on this page' in (1) by the symbol 'S'. Then what we get is : (3) 'S' is true if, and only if, 'S' is not true. This is obviously a contradiction. According to Tarski, the source of this paradox is the fact that the language for which we are giving the definition of truth is a "semantically closed" language. A semantically closed language is one that contains, in addition to its expressions, names of those expressions and semantic predicates like 'true'. This is also a language in which we can formulate the usage of the term 'true' by using its own vocabulary. This talk of semantically closed language becomes clearer if we make a distinction between what Tarski calls "object-language" and "meta-language". An object-language is the language which we are talking about, whose sentences are the subject matter of our definition of truth. Meta-language is the language in which we are talking, the language that we are using to formulate the definition. It is easy to overlook this distinction in case of natural language. In English, for example, the word 'true' itself is a part of the language and is also used as a semantic predicate of English. This is what gives rise to the Liar's Paradox.

However, in our schema (T), the definition is to be formulated in the meta-language. In 'S is true if, and only if, P', 'S' is the name of a sentence and 'P' stands for any sentence of object-language. So the meta-language must contain names of every sentence of the object-language. Since 'P' stands for sentences of the object language, the meta-language must contain the names of all the sentences of the object-language. The meta-language should also contain logical terms like 'if, and only if '. In other words, a meta-language must be "essentially richer" than the object-language. If we violate this condition, we will end up having antinomies like the Liar's Paradox.

We have been concerned with the conditions that a satisfactory definition of truth must meet. Now Tarski introduces the relation of "satisfaction"[5] to define truth. Satisfaction is a relation that obtains between arbitrary objects and sentential functions. Sentential functions are expressions like 'X is white' etc. which contain free variables. 'X is white' is not a sentence, for it contains a variable and, hence, it is neither true nor false. But we can apply the notion of satisfaction to sentential functions. For example, the sentential function 'X is white' is satisfied by snow since, if we substitute the variable X by 'snow' then the sentence 'Snow is white' turns out to be true. Of course, we have to apply a recursive procedure here. We will describe how the satisfaction of a compound sentential function is made out of satisfaction of simpler sentential functions. So once we have interpretation of predicates, we are in a position to figure out the satisfaction relation between sentential functions and appropriate objects.

So far, we have been talking about sentential functions.[6] But we are interested in defining the truth of a sentence. Sentences are sentential functions that do not contain any free variables. So while Fx ('x is white') is a sentential function, ($x)(Fx) is a sentence. This says that there is something that is white. This shows that as long as there is something which satisfies the sentential function Fx, everything will satisfy the sentence ($x)(Fx). Conversely, if nothing satisfies Fx, then nothing will satisfy ($x)(Fx).

Now we can extract a general definition of truth using this notion of satisfaction. "A sentence is true if it is satisfied by all objects and false otherwise".[7] Since our object-language satisfies the criterion of formal correctness, we already know the precise interpretations of the predicates. So, to say that the sentence ($x)(Fx) is true is to say that this sentence is satisfied by any arbitrary object. Once we have the interpretation of predicates, we can determine which simple sentences are satisfied by which things. Then we can determine the satisfaction of more complex sentences made out of negation, conjunction, etc. This shows that we can define the satisfaction of any number of sentences in an object language, provided it satisfies the criterion of formal correctness. Defining truth in terms of satisfaction proves to be materially adequate since it fulfils convention (T) as mentioned before.

Some general comments on Tarski's definition are worth mentioning here. Tarski's definition does not inform us of how we are going to determine the truth condition of a sentence. He gives us a general form a theory of truth should take which can tell us what is involved in a sentence being true, when that theory is applied to an object language.

Tarski is not aiming at discovering a new theory of truth. His claim is a modest one. He tries to capture the ordinary pre-theoretical meaning of truth, but in a precise and rigorous manner.

Tarski is suspicious of an attempt to develop a theory of truth for natural languages. Natural languages are not 'exactly specified' and 'semantically closed'. When we tried to apply a theory of truth to natural languages, that gave rise to paradoxes. According to Tarski, a theory of truth can be successfully applied only to a formalized language as envisioned by him.

I have described Tarski's theory very briefly, ignoring all the subtleties, just to set the stage for a discussion of Davidson's theory of meaning à la Tarski. Davidson exploits Tarski's theory of truth to generate a theory of meaning for a natural language.

1.3 Davidson's version of a theory of meaning à la Tarski's theory of truth

Davidson starts from the assumption that a theory of meaning must show how meanings of sentences depend on meanings of words. Otherwise we cannot explain the fact that after learning a finite number of words and a finite set of rules we can use and understand a potentially infinite number of sentences. How can a theory of meaning fulfil this task?

First, Davidson shows the futility of talking in terms of meanings as entities. Let us take the sentence 'Socrates is the teacher of Plato'. Even if we can find some entity named Socrates and Plato in the world, how can we determine the meaning of 'the teacher of'? There is no entity, according to Davidson, known as 'the teacher of'. Frege took the meaning of a predicate as 'incomplete' compared to the meaning of a name. So the meaning of 'the teacher of' is such that when this expression is prefixed to a singular term, the whole expression refers to the teacher of the person to whom the singular term refers. So once we know the meanings of individual proper names, we can prefix 'the teacher of ' to those names and we can understand the meanings of infinite number of expressions.

But here we have been equating meaning with the reference of a singular term which Frege warned us against. Frege, by his famous example of 'morning star' and 'evening star', convinced us that if we do not distinguish sense from reference we will be led to absurd results. So, we are told by Frege— as we have seen earlier in the introduction— we should start from meaning (as different from reference) of each sentence so as to show how this meaning depends on meanings (as different from reference) of its parts.

But this shift from reference to meaning, according to Davidson, does not explain anything. If we try to explain the meaning of 'the teacher of Plato' by saying that it yields the meaning of 'the teacher of Plato' when hooked on the meaning of 'Plato', where 'the teacher of ' is an incomplete expression, there is no progress. Our theory of meaning should have consequences, for any sentence of a language for which the theory is being given, of the form 's means m' where 's' is a description of the sentence and 'm' is replaced by a singular term which refers to the meaning of the sentence. Falling back on meanings as entities does not help our project in any way. Davidson thus concludes that meanings "have no demonstrated use".[8]

As we have seen a little earlier, not all words have corresponding meanings independent of their occurrence in a sentence. This is a suggestion toward holism that we will discuss later. Not only words, sentences too depend, for their meaning, on other sentences of the same language.

Our theory of meaning should have consequences for any sentence s such that 's means m'. We can replace 'm' with a sentence 'p', since, after all, when we ask for meaning we ask for a familiar expression. This 'p' is supposed to specify the meaning of 's'. 'P' can be replaced by 's' itself, if the meta-language contains the object language or we can also use a translation of s in meta-language. Since the expression 'means' gives rise to endless problems, let us replace it with a sentential connective and attach to the description which replaces s its own predicate. What we get as a result of this change is

(T) s is T if, and only if, p.

If a theory of meaning for a language L implies for every sentence s of L the above mentioned schema (T) without using any other semantic notions, we get all we wanted. Since this schema satisfies Tarskian criterion of material adequacy and formal correctness of a definition of truth, the predicate 'is T' will be applicable only to true sentences of L.

Moreover, as we stated earlier, a theory of meaning shows how meanings of sentences depend on meanings of words. This is satisfied by schema (T), for Tarski's definition is recursive in nature. It shows how truth of a complex sentence rests on truth of simpler parts.

Davidson shows the relation of truth and meaning by arguing that "to give truth conditions is a way of giving the meaning of a sentence".[9] Tarski's theory enables us to define truth for every sentence of a language. And understanding the truth condition of every sentence amounts to knowing a language. So a Tarski-style theory of truth gives us all that is required of a theory of meaning. And, at the same time, it does not use 'meaning' at all. So here we have a theory of meaning without 'meaning'. This perfectly accords with Davidson's extensional view of a theory language.

Like any other theory, Davidson's theory of meaning can be empirically tested. We can check whether T-sentences implied by our theory correspond to the linguistic behaviour of the speakers of the object language. It is to be noted that this theory of meaning does not discover anything new about the truth condition of a sentence. An English speaker does not need to take a lesson on a theory of meaning in order to know that 'Snow is white' is true if, and only if, snow is white. A speaker can use and interpret an infinite number of sentences on the basis of her knowledge of a finite stock of words. This is possible because of the speaker's "combinatorial activity" wherein the speaker uses the same word in various contexts. And a theory of meaning, by issuing all the possible T-sentences, reveals this semantic structure of a language. It shows how each simple component (word) contributes to the truth of a sentence, which plays the same role in very many different contexts (sentences). The knowledge of the contribution of each word constitutes one's mastery of a language. So our theory of meaning explains a very complicated ability, the ability to understand and use a language.

So far, we have been assuming that we already know the object language and it is a part of our meta-language. That is why it sounds apparently trivial when our theory of meaning implies consequences like " 'Snow is white' is true if, and only if, snow is white". But we can apply our theory to a foreign language as well. Our aim should be to have a theory that will specify truth conditions for an indefinitely large number of sentences of that foreign language. We have to figure out the sentences that an alien speaker holds true. Then we have to map those foreign sentences (held true by alien) on to true sentences in our language. This is a complex process. Some of the problems will be discussed later with reference to radical translation. We have to act on the basis of charity. Perhaps we will end up having more than one theory of meaning (more than one translation manual for Quine and more than one theory of truth for Davidson) for the foreign language. This is the much discussed indeterminacy of meaning.

We have seen earlier that Tarski was sceptical of having a formal theory of truth for natural languages. According to Tarski, natural languages are semantically closed and too confused and hence resist application of a formal theory. But for Davidson, to have a theory of meaning for a natural language, one needs to apply the formal theory of truth to a spoken language. Davidson's response to Tarskian scepticism sounds somewhat conciliatory. First, Davidson accepts that there is a possible danger of the appearance of semantic paradoxes, if formal theory is applied to a natural language. We can check this by restricting the range of quantifiers of the object language. Semantic paradoxes arise since the term 'true' is contained in the object language itself. But the very nature of this inquiry might be such that even though we develop a theory of truth for a foreign language, we might not be able to communicate to her this concept of truth in her language.[10]

It is true that natural language is confused. But, following Tarski, we can develop a formal language in English which is close to ordinary English and, at the same time, which satisfies Tarski's formal requirements. We can have a formal theory for this fragment of English. And then we can gradually extend this formal theory to other parts of ordinary English language— as far as possible. As Davidson has said, we are not interested in improving our natural language, but in understanding it. And having a theory couched in a rigorous form helps to achieve that purpose.

The existence of ambiguous terms poses no threat to Davidson's program. According to him, we should distinguish two different activities; one is explaining the logical form of sentences and the other is the analysis of individual words or expressions. The former is the task of a theory of meaning while the latter falls under the province of primitives accepted in a theory or language. The apparent grammatical form of a sentence does not always correspond to its logical form. A theory of meaning uncovers and explains this logical form by working within an extensional and holistic framework. A theory of meaning does not prescribe meaning, rather it explains meaning. How far a word is ambiguous or not is a subject for a lexicographer. A theory of meaning is neutral to the ambiguity of a word. So the existence of ambiguous terms is not a problem as long as it does not affect the logical form of sentences. A sentence containing an ambiguous term in an object language can be translated in a meta-linguistic expression containing an ambiguous term unless the truth definition is not empirically corroborated.

Natural language contains expressions using demonstratives. These sentences may be true at one time and false at another. How can we have a theory of meaning that is sensitive to this difference in truth values of the same sentence? Davidson suggests to take "truth as a relation between a sentence, a person. and a time".[11] So, corresponding to each expression containing a demonstrative in an object language, our meta-linguistic theory will relate the truth condition of the sentence with the appropriate time and speaker. Such a theory will entail T sentences like :

'I am hungry' is true as spoken by p at T if, and only if, p is hungry at T.

Notice that this theory is able to explain the role of a demonstrative in a sentence. A speaker, who knows the meaning of a demonstrative, knows that the same sentence can be true or false depending on the speaker and the time of the utterance of the sentence. The fact that our theory of meaning entails theorems as mentioned above shows that our theory is empirically verifiable.

According to Davidson, a theory of truth satisfying Tarski's convention T fulfils all the requirements of a theory of meaning. Davidson sets out three conditions which a theory of meaning should fulfil.[12] Firstly, as already stated, a theory of meaning must analyze the meaning of every expression by showing how that meaning is composed of a finite stock. A theory of meaning, failing to do this, will not be able to explain one's mastery of a language.

Secondly, a theory of meaning must provide a method for determining the meaning of any arbitrarily given sentence. Like any theory, a theory of meaning must be amenable to empirical check. And in so far as a theory of meaning is concerned, it can be verified by finding out whether such a theory can tell us a method of specifying the meaning of any sentence of a given language. In the case of Tarski's theory, we will have to determine whether the truth condition of a sentence follows from convention T. So not any single T-sentence will do. A T-sentence must strictly follow from a theory of truth that meets the previously mentioned condition.

Thirdly, statements of truth conditions must not use any semantic concept that is not used in stating the sentences whose truth conditions are being stated. We can state the same condition in terms of object-language and meta-language. The meta-language must not contain any semantic notion that is not already contained in the object language. This should not be confused with another condition, viz., that the meta-language must be essentially richer than object language. A third condition is needed in order to block the possibility of smuggling in some semantic notion which would involve us in circularity. If, while stating truth condition of a sentence, we use some new semantic notion (other than truth), then how are we going to define that notion? We cannot fall back on truth, for we are just in the process of defining truth. Nor can we fall back on meaning, for we are trying to generate a theory of meaning using the theory of truth. Since we are aiming at a semantics for natural language, we cannot take semantic notions for granted. We have to start from a minimal base. Truth acts as that base. If someone wants to start from any other base, then the onus is on her to show why truth conditional semantics does not work.

Needless to say, Tarski's theory of truth satisfies all the above–mentioned properties. Tarski's theory is recursive. It shows how the meaning or truth condition of a complex expression is built out of simpler component parts. Tarski's theory is empirically verifiable by comparing the T–sentence entailed by the theory with actual linguistic behaviour of the speakers. Since in Tarski's T–sentence of the form 's is true if, and only if, p', the truth condition of s is given by the sentence which replaces p and which happens to be s itself, we are not using any semantic concept in stating the truth condition that is not used in understanding s.

Davidson is well aware of the fact that there are problems in applying a formal theory of truth to a natural language. But this does not bother him. His interest is in a systematic description of natural language. And this description is "doomed to be to some extent incomplete and schematic".[13]

As stated earlier with regard to Tarski, we are not giving a particular theory of meaning for a particular language. Rather, we are putting forward a criterion that has to be met by any successful theory of meaning. We can always verify whether such a theory really works. If it works, this will be a valuable contribution to the empirical study of language.

Of course, just knowing a T–sentence is not enough to know the meaning of the sentence concerned. We have to know that the T sentence is a conclusion which is entailed by a theory of truth for a language to which that sentence belongs, or, in other words, the T-sentence must form a part of the theory which is holistic in nature. For only in this way we can ensure the recursive structure of a language. Such a proof shows how an infinite number of sentences can be built of a finite stock. It is only then we can see that how truth- value of a sentence depends on truth-value of other sentences. Thus we can do justice to the holistic structure of a language.

When Davidson says that convention T is the criterion of a successful theory of meaning, he does not mean that to test a theory of truth we need to know the meaning of each sentence. This is not permissible for we are determining meaning in terms of truth. What is required to test the theory of truth is to see whether speakers hold the bi-conditionals to be true. If a theory of truth for English generates a T-sentence of the form "'Snow is white' is true if, and only if, snow is white" and if we know that an English speaker actually holds the sentence 'Snow is white' true under the said condition, we can be pretty sure that the theory of truth has succeeded in its aim. Determining a speaker's attitude to a sentence— when that speaker is a user of a foreign language— might be complicated. But the same principle holds for domestic as well as alien interpretation.

Davidson calls his theory a theory of "Radical Interpretation". Since a theory of meaning gives meaning of every meaningful expression of a language, it yields a theory of interpretation for a speaker of that language. Like Quine, Davidson thinks "All understanding of the speech of another involves radical interpretation".[14] We tend to ignore the radical nature of interpretation in the domestic case just because of the fact that both interpreter and the interpretee share, more or less, the same assumptions about the world. The presence of these assumptions become conspicuous in the case of foreign interpretation. Also, in the case of domestic interpretation, those assumptions are not critically examined in order to expedite communication. But this does not undermine the philosophical importance of those assumptions.

So now we can put the main question of our inquiry in a somewhat different way. The question is : What is it the knowledge of which will enable us to interpret any number of expressions uttered by a speaker? It would be easier for us to interpret someone's utterances, if we had a theory of belief ascription by which we could come to know her beliefs. But this is not possible, for a speaker's beliefs and her linguistic behaviour form a circular network. In order to know one's belief, we have to know at least part of her linguistic behaviour and in order to be able to interpret her sentences we have to have some knowledge of her belief system. So a theory of belief ascription cannot act as an evidential base for a theory of interpretation.

We have seen earlier that a theory of interpretation must be amenable to empirical verification. We can see whether T-sentences entailed by our theory are held true by the speakers of the object language. T-sentences are thought to be true since the right side of the bi-conditional is considered to be a translation of the sentence mentioned on the left side. Since we are trying to explain meaning, we cannot start our journey from the notion of translation— for that would involve circularity. So Davidson reverses the direction. Davidson takes truth as primitive and explains meaning or interpretation.

Since truth is a semantic concept, it explains the semantic contribution of a sentence, and this is what Davidson is trying to explain. Our theory can still imply T- sentences of the form 's is true if, and only if, p', where 'p' is replaced by a sentence which is true if, and only if, 's' is true.

We have seen earlier that a theory of belief ascription cannot be the basis for a theory of interpretation. But we need some evidence to start with. We need some data on the basis of which we can start interpreting and then, of course, we can verify our interpretation. According to Davidson, "A good place to begin is with the attitude of holding a sentence true, of accepting it as true."[15] The attitude of holding a sentence true is also a kind of belief, but this is a belief which we can get hold of even before starting interpretation. We are assuming that the interpretee is making sincere assertions about her attitudes. This does not mean to ignore lies, irony, etc. But once we know which sentences the speaker holds true and consequently if we have sufficient knowledge about her belief system, then we are in a position to detect non-serious utterances as well. So when we have the knowledge of this attitude, we can form a T-sentence. Of course, the interpretee herself might be wrong about her attitude. But since we are not taking each T-sentence in isolation, rather, as entailed by a theory which necessitates a holistic structure, at some later stage in interpretation we can detect that the interpretee was wrong and we can make necessary adjustments. Also, we have to aim at maximizing the agreement between us and our interpretee. For we can make sense of disagreement only in the background of shared beliefs.

Thus we see that a T-sentence 'gives the meaning of a sentence' not by mentioning a corresponding meaning entity, but simply by stating the truth condition. Notice that a T-sentence does not tell us whether the relevant condition holds, nor does it inform us about how we can determine whether the relevant truth condition holds. It only tells us which condition is to obtain, if the sentence is to be true. But to be able to come up with a T-sentence is not enough to interpret a language. Because of the holistic nature of a language, we must see that the T-sentence is entailed by a correct theory of truth. By a 'correct theory of truth' we mean a theory that meets all the conditions discussed above. Only then do we know the true semantic contribution of a sentence to the whole of linguistic structure and we also potentially know T-sentences of a host of other related sentences.

The fact that Tarski introduced T-sentences to explain semantic properties of simple formalized languages does not deter Davidson from generating a theory of meaning for a natural language. Davidson endorses Tarski's characterization of the object language and meta-language distinction. He goes on saying "Now add to the meta-language Tarski's definitions leading up to and including the definition of truth, but do not *call* them definitions, and think of them as employing empirically significant expressions suitable for describing the semantics of the object language."[16] In this way we are changing our perspective of viewing a theory of truth. But Tarski's formal system itself remains unaltered. Now whether this new perspective is a valid one is a matter of philosophical debate that we will enter shortly. As explained earlier, Davidson thinks this new perspective is a valuable contribution to the philosophy of language.

According to Davidson, Tarski-style T-sentences are neither logical truths nor stipulative. By denying those sentences to be logical truths Davidson is saying that they have empirical content. They say something significant about a sentence that can be empirically verified. By rejecting them as stipulative Davidson is saying that a T-sentence does not tell us everything about the predicate 'truth'. Davidson says "He (Tarski) defined the class of true sentences by giving the extension of the truth predicate but he did not give the meaning".[17] And this is where Davidson's own contribution comes in. Davidson employs his insight about the relation between truth and meaning and extends Tarski's definition to natural language. Tarski's definition gives us the definition of the truth predicate for every true sentence of an object language. We can employ this definition and at the same time, we can acknowledge that there are other properties attached to truth. Of course, we will not use any unspecified property in our meta-language. Without losing Tarski's technical achievement, Davidson wants to have an empirical theory of natural language.

1.4 Davidson's theory of meaning is a theory of understanding—A reply to Dummett

In recent years Davidson's observations on the form of a theory of meaning have invited a great deal of interest—pro and con. Criticisms of Davidson come from different angle. Some reject Tarski's theory of truth claiming that it does not explain truth at all. Some argue that a theory of truth and a theory of meaning are totally different projects; hence Davidson's attempt to generate a theory of meaning out of a theory of truth is totally misleading. Still there are other people who are sceptical of having a Tarski-style theory of truth for a natural language. All these different kinds of attack on Davidson's project are philosophically important, and the plausibility of the Davidsonian program rests on how well Davidson can deal with them.

I will narrow down my discussion of the polemic against Davidson for several reasons. I will primarily deal with the issue as to whether we can have a theory of meaning in the form of a theory of truth. I am not, for instance, interested in theories of truth, nor in Tarski as such. It seems to me that the most important question with regard to Davidson is whether there is any relation between a theory of truth and a theory of meaning. Does a theory of truth give us everything what we want from a theory of meaning? Unlike Davidson, many philosophers have answered this question in the negative. The rest of this chapter will be devoted to a discussion and critical assessment of these philosophers.

Perhaps the most formidable and thoroughgoing opponent of Davidson's version of a theory of meaning is Michael Dummett. Dummett asks the question: Does the meaning of a sentence consist in its truth conditions? An affirmative answer to this question, following Davidson, will face formidable difficulties, according to Dummett. There are a great many sentences for which we do not have an effective procedure of determining whether they are true. If to know the meaning is to know the truth condition, then we could not explain the meaning of those sentences, since we do not know their truth condition. But, in fact, we do know what those sentences mean. In order to avoid these difficulties, Dummett thinks that we should abandon the assumption of bivalence, the assumption that each sentence is determinately either true or false independently of what we can know or cannot know. He wants to have a theory of meaning where truth is not the central notion. He advocates an intuitionistic account of the meaning of mathematical statements.

According to Brouwer, who introduced intuitionism in contemporary philosophy of mathematics, propositions about numbers can be true only if it is determined to be true by the law that generates the relevant sequence of natural numbers. This is equivalent to 'possessing a proof.' So, something has a proof in mathematics means that whenever we mention the existence of that something, mathematics provides a method of finding or constructing that something. A mathematical object exists only if it can be constructed. To say that there is a natural number x such that Fx is to say that in the derivative sequence we will have an x such that Fx. To assert x is to have a proof in the above-mentioned sense. Brouwer thinks that given a proposition 'p', there is no reason to suppose that we will be in possession either of a proof of 'p' or a deduction of the absurdity form 'p'. If the law of excluded middle is taken as true of mathematical statements, then we should have a general method for the solution of *all* mathematical questions, which Brouwer rejects outright. The fundamental idea is that, to know the meaning of a sentence is not to know its truth condition, but to know whether or not a proof of the sentence exists or can be constructed.

If we apply this theory to natural language, instead of 'proof' we will be using 'verification'. On this account, understanding the meaning of a sentence consists in the capacity to recognize whatever is counted as establishing the sentence as true when, in fact, it is established as true. We do not have to have the means of deciding the truth/falsity of the sentence right now. So in order to have the knowledge of what would verify a sentence, one does not need to know the truth condition of the sentence. It is enough if one has the means to recognize the sentence as having being verified when, in fact, it is verified. Dummett argues, as I will explain shortly, that natural language consists of sentences such that whose truth conditions can not be decided at the present moment. But we do have the capacity to recognize that they are verified when, in fact, they will be verified. So a theory of meaning, which rests on verification, will be able to explain our knowledge of the meaning of those sentences.

Of course, Dummett admits that truth will play an important role in a verificationist theory of meaning. For Dummett, a sentence's having been recognized as verified is identical with its being recognized as true. Then what is the difference between verificationist theory and the theory of meaning based on truth? When we talk of verification of a sentence, we do not have to know right now whether the sentence has been verified or not. It is enough if we can recognize the sentence having been verified when it is actually verified. So verification does not require to pin down the truth condition of the sentence in order to be able to understand the meaning of the sentence, simply because we do not know the truth condition of those sentences but we do understand their meaning. Thus, in a verificationist theory, meaning is given not in terms of truth condition, but in terms of its verificatory condition. Truth comes later, when the speaker recognizes that the sentence, in fact, has been verified. Here verification plays the central role and truth enters as an appendix to verification. Also, truth so introduced is explained in terms of a speaker's capacity to recognize certain sentences as true and not in terms of the conditions that are independent of the speaker's knowledge.

Thus, in Dummett's envisaged theory of meaning, verification— instead of truth— is the central notion. How far an intuitionistic account of mathematical statements is a valid account and whether a verificationist theory of meaning is a valid one are matters of great debate. My concern is with the viability of Davidson's program. Consequently, I will primarily deal with Dummett's negative thesis. And I will show that Dummett fails to build a strong case against Davidson. Dummett's procedure is as follows: First he sets out the condition for a successful theory of meaning. Then he shows that Davidson's project falls short of this. According to Dummett, a theory of meaning aims at explaining how a language works. "A theory of meaning is a theory of understanding",[18] says Dummett. A theory of meaning gives an account of the knowledge that enables a person to understand a language.

When Dummett talks about a theory of meaning as a theory of understanding, he does not suggest that such a theory will describe the psychological mechanism of a person who knows a language. By 'knowledge of a language' I mean the knowledge that enables a person to communicate with her fellow speakers using the language. I am using the word 'communicate' in the broad sense which can be paraphrased as 'to do whatever can be done by the utterance of the sentences of the language'. So a theory of meaning is a philosophical description of the knowledge, the possession of which enables one to have the skill to engage in linguistic communication with others. Moreover, it would be incorrect to say that one who possesses the knowledge of a language could give us an explicit formulation of the theory of meaning for that language. And the reason is that when philosophers (especially Dummett and Davidson) talk about a theory of meaning, they do not simply take up the practical project of constructing a theory of meaning for a particular language. These philosophers think that once we can lay down certain general principles on the basis of which a theory of meaning can be developed, we would have a better grip on the problems concerning meaning. This is why, in the present context, when I talk of 'a theory of meaning', I do not suggest a theory which the speakers of a language actually use in the course of communication.

Dummett explores the question whether a theory of meaning "should issue in direct ascriptions of meaning". By "direct ascriptions of meaning" he means whether a theory should generate statements like "The word/sentence x means...." Dummett thinks that if a theory of meaning does not issue in direct ascription of meaning but merely explains different contexts where the word 'meaning' occurs, then that falls short of a theory of understanding. As a passing comment, I disagree with Dummett here. A theory of meaning which issues statements like "x means ..." (where x is a word or a sentence) is not explanatory in nature. A theory of meaning is supposed to explain meaning by replacing 'meaning' with something else. How can the theory itself involve using the notion that it is supposed to explain? Two questions are involved here. First, what does any particular sentence mean? Second, what is involved in the claim that a person knows the meaning of a sentence or that a sentence x means y? A theory of meaning, in the sense in which we are concerned here, deals with the second question and not with the first one. One does not need to know a theory of meaning in order to know what a sentence means. Nor does it explain anything to say that meaning is what a sentence/word means. A theory or a definition is an attempt to clarify a concept with the help of some more familiar and easily comprehensible concepts. It eliminates the definiendum in favour of some other concepts. I am afraid that if a theory of meaning issues in direct ascription of meaning in Dummett's sense, then such a theory would lack any explanatory power. For Dummett's direct ascription theory of meaning generates statements of the form 'The sentence x means ...' But this much we know before any theory of meaning comes into the picture. Such a theory is also circular, for it involves use of 'means' and again tries to explain meaning. It is only as an answer to the latter of the two questions mentioned above that a theory of meaning becomes a theory of understanding, which aims at explaining one's mastery of language. A theory of meaning analyzes the speaker's knowledge of the meaning of a sentence, it does not stipulate meaning, it does not say which sentences should carry which meaning.

Dummett distinguishes a 'modest' theory of meaning from a 'full-blooded' theory of meaning.[19] A modest theory of meaning is one that knowledge of which would enable only that person to understand the object language if the person already possesses the concepts expressible in that object language. According to Dummett, an axiom like 'is square is satisfied by all and only square things' (which might be a part of a Davidsonian theory of interpretation) will enable one to know what it is that the speakers of the language know when they use the expression 'is square', if one already possesses the concept of squareness. A full-blooded theory, on the other hand, says that what it is to have the "concepts" expressible in the object language. The theory of meaning, according to Dummett, must not only relate squareness with the expression 'square', it must also say what it is for someone to have the concept of squareness. It must do this for all the primitive expressions of the object language.

Dummett's contention is that any successful theory of meaning should be a full-blooded one, while Davidson's version of a theory of meaning is a modest theory.[20] In Davidson's T-sentences, the axiom does not provide any explanation of the concept expressed by a primitive predicate. This kind of theory is intelligible only to a person who already possesses the concept corresponding to that predicate. Since a modest theory explains the meaning of an object language on the basis of understanding of the concepts expressed by its primitive expressions which themselves remain unexplained, such a theory of meaning fails to be a theory of understanding. This theory fails to explain our understanding of the primitive concepts.

I think that the whole charge is misleading. According to Dummett, Davidsonian modest theory does not explain our understanding of primitive concepts expressed by predicates. Also notice that, according to Dummett, to grasp a concept is to understand a corresponding word or sentence. Now Davidson's T-sentence is designed to explain the meaning of a sentence of the object language. Of course, there are certain conditions which a T-sentence has to meet. If our theory entails a T-sentence of the form '"Snow is white" is true if, and only if, snow is white' and if we *know* that this is implied by a theory which meets all other conditions, then our theory has been able to explain satisfactorily the meaning of the term 'white'. And, since to grasp a concept is to grasp the meaning of the corresponding word (according to Dummett), our theory has explained a speaker's understanding of the concept 'whiteness'.

It is not true that this kind of theory is

intelligible only to people who already possess the knowledge of the concept. Think of having a theory of interpretation for German. Such a theory would entail theorems like '"Schnee ist weiss" is true if, and only if, snow is white'. If an English speaker possesses such a theory for German, she can quite legitimately claim to understand German. Such a theory enables the English speaker to come to know the predicate 'weiss' in German. A modest theory of meaning does not presuppose the knowledge of object language, rather it explains the object language. In a sense, a modest theory presupposes mastery of some language. But this is a trivial claim, for any theory is couched in a language.

Even some interpreters of Davidson mistakenly thought that Davidsonian theory is a modest theory of meaning. Simon Evnine concludes his discussion on Dummett and Holism by admitting that "Dummett is right, therefore, that Davidson's theory is modest rather than full-blooded".[21] And the reason for this, Evnine thinks, is that Davidson rejects attempts to reduce meaning to non-semantic. I would like to make two comments here. Firstly, I think that Evnine is wrong in attributing modesty to Davidsonian theory. If a full-blooded theory is one that exhibits one's knowledge of what it is to know the concepts expressible in the language for which it is a theory, then, as I have shown earlier, Davidson's theory is a full-blooded theory— for Davidson's theory of interpretation enables one to interpret the concepts expressible in the object language. Secondly, Evnine says that Davidson eschews the attempt to reduce meaning to the non-semantic. This statement needs clarification. One of the important and interesting consequences of adopting truth conditional semantics is the avoidance of both extremes, reductionism on the one hand and semantic dualism on the other. What I am defending is a middle way that does not emphasize the one at the cost of the other. The reason why Davidson shuns any attempt to explain meaning with the help of some other semantic terms like 'sense' or 'proposition' is that any attempt to do so would get us involved in circularity. And the reason why Davidson shuns any attempt to reduce meaning into the non-semantic is that a person's belief and what her utterance means are interlocked with each other. Knowledge of the one seems to require knowledge of the other. How can we then interpret a speaker's utterances?

Here Davidson introduces his theory of truth condition. Knowledge of the speaker's holding a sentence true does not seem to require our knowledge of what the utterance made by the speaker means. So if we have a theory which will assign truth conditions to the sentences uttered by the speaker, then we can claim to interpret the speaker's language. In other words, what we end up having is a theory of meaning for that language. So we start from a theory of truth condition, and a theory of truth condition is part of what one might call a theory of reference. We are working within a theory of reference, but we end up giving a theory of meaning. We did not reduce meaning to the non-semantic in the sense that we did not reject meaning. But we did produce a theory of meaning without using semantic notions. This is what I call non-reductive extensionalism, which will be discussed in the second chapter.

As I have explained a little earlier, Dummett mentions Davidson's suggestion that a theory of meaning should imply a direct ascription of meaning. Then Dummett "legitimately converts" Davidson's T-sentence into M-sentence of the form '"Snow is white" means snow is white'. And then he complains that M-sentence is "signally unexplanatory".[22] Dummett's complain is based on a misreading of Davidson. The move from T-sentence to what Dummett calls M-sentence is not a legitimate one. The whole point of Davidson's program is to generate a theory of interpretation without using 'meaning'. He calls his theory a theory of meaning without 'meaning'. This is where Davidson finds truth helpful. Davidson wants to substitute an M-sentence by a T-sentence where the latter is better understood in terms of philosophical clarity. A couple of paragraphs back I argued that

Dummett is confused about the meaning of 'direct ascription of meaning'. I suggested that if a theory implies M-sentence, such a theory lacks explanatory power. It is no progress in understanding meaning to say that 'S means that P' means that P is the meaning of S. We can still talk of direct ascription of meaning, but not by using Dummett's M-sentences, rather through Davidson's T-sentences. We cannot expect to explain away meaning using the notion of meaning itself. But it is quite plausible to explain meaning by truth.

Dummett introduces the distinction "between knowing, of a sentence, that it is true, and knowing the proposition expressed by the sentence."[23] Dummett cautions us that he is not indulging in an entitative notion of proposition. He is only making us aware of the fact that there are cases where a person knows a sentence to be true without knowing the proposition expressed by that sentence. And, according to Dummett, the necessary and sufficient condition of one's knowing the meaning of 'Snow is white' is that she knows the proposition expressed by the sentence. Dummett gives the example of 'The Earth moves'. If a person has some knowledge of the verb 'means' and if she knows that 'The Earth moves' is an English sentence, she knows the corresponding M-sentence '"The Earth moves" means that the earth moves' to be true. But she might not know what 'The Earth moves' means.

I want to raise a couple of points here. First, Davidson's T-sentences do not tell us *that* a sentence is true. I mean, T-sentences are not devises by which we can determine whether a sentence is true or not. It only informs us about what is involved in the claim that a sentence is true. Knowing that a sentence is true and knowing what is involved in a sentence's being true are two different things. Consider Dummett's example of 'The Earth moves'. It is true that one might know the M-sentence to be true without knowing what 'The Earth Moves' means. But this is not Davidson's position. As I have argued earlier, Davidson's motive is to "sweep away" 'means that' and introduce a sentential connective. Dummett thinks that Davidson's theory of interpretation generates M-sentences which it does not. Davidson himself asserts that M-sentences will not be of any help to us.[24]

Let us take the T-sentence corresponding to Dummett's example which will go like this:

'The Earth moves' is true if, and only if, the earth moves.

Remember, this T sentence does not tell us that 'the earth moves' is true. We do not know whether 'The Earth moves' is true or not, at least we cannot tell from this T-sentence alone. The T-sentence informs us what situation would obtain for the sentence being true. If a person knows this T-sentence, she knows under what condition the sentence would be true. She does not know whether the sentence is true or not at present time. But she knows what condition makes the sentence true. This is a valuable piece of knowledge for understanding the meaning of a sentence. One who knows the truth condition of a sentence knows the semantic contribution or meaning of that sentence provided the T-sentence meets all other conditions set forth. The T-sentence '"Snow is white" is true if, and only if, snow is white' and the M-sentence '"Snow is white" means that snow is white' do not belong to the same category. If meaning is what we are going to define, then the M-sentence does not help. This is precisely why Davidson introduces T-sentences. A theory of T-sentences for a language gives us what we expect from a theory of meaning. And this too, without presupposing meaning. We do not need a distinction between knowing the truth and knowing the proposition. Since a T-sentence gives us direct insight into what is involved in a sentence being true, this exhausts our knowledge of what that sentence means— irrespective of whatever proposition the sentence expresses.

But, Dummett might argue, knowing a T-sentence is not enough to grasp the meaning. This is true. Davidson's T-sentence requires us to see the T-sentence as implied by a theory of truth for the object language. A T-sentence is a part of a theory that systematically presents truth conditions of all other sentences of the language concerned. This is how we can also show how the meaning of a compound expression depends on the simpler parts. Dummett raises the same objection again in a different way. He thinks that to know the T-sentences for these simpler parts. A person knows '"The Earth" denotes the Earth' is true even if she does not know what 'The Earth' means. My point is, just if a person knows that this T-sentence is entailed by a theory of truth and thereby knows how this T-sentence is related to other T-sentences, she can claim to understand a big chunk of the language concerned. In that case, she can use this language while communicating with other speakers. A theory of truth, in this sense, becomes a theory of understanding. To understand a language is to use it in an appropriate way. And to use a language in an appropriate way is to know what constitutes the truth conditions of one's and her interlocutor's utterances.

There is no circularity here. In the case of radical interpretation we have seen how we can gradually develop a theory of truth for a foreign language from minimal evidence. We have to work under certain constraints. We have to maximize consistency in our interpretation. We are not justifying T-sentences with reference to our knowledge of the meanings of the sentences concerned. We are justifying T- sentences by looking at how well they fit with the available evidence— both linguistic and otherwise.

At one point Dummett admits that Davidsonian modest theory of meaning can interpret one language but only "via an understanding of another ... it does not explain what it is to have a mastery of a language, say one's mother tongue, independently of a knowledge of any other."[25] Notice that a theory of meaning is not concerned with the actual process of language acquisition. To echo Dummett's words, a theory of meaning is a theoretical representation of a practical ability, the ability to speak and understand a language. Since it is a theoretical presentation and since we are talking about a language, the object language/meta-language distinction comes in. It is true that when one learns one's mother tongue, she does it independently of any knowledge of any other language. But when we, philosophers of language, try to theorise about that knowledge of one's mother tongue, our knowledge of the theory should be rich enough to explain that knowledge of language. Of course, this object— language/meta-language distinction is relative. The same language can be treated as object language or as meta-language in different contexts. If our theory of meaning can interpret one's knowledge of mother tongue employing all the concepts available in the meta-language, the theory achieves its purpose. It is a virtue of our theory that makes us aware of this meta-language/object language distinction, which was obscure in many earlier works.

As mentioned earlier, according to Dummett, a theory of meaning is a theory of understanding. I agree with this. A theory of meaning represents a speaker's knowledge of her language. But a theory of meaning does not describe the psychological mechanism involved in knowing a language. We are not concerned with the actual occurrence of psychological events that a person experiences in speaking and understanding a language. We are also not concerned with a theory of meaning for any particular language. We are trying to formulate the general form a theory of meaning should take for any natural language. Even if two speakers differ in their respective psychological histories of linguistic behaviour, our theory of meaning would represent their knowledge of language in an identical manner.

However, Dummett's point is that if we take truth as the central notion in our theory of meaning, such a theory will consist of two parts.[26] The core of the theory will be a theory of truth that will specify the truth conditions of each sentence. Dummett calls this theory of truth condition "a theory of reference", for in it we will also find, other than theorems stating truth condition of sentences, axioms assigning appropriate references for the words involved. Then we will have a theory of sense which explains the content of a speaker's knowledge of reference by showing how one's knowledge of different kinds of linguistic acts like requests, wishes, etc., are related to one's knowledge of the sense expressed by those sentences. There is another supplementary part of a theory of meaning. This is a theory of force. The theory of force will give an account of various kinds of linguistic acts performed by uttering sentences expressing wish, command, request, etc. This part will explain "conventional significance" of these different utterances.

I am not comfortable with Dummett's tripartite division of a theory of meaning. I do not see what role a theory of sense plays. According to Dummett, a theory of sense "will lay down in what a speaker's knowledge of any part of the theory of reference is to be taken to consist, by correlating specific practical abilities of the speaker to certain propositions of the theory."[27] So a theory of sense explains a speaker's knowledge of the theory of reference. A theory of reference is a theory of truth that sets out truth condition for every sentence. Now, if a theory of truth satisfies the conditions previously discussed, it explains a speaker's knowledge of reference. I do not see how a theory of sense comes in here. Dummett talks of a theory of sense relating practical abilities of a speaker to propositions of the theory of reference. If by "specific practical abilities" Dummett means the ability to perform linguistic acts like assertion, request, etc., then this falls within the scope of a theory of force. Though I do recognize the importance of a theory of force, I do not think we need a theory of sense to connect a theory of reference to a theory of force. A theory of reference (truth) itself is capable of doing this job.

Anyway, even if we accept Dummett's three-fold division, the main issue remains unaffected. And this is : Can we accept truth as the central notion of a theory of meaning? Dummett accepts the intuitive obviousness of the notion of truth as an explanatory device for meaning. One of the reasons for this obviousness is what Dummett calls "equivalence principle". This is the principle that any sentences s is equivalent to the sentence 'It is true that s'. Notice that the equivalence principle explains truth where 'true' appears within the object language itself. From Tarski we learned that such a "semantically closed" language will not serve our purpose.

It is true that certain sentences of a language, which Quine calls "theoretical sentences", can be explained by referring to other sentences. Here the notion of truth helps us to see why this kind of explanation works. The truth conditions of higher level sentences rest on the truth conditions of simpler sentences. A new higher level sentence can be verbally explained by looking at how its truth condition is constituted out of truth condition of some other sentences. So here is another reason why the notion of truth seems to help in determining the meaning of a sentence.

Nonetheless, Dummett is sceptical of the explanatory power of truth. A theory of meaning which rests on truth will have to explain a speaker's knowledge of the truth condition of a sentence. A speaker's knowledge of the truth of a sentence consists in recognition of the truth of a sentence only when the relevant condition obtains. So, if a speaker possesses a mechanism by which she can recognize whether the condition of the truth of a sentence holds, she can claim to know the truth condition of the sentence and consequently she knows the meaning of that sentence as well. But the problem is that "natural language is full of sentences which are not effectively decidable, ones for which there exists no effective procedure for determining whether or not their truth conditions are fulfilled".[28] Sentences which involve quantification over an infinite or unsurveyable domain, subjunctive conditionals, sentences referring to regions of space and time which is in principle, inaccessible, are some examples. The fact that we might come to know the truth condition of the undecidable sentences in future does not help. For, at present, we cannot equate our capacity to recognize their truth conditions with what those conditions are.

Dummett traces back the origin of the notion of truth in an act of assertion. An assertion is called 'true' or 'false' in the primary sense of these terms. And an assertion is judged by an objective standard of correctness. Another distinction is closely related with the notion of truth : the distinction between the truth of what someone asserts and the ground or evidence one has for that assertion. An analysis of future-tense sentences as constituents in compound sentences reveals, according to Dummett, the necessity of making a distinction between truth conditions and assertibility conditions. From this Dummett concludes that the notion of truth "must be capable, in turn, of yielding the more primitive notion of the correctness of an assertion".[29]

Before we go further, I would like to take up the case of future-tense sentence which, according to Dummett, is a case of undecidable statement. Here it is impossible to establish the truth condition of a sentence at the time of utterance, but it is possible to determine the assertibility condition. Let us take an example: 'Unless people become aware of the environment, the government will set up the nuclear plant'. The consequent clause is a future-tense sentence. Now Dummett's point is that we are not in a position to conclusively establish the truth of this sentence right now. I agree with this. But this does not threaten the truth conditional theory of meaning. This theory will imply a T- sentence for this future-tense sentence which will go like :

'The government will set up the nuclear plant' is true if, and only if, the government will set up the nuclear plant.

Granted that at the present moment we do not know whether the government *will* set up the nuclear plant or not, notice the bi-conditional 'if, and only if'. The T-sentence is not saying that the sentence is true. It only describes the condition under which the sentence is true. We do not know whether that condition will obtain. But that does not interest us. If we know what would make the sentence true, that is enough. And, at present, we know this much, that such and such condition would have to obtain for the sentence to be true. In this sense we already know the truth condition of a future-tense sentence. Though we do not know whether or not the government will set up the nuclear plant, we already know the condition that would make the corresponding sentence true. And if we know this much, we can claim to know the meaning of that sentence, provided the theory of truth satisfies other conditions.

Next Dummett takes up the case of subjunctive conditional sentences. This type of sentence is not effectively decidable. An example of a subjunctive conditional would be : 'If the vase were to fall, it would break'. The reason why we tend to think of this sentence as effectively decidable is that we equate the truth of this sentence with the truth of another corresponding sentence which is not an overtly subjunctive conditional, like the sentence 'The vase is fragile'. And then, on the assumption of bivalence, we conclude that the subjunctive conditional must be either true or false. We explain the truth of the sentence 'The vase is fragile' with reference to the truth of the corresponding subjunctive conditional. Dummett thinks that this whole move rests on a realist assumption that each sentence is determinately either true or false.

I do not want to enter into the debate of realism versus anti-realism in contemporary philosophy of language, for this deserves to be a subject matter of a separate project. Nor do I want to discuss the issue of bivalence. But, unlike Dummett, I think that the case of a subjunctive conditional is not undecidable in the sense of the term 'truth condition' that I have explained earlier. By 'undecidable' I mean there exists no effective procedure for determining their truth condition. In fact, Dummett himself mentions two models of explaining the knowledge of the truth condition of a sentence.[30] One is the knowledge or the ability to state the condition and the other is the ability to observe whether or not a sentence is true. It seems to me that Dummett interprets truth condition in the latter way and then shows the futility of truth conditional semantics. But I have interpreted truth condition in the former way and this does not pose any problem (at least in our present cases). I think that Davidson intends to take the term 'truth condition' in this way, which will generate a theory of interpretation for a natural language. The subjunctive conditional 'If the vase were to fall, it would break' is decidable, since we know what condition would have to obtain in order for the sentence to be true. Of course, this requires that we have a theory of truth for the language to which this sentence belongs.

1.5 Davidson's theory of meaning is an interpretative theory – A reply to John Foster

Along with Davidson and Dummett, J. Foster believes that a theory of meaning must suffice for one's mastery or understanding of a language. Foster calls such a theory an "interpretative theory."[31] As I have mentioned earlier, a theory of meaning does not aim at producing a manual for language students. We want to achieve some philosophical insights into the nature of language and meaning. And the nature of language and meaning are best manifest in a speaker's linguistic behaviour. So the idea is that if we have a theory of meaning which can adequately explain a speaker's knowledge of language, such a theory will be able to throw light on the nature of meaning and working of a language. This is why a theory of meaning must be an interpretative theory. i.e., a theory which, if one possesses, will enable her to interpret the sentences of the language to which that theory is applied. I agree with this claim.

Next Foster argues that Davidsonian theory is not interpretative in nature. His reason is as follows. Let us assume that we have a theory Ø which is a theory of truth for a language L. So Ø will imply T-sentences for each and every sentence of L. Consider, for example, that there is a two-place predicate P that stands for 'a part of' in the language L. What would happen if we have a predicate P_1 that is coextensive with P but has a different sense? In a sentence that involves the use of P, we can safely substitute P by P_1 without altering the truth of that sentence. Then it is quite possible to interpret the sentence involving P to mean whatever it would mean if it involved P instead of P_1. In other words, if truth is all that matters, then we cannot distinguish two sentences having different meaning but possessing coextensive predicates. Thus we have importantly different interpretations of a sentence with all of which Ø is consistent. Hence "knowing the facts which Ø states does not suffice for so much as an approximate understanding of a single sentence".[32]

Notice that Foster is not referring to the thesis of indeterminacy when he speaks of "different interpretations" being consistent with Ø. We end up in indeterminacy when we have more than one set of T-sentences which are not compatible with each other, but which fit in the totality of evidence. Foster's alleged "different interpretations" exist *within* a single theory of truth. These "different interpretations" crop up since fixing the truth condition of a sentence does not give its meaning, according to Foster.

Let us analyze Foster's own example. The T-sentence for the expression 'The Earth moves' will be like:

'The Earth moves' is true if, and only if, the earth moves.

And the T-sentence for the expression 'The Earth moves and ... is a part of ...' will be like this:

'The Earth moves and ... is a part of...' is true if, and only if, the earth moves and ... is a part of....

It goes without saying that the two sentences 'The Earth moves' and 'The Earth moves and ... is a part of ...' differ in meaning. The latter contains more than the former. Foster's claim is that a theory of truth is insensitive to this difference. I do not share Foster's opinion. Our aim is to explain what is involved when a sentence means whatever it means. To do this, we cannot use meaning itself. Truth can help us. Our theory Ø implies two different T-sentences for two sentences whose truth conditions are being defined. Since the latter is a compound sentence, knowledge of its truth condition presupposes knowledge of the truth conditions of its components. And the theory Ø provides us with T-sentences for those components as well. Since our theory is sensitive to the holistic structure of the language, the T-sentences specifying truth conditions of all those different components form a consistent system. If any T-sentence puts truth conditions on a sentence in an arbitrary fashion, it will find itself alienated from the rest of the system. This is a self-correcting mechanism.

The fact that the two sentences mentioned above differ in meaning is manifest in their having two different T-sentences. If we substitute a predicate by another which is coextensive with the former but different in meaning, that should put strain on the holistic interconnections held by different sentences within a system. We have to look at other sentences to figure out the meaning of that substitutional predicate. We might have to make certain adjustments in our system. Admittedly, in the case of natural language, this is going to be messy. Nonetheless, in principle, it is possible. Consider the two expressions, 'Socrates' and 'The teacher of Plato'. They are coextensive but differ in meaning (in Fregean "sense"). A theory of truth will contain large numbers of bi-conditional T sentences containing these expressions. And these expressions constitute a holistic network. The fact that they differ in meaning will be manifest in the fact that the moment we try to substitute one by the other, we will have sentences that will be inconsistent with other related T-sentences. We might have to change the inferential connections between the T-sentences. So Foster's apprehension that we might interpret P to mean whatever is meant by P_1 is ill-grounded. Holistic elements in a linguistic structure will prevent us from doing that. Since theory Ø works under holistic constraints, it is interpretative in Foster's sense. If P is substituted by P_1 and this does not affect anything anywhere in the whole linguistic network even if P_1 differs in meaning from P, then, I am afraid, that the claim that P and P_1 have different meaning sounds untenable.

Next Foster explains Davidson's revised thesis and tries to show that even this will not help. In order for the bi-conditional in a T-sentence to be true, and, moreover, if the T-sentence is supposed to give meaning, the sentence used on the right hand side must be a translation of the sentence mentioned on the left hand side. So if one knows a T-sentence and knows that it is implied by a T-theory (theory of truth), it suffices for one's knowledge of language. Also, a theory of truth must satisfy certain formal and empirical constraints— as discussed earlier.

Foster claims that even if one knows the facts theory Ø (theory of truth) states and also knows that it is a truth theory, it does not suffice as a mastery of a language.[33] Foster tries to prove his point by formulating a counter-example. He talks about foreign interpretation. We can formulate a theory of truth for English that is couched in German. This theory will represent a German speaker's knowledge of English. Such a theory will issue T-sentences like '"Snow is white" ist wahr wenn und nur wenn Schnee weiss ist'. Now we can have a similar theory of truth for English couched in French. Foster thinks that both these theories state the same facts. This is ambiguous. Both these theories are theories about English, but they convey different linguistic facts to German and French speakers simply because one is in German and the other is in French. If $Ø_1$ is the reformulation of Ø in French, then they do not necessarily express the same facts. Difference of meta-language is significant when that meta-language happens to be one of the natural languages. Anyway, if a German speaker knows T-sentences as mentioned above and also knows that those T-sentences are issued by a theory of truth for English, she knows all there is to know in order to know English. It is true that the right hand side sentence is a translation of the left hand side sentence. But this is a happy consequence. The German speaker does not need to start already armed with a notion of translation. Such a theory is genuinely interpretative, for directly from her own mother tongue— which also happens to be the language of the theory, she can go on interpreting the object language.

1.6 Davidson's theory of meaning is not at variance with the original Tarskian notion of semantics— A reply to Brian Loar

Like Foster, Brian Loar also thinks that if one knows only the T-sentence 'S is true if, and only if, P', she does not thereby know what S means. And I agree. That person must also know that S is the name of an expression and that the T-sentence is implied by a truth theory which possesses a holistic structure. This is called (TT) principle by Loar.[34] We have discussed this issue earlier. Now Loar thinks that (TT) is meta-linguistic with respect to the object language and "is radically at variance with the original Tarskian position that semantics treats of certain relations between the linguistic and the extra-linguistic...".[35]

I do not share Loar's opinion. While we are developing a theory of meaning, we should be careful about different levels of talk we engage in. When we talk to each other, we use language to refer to something extra-linguistic. Now, in semantics, we study the language itself and its relation to something extra-linguistic. Notice that when we are talking about having a theory of meaning, we are not constructing a theory of meaning for a particular language like English, German, etc. We are trying to give a general form that any theory of meaning should take. So at this meta-level we are theorizing about a theory. No wonder then that the (TT) principle is meta-linguistic. But this does not threaten the Tarskian vision of semantics as a study of the relation between language and something extra-linguistic. We still hold this Tarskian view of semantics. But instead of asking directly what meaning is, we ask ourselves : What form a theory of meaning should take?

Philosophers of language do not aim at specifying the meanings of every expression of a language. They aim at clarifying the notion of meaning and workings of language. This is why we talk of the *form* of a theory of meaning instead of a theory of meaning for a particular language. This is in no way at variance with Tarski's view of semantics. Once we decide the form of a theory of meaning, we can apply that form for giving a theory of meaning for a natural language and that theory of meaning will relate the sentences of that language to something extra-linguistic. There is no conflict between (TT) principle and Tarski. The (TT) principle formed the main project in a bit different way from Tarski, but they are one at bottom.

Loar finds truth conditional semantics

problematic when we interpret "simple signals", like a certain type of hand wave which conveys a meaning to a group of people who are familiar with that kind of gesture. The meaning of a certain gesture means what a corresponding sentence means. And if we try to interpret the meaning of that signal by referring to the truth condition of the relevant sentence, "you get the 'grass is green' problem with a vengeance. No consideration of structure or simplicity could rule out arbitrary true equivalences".[36]

It is true that in a particular community people quite often communicate with each other by using different signals. Whether that non-linguistic communication is dependent on linguistic use is a matter of further discussion. But, for a student of philosophy of language, 'meaning' in the context of verbal communication and knowing a language are the main concerns. A simple smile of a beloved might 'mean' something very important to a lover or observing hundreds of people dying in a war might reveal a new 'meaning' of life to a person. But, I am afraid, these kinds of 'meanings' fall outside the scope of the philosophy of language in the way we are pursuing it here. So, explaining the meaning of bodily signals does not concern my present project.

Loar refers to the 'grass is green' problem. Some people think that if to generate a theory of meaning all we need is to have a theory of truth which will issue T-sentences, then there is no way to rule out the possibility of a T-sentence of the form :

> 'Snow is white' is true if, and only if, grass is green.

With regard to a discussion of Katz's criticism of Davidsonian extensionalism in the second chapter, I will show why this apprehension is not well-grounded. I do not want to repeat all that here. My point is that, if a theory of truth meets all its requirements, having a holistic structure in this case, then it cannot generate such a T-sentence (assume, our object language is English). If it does at all, then it is clear that the language for which a theory of truth is being formulated is not English. And, if it is not English, then there is nothing wrong with the T-sentence, for, in some language that T-sentence might be held true. This is, at least, logically conceivable. Obviously, in that language words like 'snow', 'white', 'grass' and 'green' will have completely different meanings.

I.7 Davidson's theory of meaning is modally projectible — A reply to Kenneth Taylor

Kenneth A. Taylor thinks that truth conditional semantics fails to be a theory of meaning.[37] A theory of meaning must be "modally projectible". Since a theory of meaning explains meaning of each sentence of a language and a language potentially contains an infinite number of sentences, our theory must project meanings of those sentences on the basis of some finite evidence. The theory must be put in a finite form, which, at the same time, will be able to give the meanings of an infinite number of sentences. This is what Taylor means by projective character. And a theory of meaning must be modally projectible means that such a theory "must provide criteria by which to delineate, within the range of possible circumstances, which of those circumstances would, were they to obtain, suffice for the truth of any given sentence of the relevant language".[38] It goes without saying that we quite often use sentences that refer to possible circumstances. And, if a theory of meaning is to be a theory of interpretation, it must be able to interpret those sentences. So I agree with Taylor's modal projectibility requirement (remember, Dummett raises a similar point with reference to undecidable statements).

But why does Taylor think that Davidson's theory fails to be modally projectible? The answer is: Davidson's theory leads to indeterminacy of interpretation. Taylor's main premise seems to me is that once we accept indeterminacy, there is no way we can determine which particular circumstance (out of a set of possible circumstances) would obtain if the sentence were true.[39] Though the principle of charity might minimize the amount of indeterminacy, it is not ruled out altogether. And, as long as indeterminacy is there, the theory ceases to be modally projectible.

Taylor's argument involves a misinterpretation of the indeterminacy thesis. Indeterminacy of interpretation does not suggest that it is impossible to interpret sentences, whether factual or modal. Nor does it mean that there is nothing to interpret. What it means is that we can come up with more than one set of interpretations for the same set of sentences based on available evidence. A theory of meaning, which accepts indeterminacy, can very well provide criteria for determining the relevant possible circumstances that would make a sentence true. The interesting point is that we will have different sets of criteria and, as a consequence, we will end up having different circumstances which would make the same sentence true or false. But there is no contradiction here. Because now we have two different theories of interpretation having different criteria for determining relevant possible circumstances. So the truth of a sentence turns out to be relative to a theory of interpretation within whose framework we are working. Whether this picture is a valid one is an issue worth considering (I will discuss this issue in the fourth chapter). So, indeterminacy does not suggest a denial of modal projectibility, it only means that there can be more than one way of modal projectibility for the same language— each of which is valid in the face of objective evidence. It is not the case that we can never determine which particular circumstance would obtain if the sentence was true. What happens in indeterminacy is that it is possible to pick up more than one mutually incompatible set of circumstances that would obtain if the sentence were true.

Taylor thinks that if we rest our theory of meaning on truth, then we cannot distinguish between two predicates 'smite' and 'white' where 'x is smite' is defined as 'x is white and grass is green'.[40] For 'smite' and 'white' are coextensive but they do differ in meaning.

Notice that the knowledge of the predicate 'smite' presupposes the knowledge of the two sentences 'x is white' and 'grass is green' and also the knowledge of the truth functional connective 'and'. We have said earlier that a theory of truth shows how the truth of a complex expression rests on the truth of simpler parts. So the truth of 'x is smite', depends on the truth of 'x is white' and 'grass is green'. We have also said that just knowing a T-sentence is not enough to know the meaning. She must know that the T-sentence is implied by a theory of truth that satisfies all the formal and empirical constraints. Now, if one knows the T-sentences like 'x is white', 'x is green' and 'x is smite', she can clearly make a distinction between two predicates like 'white' and 'smite', provided she knows that these T-sentences are implied by a truth theory. If she cannot distinguish those two predicates given all other factors, then that would put pressure on the holistic nature of language. If a person knows the truth condition of 'x is smite' but cannot distinguish 'smite' from 'white', she is being inconsistent in using these two predicates which holism will not allow her to do. So a theory of truth can distinguish these two predicates if it meets all the requirements.

1.8 On the plausibility of the Davidsonian project

What has bothered many people is Davidson's attempt to bridge the gap between a semantic theory for formal languages and formal semantics for natural languages. Davidson's theory, according to his own admission, is descriptive. It aims at describing the logical form of the sentences by giving a theory of truth for the sentences which constitute a language.

Two kinds of questions can be asked about the Davidsonian programme: i) Do the natural languages have the kind of systematic logical form which it must have in order to be captured by a truth-theory? and

ii) Even if a truth conditional semantics succeeds in describing the logical structure of the natural language, does it not at best give us a mere paraphrase, rather than interpretations of the expressions of that language?

Regarding the former question, I think that the very attempt to develop a theory of meaning presupposes that natural language serves certain shared purposes and that it has an identifiable structure suited to serve such purpose. When I call this a 'presupposition', I do not mean it as a dogmatic assertion but a common ground on the basis of which we can start theorizing, an experience that is shared by speakers in their pre-theoretic lives. The shared experience I am referring to is the successful linguistic communication between the speakers of a linguistic community. It is only by accepting this phenomenon that we can ask ourselves : What is it the knowledge of which enables me to communicate with other people, to know what their utterances mean, etc.? If there were no systematic pattern in what the speakers say to each other, if everything was random, that would make our linguistic communication impossible. Successful communication would be a matter of chance, and not a matter of regularity, which is furthest from the truth (at least in the majority of the cases). So, even if the fact that there is a logical structure in a natural language is a presupposition, it is a presupposition which we can rely on.

With regard to the second question, I have

been trying to convince the reader that if we put enough constraints on a truth theory then that would enable one, if she knows the truth theory, to interpret the expressions of the object language. Remember the objections of Foster, Loar and others, who claim that truth conditional semantics gives rise to irrelevant and bizarre T-sentences. I have tried to show that a theory satisfying the formal and empirical constraints can block the possibility of such bizarre T-sentences. Notice that the constraints I am talking about are constraints not of the object language, but of the meta-language, i.e., the language of the theory. So, even if, ultimately, we are concerned with interpreting the object language, our first step is to make the theory strong enough— which would result in interpreting the expressions of the object language. So our focus is on the form and content of a theory, since we must have a theory which will avoid generating the bizarre T-sentences. This is the point Howard G. Callaway mentions when he says that "it is not the syntactic language itself which calls for interpretation but rather discourse conducted in the syntactically specified language."[41]

So now we have two levels of language, one is the object language and the other is the meta-language. We can also talk of two kinds of theories, theory expressed in the object language and that expressed in the meta-language. The object language expresses a theory in the sense that it exhibits the belief-system of the native. In order for a semantic theory to be interpretative in nature, there should be a match between the theory of the meta-language and the theory of the object language. One way of doing this is by showing the pattern of inference holding among the sentences of the object language. This, in its turn, will ensure that such a theory is interpretative in nature. This will also block the possibility of the bizarre T-sentences. If our theory of T-sentences can show that a given T-sentence relates two or more than two sentences (of the object language) on the basis of the evidence about the pattern of inference among those sentences, that would block the possibility of the above–mentioned bizarre T-sentences, for there lacks any inferential relation between the sentences 'That is snow' and 'That is grass' given the interpretation of the words 'snow' and 'grass' in ordinary English. It is not that first we have the knowledge of the inferential pattern of the sentences of the object language and then, accordingly, we select the T-sentences. This would be question begging, for if we do not know how to interpret the sentences, we cannot determine their inferential relation either. Both interpretation and exhibition of inferential pattern will go hand in hand. If the theory takes the inferential pattern into account, it can not generate those bizarre T-sentences.

Notice that I have been putting more and more constraints on the theory of truth to generate a theory of meaning. Let me explain the rationale behind this strategy. My approach (which is Davidsonian in spirit) might be called an indirect approach to meaning. I am not trying to *define* or *analyze* meaning. It is perhaps trivially true that a theory of meaning is about meaning. But since I have been defending Davidson's thesis that a theory of truth can generate a theory of meaning, my aim is to show that a theory of truth can explain the phenomenon for which we invoke meaning. That phenomenon is one's knowledge or understanding of a language. So it is rather misleading to say that a theory of truth gives or defines meaning. Davidson's claim is that if one knows the theory of truth, then one is able to understand the language for which the truth theory is given. And, since part of one's understanding a language consists in understanding the meanings of the expressions of that language, a theory of truth can shed some light on the concept of meaning. This explains why I have been trying to put enough constraints on a theory of truth, since, by doing that, I can show that a theory of truth suffices for one's understanding of a language.

In this chapter I have explained Davidson's version of a theory of meaning and I have tried to defend it in the face of some criticisms. Many of the criticisms arise out of misinterpreting Davidson's program. Some points raised by certain critics can be accommodated within a truth conditional semantics. Of course, I am not under the illusion that all problems toward giving a theory of meaning à la Davidson have been solved. The problems are multiplied especially since the subject matter of our investigation is natural language that often seems to escape rigorous regimentation.

As I have said earlier, our aim is not to improve natural language but to understand it. So there is no point in lamenting over the fact that natural languages lack precision. We have to take this somewhat messy character of a natural language for granted. In spite of its messy character, there is a considerable portion of natural language that is amenable to a formal theory of truth. How far such a formal theory of truth can be extended to other parts of language— for example— belief sentences, adverbial sentences, etc.— is a matter of further discussion. Philosophers, including Davidson himself, have worked toward that aim. Still, much more needs to be done to prove convincingly that a theory of meaning can be given by applying a formal theory of truth to a natural language. Davidson's main contribution, it seems to me, lies in making us aware of how a theory of truth can generate a theory of meaning. Some critics have tried to minimize the importance of this insight by calling it a platitude. Even if it is a platitude, it is a platitude that cannot be ignored. And Davidson has shown how we can gain important philosophical insights into the nature of meaning and language in general by working on the basis of this so-called 'platitude'. Hence, contrary to some people's belief, Davidson's program is not in ruins; rather, it is a valuable contribution to the study of philosophy of language.

I have defended Davidson's attempt to explain meaning in terms of truth. Truth is the product of the relation of a sentence to what it describes. Defending this distal theory requires embracing an extensional approach to meaning in a natural language. On extensionalism, we do not explain "meaning" either in terms of mental ideas or Fregean "sense". Here we explain "meaning" in terms of the relation between the sentence and the external objects or events which the sentence describes.

In the next chapter I will discuss what extensionalism is and why it is better to approach linguistic meaning from an extensional viewpoint.

NOTES

[1] W. V. Quine describes this process in detail in *The Roots of Reference*, La Salle, Illinois: Open Court, 1973.
[2] Tarski, Alfred., "The Semantic Conception of Truth" in *Semantics and the Philosophy of Language*, Ed. by Leonard Linsky, Urbana:, The University of Illinois Press, 1952, p. 13.
[3] Ibid p.16.
[4] Ibid, p. 19.
[5] Ibid, p. 20.
[6] Ibid, p. 24.
[7] Ibid, p. 25.
[8] Davidson, D. *Inquiries into Truth and Interpretation*, Oxford, Clarendon Press, 1986, p. 21.
[9] Ibid, p.24.
[10] Ibid, p. 29.
[11] Ibid, p. 34.
[12] Ibid, p.56.
[13] Ibid , p. 59.
[14] Ibid , p. 125.
[15] Ibid , p. 135.
[16] Davidson, D. "The Structure and Content of Truth", *The Journal of Philosophy*, Vol. 87, 1990, p. 293.
[17] Ibid, p. 294.
[18] Dummett, M.A.E., "What is a Theory of Meaning?" in *Mind and Language,* Ed. by Samuel Guttenplan, Oxford, Clarendon Press, 1975, p. 99.
[19] Ibid, p. 102.
[20] Recently Dummett admitted that he was wrong in thinking that Davidson's theory is a modest theory. See his *The Logical Basis of Metaphysics*, Cambridge, Mass., Harvard University Press,1991, p.110.

[21] Evnine, Simon, *Donald Davidson*, Stanford, Stanford University Press, 1991, p. 133
[22] Dummett, M. A. E., "What is a Theory of Meaning?", p. 105.
[23] Ibid., p. 106.
[24] Davidson, D., *Inquiries into Truth and Interpretation*, p.20.
[25] Ibid p. 114.
[26] Dummett, M. A. E., "What is a Theory of Meaning? (II)" in *Truth and Meaning,* Ed. by Gareth Evans and John Mcdowell, Oxford, Clarendon Press, 1976, p. 74.
[27] Ibid p. 74.
[28] Ibid, p. 81.
[29] Ibid, p. 88.
[30] Ibid, p. 98.
[31] Foster, J. A., "Meaning and Truth Theory" in *Truth and Meaning*, Ed. by Gareth Evans and John Mcdowell, p. 2.
[32] Ibid p. 13.
[33] Ibid, p. 19.
[34] Loar, Brian, "Two Theories of Meaning" in *Truth and Meaning,* Ed. by Gareth Evans and John Mcdowell, p. 143.
[35] Ibid, p. 144.
[36] Ibid, p. 144.
[37] Taylor, Kenneth, A, "Davidson's Theory of Meaning", *Philosophical Studies,* Vol. 48, 1985, p. 92.
[38] Ibid, p. 93
[39] Ibid, p. 97.
[40] Ibid, p. 98.
[41] Callaway, Howard G., "Semantic Competence and Truth Conditional Semantics", *Erkenntnis* 28, 1988, p. 13.

CHAPTER 2
EXTENSIONALISM

This chapter discusses the issue of extensionalism. First I delineate the use of the term 'meaning' with which I am concerned in the present work. Then I will explain Frege's attempt to explain semantics in terms of two notions that he introduces: i) Sense and ii) Reference. I will explain and defend the Quine-Davidson polemic against Fregean attempt to generate a theory of meaning out of a theory of 'sense'. My defense of truth conditional semantics leads me to embrace extensional approach toward a theory of meaning, but I qualify my extensionalism by denying any reductionist approach.

Then I will take on the critics of extensionalism. I will start with Noam Chomsky. Although the Quine-Chomsky debate is quite old, I will discuss it because some of the contemporary critics of extensional semantics seem to take Chomsky's criticism of Quine for granted. In my discussion on Chomsky, I will show that Chomsky's dissatisfaction with the Quinean model of language arises, to a large extent, from a misinterpretation of Quine's writings. The three points which I will specifically deal with are: i) there is nothing wrong in using 'language' and 'theory' interchangeably in the present context of a theory of meaning which I am defending; ii) extensional semantics is not at variance— but rather compatible with— what Chomsky calls "creativity" of human knowledge of language; and iii) the alleged inconsistency between Quine-I and Quine-II appears due to Chomsky's misinterpretation of Quine's model of language learning.

While arguing against Jerrold Katz, I will show that my version of extensionalism does not espouse any reductionist attempt to go from meaning (sense) to reference. I am only opposing Fregean 'sense' because of its irrelevance to a theory of meaning. I am not opposing the existence of the knowledge of the underlying grammatical structure internalized by the speaker as such, but I do deny their explanatory role for developing a theory of meaning. Katz criticizes Davidsonian extensionalism, for it generates bizarre T-sentences of the form "'Snow is white' is true if, and only if, grass is green". I will argue that if the theory of T-sentences is holistic in nature, then we can block the possibility of such bizarre

T-sentences. Katz gives us a revised version of intensionalism, which, I will show, suffers from its own problems.

I accept Charles Taylor's observation that i) language brings things out in the "public space", ii) language involves "different ways of disclosure", and, iii) language constitutes some essentially human feelings. And I will argue that none of these observations go against the claims of extensional semantics. The extensional approach toward a theory of meaning does not reject what Taylor calls "expressive dimension" of language. I will show that if we do not start taking an extensional approach while interpreting a language, we get trapped in a vicious circle.

2.1 Why an Extensional Theory of Meaning?

To know a language is to know the meanings of the expressions of that language. But what is it to know the meaning of an expression? We can give an answer to this question only if we know what meaning is.

We use the term 'meaning' in very many different contexts, for example :

(a) Her smiling face means she is happy.
(b) I cannot find any meaning in my life.
(c) 'Tisch' in German means table.

In these three statements, the term 'meaning' occurs in three different senses (though one might find some connection among them). `Meaning' is sometimes used as an attribute which a string of sounds or letters (it depends on whether we are talking of spoken or written language) is said to possess or fails to do so. But 'meaning' is also sometimes used as a verb where something means something else. In any case, meaning is normally explained in terms of a relation that holds between at least two members. As one interested in the philosophy of language, I am primarily concerned with linguistic meaning exhibited in (c). It is true, of course, that 'meaning' of (a) and (b) also gives rise to important philosophical problems.

'Meaning', in one of its most fundamental senses, is inextricably related to language. It is the possession of meaning that determines which strings of sounds constitute expressions of a language and which do not. Since there is more than one language, when we talk of meaning we should qualify it by saying 'meaning in such and such language'. For it is often the case that the same utterance might have different meanings in different languages or a meaningful expression in one language might turn out meaningless in another language.

This does not mean that we will have different theories of meaning for different languages. It is undeniable that meaning is what it is, in so far as it is understood and expressed by native speakers of respective languages. And, as theorists of meaning, our aim is to make sense of the fact of understanding or knowing the meaning of an expression that any speaker of any language exhibits. Every native speaker claims to know the meanings of various expressions of her own language and uses them accordingly. But what is that the knowledge of which enables a speaker to know the meanings of those expressions? Philosophy of language tries to answer this question by producing a theory of this practical ability of a speaker, i.e., the ability to understand and communicate the meanings of the expressions of her language.

So at present we are concerned with meaning as it is associated with different expressions of a language. Any language consists of different kinds of expressions, for example, indicative, imperative, exclamatory, etc. Any successful theory of meaning must be able to explain, meanings of these varieties of sentences. Let us begin this task with an analysis of the meaning of indicative sentences. I choose indicative sentences as our starting point for two reasons. Firstly, indicative sentences constitute a substantial part of our language. If we can develop a theory of meaning for indicative sentences, we can claim to have succeeded in taking a big step towards our aim. Secondly, it seems to me that meaning of an interrogative or imperative sentence depends on the meaning of the corresponding indicative sentence. So if we succeed in coming up with an analysis of the meaning of indicative sentences, then we can try to derive a theory of the meaning of interrogative and imperative sentences from that of indicative ones.

Also our analysis of meaning will start from the meaning of a sentence and not from the meaning of a word. Our aim is to explain the verbal behavior of a speaker. And the primary unit of that behavior by which a speaker expresses a meaning is nothing less than a sentence. This sentence might be a holophrastic one. Meaning is expressed only through a complete sentence and it is only in the context of a sentence that a word gains its meaning. The meaning of a word consists in what it contributes to the meaning of the sentence where it occurs. This does not require that we have to learn the meaning of each sentence in isolation. That would lead to difficulties, since a language consists of infinitely large number of sentences. After learning the meanings of 'Bring the cow', 'Feed the cow' and 'Bring the horse', we do not have to have a separate lesson to learn the meaning of 'Feed the horse'. We know the meanings of words in so far as they contribute to the meanings of sentences containing them and then, by means of combinatorial activity, we come to know the meanings of new sentences. It is true that we can focus on individual word meaning, but that is possible only by abstraction.

This shift of attention from word meaning to sentence meaning is referred to as the second milestone of empiricism by W. V. Quine.[1]

Gottlob Frege realised this and emphasised the primacy of sentential meaning. Another of his major achievements was his discovery of the distinction between sense (meaning) and reference. In the next few paragraphs I will briefly explain Frege's argument for 'sense' as different from 'reference' in order to facilitate my criticism of 'sense' because of its inability to explain meaning. Frege introduces the distinction between sense and reference by analyzing the notion of identity. He asks the question : Is identity a relation between objects or names of objects?[2] His reason for choosing the latter is as follows. Let us take two sentences 'a = a' and 'a = b' where 'a = b' is true. The sentence 'a = a' is valid a priori. But a sentence of the form 'a = b' contains an extension of knowledge which may, in some case, be a valuable scientific discovery. We can think of Frege's example of 'morning star' and 'evening star' here. If identity were a relation between objects, then there would be no difference between 'a = a' and 'a = b', for both 'a' and 'b' refer to the same object. Knowledge of 'a = a' does not necessarily lead to the knowledge of 'a = b'. A person might know the former without knowing the latter. The knowledge of 'a = b' involves a discovery, it constitutes an advancement of knowledge. There is a significant cognitive difference between 'a = a' and 'a = b'. In order to explain this cognitive difference, we have to conclude that identity holds between signs or names of objects and not between objects themselves.

But if both 'a' and 'b' refer to the same object, how can we explain the fact that there is a difference in cognitive values of two sentences 'a = a' and 'a = b'? Here Frege introduces the notion of sense. Though both 'a' and 'b' have the same nominatum, they are presented to us differently, one as 'a' and the other as 'b'. In other words, they have different senses. Frege defines sense as "in which is contained the manner and context of presentation."[3] The same sense can be represented by different expressions within a language or in different languages.

Frege identifies the sense of a declarative sentence with what he calls a 'proposition'.[4] Elsewhere[5] Frege defines thought as the sense of a particular type of sentence, viz., declarative ones. So for Frege 'proposition', 'thought' and 'sense' are closely related.

Frege claims to prove that the proposition or thought of a sentence is to be identified with the sense a sentence expresses and not with its nominatum. Frege's proof works by alluding to the cognitive difference between two sentences when in one of them a word is substituted by another word having the same nominatum but different sense. Frege equates the nominatum of a sentence with its truth-value.

First, Frege denies that thought can be equated with reference to external objects. Then he goes on to deny that thought can be identified with ideas. By 'ideas' he means features of the imagination, sensation, feeling, etc. Here Frege's main reason seems to arise out of the objectivity and communicability of thought. Ideas are typically subjective and unsharable. But thought exists independently of its bearer. If thoughts were entirely dependent on a subject, then, as Frege said, there would be no "the Pythogorean theorem" but only "my Pythagorean theorem" and "her Pythagorean theorem."[6]

Unlike ideas, thoughts are something that we share and can possess at the same time. The very existence of a common science and pursuit of a common truth relies on the public shareability of thought.

Frege concludes that "the result seems to be thoughts are neither things of the outer world nor ideas."[7] Frege had to accept a third realm which is neither mental nor material. Thoughts are there in that realm whether we know them or not. We come to recognize some thoughts as true, but we do not make them true. Thoughts are timelessly true.

I do not think that we can have a viable theory of meaning based on Fregean notion of sense. The way Frege defines sense exhibits the legacy of intensional semantics in his theory. By 'intensional semantics' I mean a semantics that tries to explain meaning by taking refuge in intensional notions like 'sense' or 'proposition'. I accept Quine's arguments against intensional semantics. In the following paragraphs I will explain Quine's reasons (with some of which Davidson has explicitly expressed his sympathy) for rejecting intensionalism in a theory of meaning.

First, the seeming innocence of notions like sense or proposition is deceptive. If we go on analyzing these concepts and situate them in our linguistic behavior, we can see how notoriously difficult it is to comprehend these notions. Perhaps the most common method of knowing the meaning of an expression is to look at the dictionary. The dictionary gives us the pair of expressions that are said to have the same meaning. The dictionary does not determine meaning. It merely reports which expressions can be used *salva veritate* by the native speakers of the language. We might think of a grammarian as the one who determines the meaning of a sentence by determining which particular sequence of phonemes will be considered meaningful and by giving a syntax of forming a large number of meaningful sentences out of a finite stock of words. So the grammarian's task seems to be that of determining which sequences in a language can be considered to have a meaning. It seems to me that the grammarian's task comes conceptually prior to that of a lexicographer. Talking of having the same meaning presupposes that expressions do have meaning. And it is the task of the grammarian to determine which sequence of phonemes will have meaning.

Now how does the grammarian set out in this task when she is faced with a new language? She will listen to many sentences uttered by the native speakers of that language. Since it is possible to construct a great many sentences out of a limited number of meaningful units, the grammarian has to break down the long sentences into smaller units. But the problem is that the grammarian will come to hear two long utterances that have very similar acoustic make-ups. How does he know whether these two have the same meaning or not? Here the notion of a phoneme might help. Two highly similar sounds will be considered as the same phoneme, if, by putting one instead of another in the same utterance, the meaning of that utterance does not change. This might help the grammarian to choose the particular phonemes. But one can see immediately that this notion of a phoneme requires an understanding of the meaning of the expressions of the language for which we are trying to set up a grammar, i.e., trying to determine the meaningful segments of that language.

The point is that it is true that the utterances of the speakers of the language have meaning long before the grammarian has started setting up a grammar for the language. The grammarian only reproduces the structure of that language in formal terms. And it is notoriously difficult to explain how the grammarian does start accomplishing her task without involving a prior notion of meaning of that language.[8] This same problem will arise if the grammarian rests her explanation on the notion of a morpheme.

How can we explain the task of a lexicographer? It can occur within the same language or in between two or more languages. Let us first deal with the sameness of meaning within a language. We can say that two expressions have the same meaning if they are interchangeable *salva veritate*, without changing truth-values of the sentences where they occur. There are two problems with this. First, interchangeability *salva veritate* is a weak criterion of determining synonymy. Obviously "'Bachelor' has eight letters" cannot be re-written as "'unmarried male' has eight letters", even though 'bachelor' and 'unmarried male' are considered synonymous. Secondly, if we define synonymy in terms of truth, then, according to Davidson's distal theory, sentences are tied directly to external objects or events. If so, then we are talking within a theory of reference and not about Frege's 'sense' which was disengaged from reference.

If we try to define synonymy in terms of analyticity by saying that synonymous expressions are analytically true, then the problem is that analyticity involves meaning. For we think of analytic truth as a truth of language, how we use certain expressions. This is why if we deny an analytic sentence, we get involved in self-contradiction.

The situation is no better if we consider synonymy between two languages. How is a lexicographer going to determine which expression of her language is synonymous with which expression of the foreign language? This picture is similar to that of a field linguist engaged in a radical translation of a foreign language into the linguist's language as conceived by Quine (I will discuss this later in detail). If we define synonymy in terms of 'uttering under the same condition' where by 'same condition' we mean the same external object or event, then again we seem to conflate sense with reference about which Frege warned us.

If, for a moment, we concede that Quine's reasons for showing the inconsistency in these notions are wrong, this won't get us anywhere. We want a theory of meaning to explain what it is for a sentence to mean what it means when uttered by a speaker. It is no help to say that to mean is to express a sense or proposition. What is involved in expressing a sense or proposition? A description of the speaker's psychological mechanism won't do, for as we have seen earlier, Frege denies sense to be equated with mental idea. Frege defines 'sense' as the "mode of presentation". So two expressions have two different 'senses' means that the two expressions are present to the speaker in two different ways. This is true, perhaps trivially. The fact that two expressions with different meanings are present to a speaker in two different ways does not explain what it is that we know with reference to which we can see the difference in meaning in these two expressions.

Moreover, we want to explain meaning. Frege introduces sense to explain meaning. It is important to notice the way Frege defines sense. Sense is not to be identified with mental ideas or image. Now, if to know the meaning of an expression is to know its sense, how can we know what sense is being expressed when a speaker utters a sentence? Obviously we cannot directly look at the speaker's inner mental realm for two reasons. First, we are not telepathic beings, otherwise language would be redundant. Second, even if we could know what was going on in the speaker's mind (whatever that is), it does not help, because sense is not to be identified with one's mental idea or image. If we try to determine the sense by looking at the external world, then we seem to conflate sense with reference.

The problem is that we cannot know what sense a speaker expresses by her utterance unless we know what the utterance means. And Frege probably would say that we cannot know what an utterance means unless we know what sense is being expressed. So there is a circle here. Explaining meaning without introducing sense will result in breaking this circle. Davidson introduces truth conditional semantics to break this circle, which I have defended in the second chapter.

A theory of meaning for language L is supposed to give meaning of any sentence s of L such that 's means that p'. Since we want to explain meaning, we need something to put in place of 'means' in 's means that p' which will do the same job as 'means' does. If we put 'sense' there, due to the reasons mentioned earlier, we are not better off in so far as our theory of meaning is concerned. The moral is that introducing Fregean sense does not help. It only fosters "the illusion of explanation"[9], according to Quine. It does not give us the knowledge that we want from a theory of meaning in a non-circular manner.

Quine's second point is that our knowledge of meaning must be based on behavioral dispositions. A disposition, for Quine, is a physical trait that includes linguistic trait as well. The feature that makes a physical trait dispositional in nature is its implicative causal mechanism. Let us take the example of solubility in water in order to explain the dispositional character. 'Sugar is soluble in water' means that if we put sugar in water it will dissolve. So the phenomenon of solubility in water can be explained in terms of what happens with the structure of particles in water. And we can single out this solubility in water only by its behavioral symptoms.

Similarly, when Quine talks of verbal disposition, it is a physical trait in the sense that it consists in emitting certain utterances. And we can determine each verbal disposition on the basis of the overt verbal speech. Language is a mode of social communication. Inter-subjectivity is not only a feature of, but constitutive of, language. So the study of language is the study of human behavior, of how people interact with each other using the medium of language. And verbal dispositions, of which speakers can be aware of while communicating by language, must play a prominent role in explaining what goes on in linguistic communication and, consequently, what goes on in understanding the meaning of a sentence. Any linguistic communication presupposes an awareness on the part of the speakers as to what sentences a speaker will assent to, given that the speaker has already assented to some sentence s. If we find that the speaker does not assent to certain sentences which she should, given her assent to sentence s, this would make us rethink our interpretation of what the speaker meant when she uttered s. And since it is the verbal disposition which speakers can be mutually aware of while communicating by means of language, any theory that attempts to explain one's understanding of the meaning of a language must rest on verbal dispositions. And this excludes the employment of "sense" and other kindred notions, for they seem to play no role in linguistic communication. If we insist on using the notion of sense but somehow rest it on verbal dispositions, this only shows our philosophical lavishness in entertaining reified notions, and that, too, without any purpose.

Thirdly, the fact that meaning is grounded on verbal disposition can be shown by looking at the ways we learn a language.[10] The initial method, for Quine, is ostension. A child is exposed to an environment where she learns to associate holophrastic sentences to non-verbal stimuli. The child learns this from the elders under publicly recognizable circumstances. Sentences learned this way are called "observation sentences" by Quine. Examples of observation sentences are 'This is red', 'It is raining', etc. Truth-values of these sentences depend on the circumstances obtaining at the time of utterance of those sentences. Also, learning these sentences depends on inter-subjectively observable situations. This means that both the child and the elder must share the same circumstance. The child must utter 'This is red' in front of a red object and the elder must be able to see both the child and the red object in order to reinforce or correct, if necessary, the child's learning. This inter-subjective observability is important for language learning at this primitive level, since this is what enables a child to learn when to assent to an observation sentence.

The next stage in learning is what Quine calls "analogic synthesis". At this stage the child learns new sentences composed of parts which have occurred in other sentences which were learned by ostension. The child learns this by comparing the ways those parts have occurred in previously learnt sentences. The basic idea behind analogic synthesis is that most sentences a person learns are built of parts of other sentences which the person has already learned. The child carries its knowledge of observation sentences to theoretical (non-observational) contexts. First, the child learns observation sentences in well-understood ways. Then the child carries this knowledge to a theoretical context by establishing a linkage between the observational and the non-observational part. This the child does by comparing the roles the words play in observation sentences with the newly faced theoretical contexts. A simple example might help to clarify this point. Consider the case where the child knows the meaning of the two sentences ‘Bring the cow’ and ‘Feed the horse’. Now, by analogic synthesis, the child will be able to learn the sentence ‘Feed the cow’ though she has not been exposed to learn this sentence ostensively.

Admittedly, this whole procedure is much more complex. And Quine explains this with necessary detail in his *The Roots of Reference*. I am at present concerned with explaining one’s knowing the meaning of a sentence, or, to put it broadly, one’s knowledge of a language, thereby showing the logical connection between different notions involved. Experimental findings of language learning mechanism can perhaps be used to verify our reconstruction. But my approach is speculative— to have a better philosophical understanding of the phenomenon of meaning. So even if Quine’s description of language learning is an idealized account, this is not a vice, but it might rather help us to isolate the factual questions which bear on our purpose.

Frege introduced the notion of sense in order to explain the objectivity and communicability of meaning. I agree with Frege’s emphasis on the objectivity of meaning. I think that any theory of linguistic meaning must explain how speakers can communicate the meanings of their utterances without any residue. Frege talks about conveying the same information wherein the sense of an expression is expressed. Frege might argue that since truth/falsity are primarily related to indicative sentences, when we talk of information we mean the cognitive significance expressed by that sentence. But, as we shall see later, the cognitive significance of a sentence is closely connected with the cognitive significance of other séntences. Change in one sometimes necessitates change in others. And if we start talking of the closely interrelated fabric of sentences, we will end up discovering the possibility of alternative systems of sentences that describe the same phenomenon, but are incompatible with each other. In such a situation it is not clear what role Frege's sense might play. Perhaps what Frege calls sense becomes diffused over a number of sentences within a system and perhaps alternative senses arise out of an alternative fabric of sentences.

My opposition to Fregean 'sense' does not arise solely from a dream of minimalist ontology. My concern is with having a philosophically cogent theory of meaning for a natural language. Language is inter-subjectively available social behavior. Everything concerning meaning must, ultimately, be related to this shared behavior. Though Frege was aware of this commonality, his theory of meaning fails to do justice to it. His misunderstanding arises from a faulty notion of unanalyzed and determinate meaning. I am not going as far as to claim that meaning is identical with neurophysiological process. My claim is simply this : Since language is an inter-subjective social phenomenon, any theory of meaning must be ultimately explicable solely in terms of observable behaviour of a speaker. Part of that observable behavior consists in using expressions in appropriate contexts. And appropriate contexts have to be determined with reference to the knowledge of the native speaker. But there is no circularity here. I do not claim that when a child comes to know a language, she takes lessons of a theory of meaning for that language. A theory of meaning is an explicit philosophical representation of one's mastery of language or, as Davidson puts it, a theory of meaning suffices for one's knowledge of language. And the only evidence available— against which we can check our theory— is the observable behaviour of a speaker. If our theory of meaning for English issues a T-sentence like "'Snow is white' is true if, and only if, grass is green", then we see that there is something wrong with our theory, for if we look at the way native speakers of English use the sentence 'Snow is white' we find that they do not use 'Snow is white' under the condition of grass being green. So the consequence of a theory of meaning must be supported by the actual use of the native speakers.

Similarly, when a child learns a language, it is irrelevant, if not misleading, to find out what 'sense' a speaker attaches to her utterances. If I want to teach the child the meaning of the word 'table', Fregean intensionalism requires me to teach the child the sense expressed by the word 'table'. But how do I do that? If sense is different from mental ideas and referred objects as well, as Frege holds, then the only way I can communicate the sense to the child is if the child and I have some direct insight into the 'third realm' of sense. But if the process of language learning, as I have described earlier following Quine, is true even in its broad outlines, then it seems that to learn the meaning of the word 'table' the child does not— and need not have— a direct insight into that third realm. We can represent the child's knowledge by formulating a relevant T-sentence and then putting that T-sentence in a broader perspective of other related T-sentences, as I have shown in the first chapter. Even sentences containing evaluative terms can be explained without taking refuge in sense. Take the sentence, for example, 'P is good'. Notice that our theory of meaning is not prescribing the meaning of the sentence, it is only reporting, in a systematic manner, a speaker's mastery of a language. So it is not our worry to define goodness, so that we can use the word 'good' appropriately. As a semanticist, my task is to represent the speaker's knowledge of the word 'good' in my theory of meaning. And this can be done by forming a T-sentence of the form " 'P is good' is true if, and only if, P is good" and by accommodating this T-sentence within the theory of meaning that satisfies all formal and empirical constraints mentioned before. One might argue that when we observe a speaker's verbal behaviour, we also observe the speaker expressing sense and while a child learns a sentence we teach the child to attach appropriate sense to the sentence. Recall that Frege defines sense as "the mode of presentation" of the object (reference). So, to observe the speaker expressing the sense, is to observe the speaker expressing "the mode of presentation." This "mode of presentation" cannot be explained in terms of the speaker's mental ideas, according to Frege, for then meaning would turn out to be subjective. I suggest that this "mode of presentation" can be adequately explained in terms of truth conditional semantics. Knowledge of "the mode of presentation" of the word 'table', for example, consists in knowing what sentences does the speaker assert about table, what characteristics does the speaker ascribe to table, etc. In other words, if we can list the sentences the speaker asserts (potentially) about a table, we can claim to describe the 'mode of presentation' of the word 'table' whenever the speaker utters 'This is a table'. We can achieve this goal by ascribing a bunch of T-sentences to the speaker. That group of T-sentences will constitute a coherent network which the speaker can enlarge through her language learning.

I expressed scepticism about the notion of sense in its capacity to explain meaning. Notice, I am only opposing sense the way Frege thought about it, as an explanatory device for meaning. There might be other forms of intensionalism that I am not considering here. But can we have a cogent theory of meaning without talking about Fregean sense or proposition? My answer is 'yes'. The Quine-Davidson program is an attempt in that direction. Let me call the view of meaning that I am trying to support an extensional view in order to contrast it with the Fregean tradition.

As I have briefly mentioned earlier, according to Frege, there are two significant aspects of the semantic contribution of a sentence: i) What the sentence says (sense), and, ii) What the sentence is about (reference). The former relates the sentence to the mind of someone who understands it and the latter relates the sentence to its truth-value. So, if we want to have a theory of the working of a language, following Frege, we will have a two-tier theory. Firstly, we will have a theory that will explain the speaker's understanding of a sentence; it will give an account of what it is that a speaker knows when she knows what the sentence says, i.e., its cognitive significance. Secondly, we will have a theory that will specify the truth condition of the sentence. It will give an account of what it is for a sentence to be true.

So, according to this account, a theory of meaning consists of two components: i) a theory of understanding of the sentences of the language, and

ii) a theory of truth condition of those sentences. Following E. Lepore and B. Loewer, we might call these theories "Dual-Aspect Theories of Meaning" (DAT).[11] In contrast to this, the theory that I am trying to explain and defend employs a single notion for both understanding what the sentence says and also what the sentence is about. I will call this theory the "Single Aspect Theory of Meaning" (SAT). SAT claims to explain the relation between the speaker and her understanding of the sentence and the relation between the sentence and the world as well by advocating that a theory of meaning should take the form of a theory of truth for the sentences of the object language. My strategy is to show that SAT, in the form of truth conditional semantics, is able to give an adequate account of what it is to understand the cognitive significance of a sentence. If I succeed in this, then SAT can claim to be a valid theory of meaning for a language.

Consider three friends, Tom, Dick, and Larry. Tom and Dick understand German while Larry does not. Tom utters "Es regnet". Since Dick knows German, he understands that it is raining. But Larry does not know what Tom is talking about. Probably Larry knows that Tom makes an assertion and that Tom's assertion is true. Still, Larry does not know how to interpret 'Es regnet'. Previously I have said that a theory of meaning for a language L should be such that if one possesses such a theory, that would enable her to interpret the sentences of L. So the question in the present example is : What more Larry should know in order to be able to interpret Tom's utterance, i.e., to be able to say that Tom means that it is raining? A plausible answer is that if Larry knew that 'Es regnet' is true if, and only if, it is raining, he would have the same belief as his German-knowing friend Dick has. In other words, if Larry is armed with a theory of truth condition for German, he would be able to interpret the German sentences exactly the way Dick does.

So a theory of truth for a language can serve as a theory of understanding of that language. It gives an account of what one understands when one understands a sentence. It gives an account of one's knowledge of what a sentence says; it explains one's understanding of the cognitive significance of the sentence. Needless to say, since this theory of truth condition specifies the truth condition of the sentence, it gives an account of what the sentence is about; it explains the relation between a sentence and its reference as well. So now we have a SAT which performs both the tasks of a theory of meaning which DAT proposed. SAT is able to give an adequate account of the two components of DAT. Therefore, the criticism that SAT is incomplete and hence fails to be a theory of interpretation does not withstand our scrutiny DAT remains invincible.

It is not my aim to perform a logical trimming of natural language so as to be able to substitute natural language by an ideal language that will follow the pattern of formal logic and mathematics. Echoing Davidson's words, it is not my aim to improve natural language, but to understand it. So all the ambiguities and imprecisions of a natural language do not bother me. I am not worried about how to remove this chaotic character of natural language. I take these as facts given to us as speakers. My understanding of a theory of meaning consists in a systematic presentation of the principles on the basis of which a speaker could know and use her language in communication. And one of those principles is what I have called 'extensionalism'. Although the theory I am explaining and defending is basically an empiricist theory of linguistic meaning, I do not use the word 'empiricism', since I want to distinguish the views that I have expressed here from those of John Locke who explained meaning in terms of ideas and who is also an empiricist. I have used the word 'extensionalism' in order to differentiate the observations which I have supported here from those which explain meaning by introducing intensional notions like 'sense', 'proposition', etc. Earlier in the first chapter I have defended the theory of meaning in the form of a theory of truth. Since truth is a part of extension, I have called my approach toward a theory of meaning 'extensionalism'. My 'extensionalism' is more heuristic than substantive. This is why I make a distinction between the thesis that language (meaning) is extensional and the thesis that language can be approached extensionally and I expressed my sympathy for the latter thesis, not for the former. My extensionalism is a strategy of dividing and conquering.

By supporting extensionalism I do not want to commit myself to physicalism. I do not mean to suggest that physical science is the paradigm of knowledge and we should trim our ordinary language to serve the purpose of physical science. I am not studying language to make it fit for physical science, so that whatever does not come under the domain of physical science can be dispensed with.

While arguing against the introduction of intensional entities to explain linguistic meaning, I have emphasized the verbal behavior of the speakers of a language. This should not be understood as an advocacy of behaviorism as a general theory of mind and its activities. My claim is a modest one. I want to explain meaning as we find it in the behaviour of language–users. And, for the reasons explained above, we have to rest our theory on overt verbal behaviour of the speakers. Mastery of a language is determined by one's verbal reaction to non-verbal stimuli and to other people's verbal behaviour. We learn language on the basis of shared stimulation and by being corrected or reinforced by others. We have no other choice.

In traditional philosophy, a theory of meaning was supposed to explain notions like significance (possessing meaning), synonymy (having same meaning), etc. We have seen earlier that it is impossible to define them in a non question-begging manner. Nonetheless, we cannot ignore these linguistic phenomena. They cannot remain unexplained and I think that they can be explained with reference to the external world. So an extensionalist views a language as consisting of a triad relation: speaker-sentence-world (that which is described by the sentence). In order to understand a speaker's utterance, we do not have to fall back on the sense a speaker attaches to it or on the proposition expressed by it.

From what I have said so far, it is clear that a theory of meaning (where 'meaning' is in Frege's "sense") loses all its importance and a theory of reference comes to the focus. The main concepts of a theory of reference are truth and extension. Notice that all these referential notions are inseparably connected with the external world. And the external world is the only shared area to which both the speaker and the hearer can refer. Thus significance and synonymy can be explained by notions like truth and extension that describe a certain relation between an expression and the corresponding world. The external world becomes the alpha and the omega in our theory of language.

I am not reducing meaning to reference. I deny only the capacity of Fregean sense to generate a theory of meaning. Instead of asking the question 'What is meaning?', we ask ourselves 'How can we develop a theory of meaning?' First, we set out to explain what a theory of meaning is supposed to do. Then the problem is actually to generate a theory that will do the assigned job in a non-circular way. Davidson proposes that this goal can be achieved by giving the theory of meaning the form of a theory of truth. This is an extremely clever move, for here we get what we want from a theory of meaning without taking refuge in Fregean sense.

2.2 An argument against Gricean theory of meaning

Let me make a brief comment on another approach to the problem of explaining meaning. This approach started with Paul Grice and is developed further by John Searle and others. I just want to show why the Gricean attempt to explain meaning is heading in a wrong direction. In one of his most famous articles Grice[12] starts his analysis by distinguishing 'natural' sense and 'non-natural' sense of the word 'meaning' (Grice, of course, admits that this distinction is not a watertight one). As an example of natural use of 'meaning' he mentions 'Those spots mean measles' and as an example of non-natural use of the word 'meaning' he mentions 'Those three rings on the bell (of the bus) mean that the bus is full' and 'That remark "Smith couldn't get on without his trouble and strife" meant that Smith found his wife indispensable.' Since, at present, I am concerned with linguistic meaning, natural meaning falls outside the scope of our present discussion, though it might be an interesting project to study whether there can be an explanation of meaning which is applicable to both natural and non-natural use of meaning.

After examining some options Grice comes to the conclusion that "A meant something by x" is (roughly) equivalent to "A intended the utterance of x to produce some effect in an audience by means of the recognition of this intention."[13] So to know the meaning of x is to know the intention (intention with 't' and not 's') of the utterer of x which the utterer wanted her interlocutor to recognise. Knowledge of the meaning of an utterance is explained by knowledge of the intention of the speaker. But one might ask: How can we explain one's knowledge of the intention of her interlocutor? Grice does not mean to suggest that there is some telepathic way of knowing somebody's motives and intentions. We can grasp one's intentions by what she has uttered and sometimes by her extra–linguistic behaviour. To know what one intends, we have to know what one means by her utterances. And, according to Grice, to know what one means by her utterances, we have to know the speaker's intention. It seems we are trapped in a circularity here. Davidson noticed this circularity and tried to get rid of this by turning to truth.

The same question can be asked when a child acquires a language. If to know the meaning is to recognise the intention of the utterer, how can a child know the meaning of the utterance of an adult speaker since the child does not already possess the knowledge of the language? If this 'intention' is used to denote a psychological phenomenon uniquely owned by a speaker, then, as Frege has shown earlier, it destroys the objectivity and communicability of meaning. If, on the other hand, 'intention' is meant to suggest something like Fregean 'sense', then, as I have shown earlier, this is philosophically futile.

With regard to the charge of being intensionalist, Grice comments that "one should at least *start* by giving oneself a free hand to make use of any intensional notions...."[14] But if what I said earlier is true, then we do not and need not make use of intensional notions to start explaining meaning. Grice even hinted at the possibility of reconciliation of intensional and extensional notions in a theory of language. He talks of the possibility of "deriving"[15] intensional concepts from extensional ones. Davidson's program might be interpreted as working toward that aim. Davidson frequently uses intentional notions like 'belief', 'attitude', etc., working within an extensionalist framework where the notion of truth is the central one. But, as we have seen earlier in our discussion of Davidson, in that project the intensional notions by, themselves, hardly play any significant role. They lose their explanatory power.

This emphasis on sensory evidence of external world can be viewed as a legacy of traditional empiricism. It is not unlikely, therefore, that many philosophers have objected to this kind of empiricist theory of language. In the garb of rationalism of one form or other, these philosophers have tried to reach the conclusion that an extensional view is either false or inadequate to explain many aspects of a natural language. In the following pages, I will discuss three such attempts and I will show that none of them has succeeded in their aim.

2.2.1 Is extensional semantics too narrow to explain the totality of speaker's verbal behaviour? —A reply to Noam Chomsky

Noam Chomsky[16] is one of the best known

critics of this extensionalist approach to language. Chomsky has tried to revive the Cartesian doctrine of innate ideas, though from a different perspective. According to Chomsky, the aim of linguistics is to discover some universal and essential properties of human language. Chomsky believes that there are some phonological, syntactic and semantic units which are 'universal' in the sense that they can be identified when they occur in any particular language and they can be defined independent of their occurrences in any language. This leads to the view that in spite of so many differences between different languages in their 'surface structures', all languages have close affinity insofar as their 'deep structures' are concerned. All languages apply the same formation rules in the construction of grammatical sentences.

It is important to remember what exactly Chomsky means by 'surface structure' and 'deep structure'. Many people were misled into believing that it is the 'deep structure' which is important and revealing and worth studying, whereas 'surface structure' is superficial and unimportant. Due to this confusion Chomsky gave up the old terminology and introduced the expression 'initial phrase–markers' instead of 'deep structure'. If we apply the rules of grammar to the words in a sentence, we can analyze the words into some absract phrases that are called 'phrase– markers' in technical literature. The sentence

'John is the man who murdered Dorothy' can be analyzed into 'John' as a proper name, 'is' as the verb phrase, 'the' as determiner, 'man' as noun, etc. Thus for any well-formed sentence, we can transform it into a structure consisting of phrase–markers. The transformational component of the syntax of a language transforms, step by step, the initial phrase markers into a phonologically represented sentence with its phrase–markers. It is the latter complex that is called 'surface structure' and the initial phrase–markers are called 'deep structure'. Here 'deep structure' refers to the abstract level of initial phrase markers that regulate the organization of grammar.

But what is the cause of this affinity of different languages? Chomsky thinks that the only proper explanation is to assume that human beings are born with certain dispositions that he calls 'language faculty'. This language faculty is not gained from experience. Had it been gained from experience, it would not be able to explain the universal feature of the 'deep structure' of a language.

The innateness of this language faculty can be shown to be valid by a consideration of the language-learning process of a baby. Chomsky believes that children are not born with a predisposition to learn any particular language. All children— irrespective of their race and parentage— are born with the same potentiality of learning languages. The children become native speakers of that language which they hear being spoken in their own community in which they spend their early years.

But how does a child manage to use and interpret new words and new sentences, which he has never used or heard before? Only by assuming that children are born with a knowledge of some principles of universal grammar and predisposition to apply those principles for creating and interpreting unheard sentences, we can give a satisfactory explanation of the creative capacity of children. Hence, for Chomsky, knowledge of language in the sense of universal grammar is present among babies, though babies do not have the explicit knowledge of the "surface structure" of the language.

Chomsky accuses Quine of conflating "language" and 'theory'. Quine uses these two terms interchangeably, but according to Chomsky "one could not doubt that a person's language and his 'theory' are distinct systems."[17] Chomsky is not happy with Quine's definition of language as a 'complex of dispositions to verbal behavior' as well as his (Quine's) description of how a language is learned. Quine's theory, according to Chomsky, would render language "not only finite but also extremely small",[18] which is contrary to facts. Quine's acceptance of 'quality-space' is interpreted by Chomsky as acknowledging an innate mechanism resulting in a radical departure from traditional empiricism. I would like to make certain comments on each of these observations made by Chomsky.

I do not find anything wrong in using the two terms 'theory' and 'language' interchangeably. A theory is a set of sentences conjoined to explain a certain phenomenon. The phenomenon that we are presently concerned with is meaning of a natural language. As I said earlier, an extensionalist views language consisting of a relation of speaker-sentence-world. It is true that not all sentences are directly hooked onto the world. But those sentences rest on or have inferential connections with sentences that are directly related to reality. Any recondite report must be amenable to reports of sensory experience of the external world. For this is the only point which we can share with each other. A philosophical discussion of meaning is a meta-level study. We are talking about language and not about the world which is being described by language. But, since on an extensional view, there is no direct route to meaning other than via the external world, our theory of meaning and theory of world converge. This close relation of meaning to ontology is an important consequence of extensionalism. Language gives the semantic value to the sentences. Theory gives truth conditions to them. Some sentences gain truth conditions directly with reference to the world while truth-values of some other sentences rest on the former. The meaning of a sentence is determined by its referential function and the referential apparatus is inalienably related to the external world. Semantics, viewed in this way, gives rise to a theory of the world.

However, this does not mean that any two speakers of the same language cannot disagree in their respective beliefs. Disagreement at the level of sentences directly hooked on to reality is highly unlikely. Disagreement at this level implies speakers are using same words in different ways. If I say 'Snow is white' and you say 'Snow is green', then it is clear we are not using the words 'snow' or 'green' in the same way. Disagreement at the higher level may be due to disagreement about inferential relation that sentences hold among each other. Thus we can very well avoid this absurd consequence of which Chomsky is apprehensive, maintaining the interchangeability of 'theory' and 'language' at the same time.

Chomsky attributes to Quine the view that language is a finite network of related sentences. According to Chomsky, Quine's enumeration of language acquisition leads to this absurd conclusion about the finitude of linguistic network. It seems to me Chomsky's arguments involve a misinterpretation of Quine.

I accept (along with Quine) what Chomsky refers to as 'creativity' of human language. Whether this 'creativity' is a distinguishing feature of human language which sub-human communication system lacks is a different question. It is an undeniable fact that human beings can create and use new sentences as a result of combinatorial activity. Any philosophical conception of meaning must take this feature into account. Extensionalism does this quite ably.

As stated earlier, the first method of language acquisition is through conditioning of an utterance with non-verbal stimuli. If this were the only possible mechanism, Chomsky's conclusion would have some justification. But we accept another stage where we can build new sentence from already learned ones by 'analogic synthesis'. We can use this new sentence under appropriate condition without being taught to do so. An example can make this point explicit. After learning the sentence 'Bring the cow', 'Feed the horse' one can use the sentence 'Feed the cow' in appropriate conditions, though one has not learned the sentence through proper conditioning. Even if at this stage we can create new sentences by permutation and combination, these sentences remain directly hooked on to non-verbal stimuli.

At a next stage our linguistic capability becomes free from this restraint. We come to be able to relate sentences to other sentences without actually looking at the non-verbal stimuli. This is where the inferential links between different sentences come to be recognized. If I know that Jones teaches only one language in the school where he works and also if I know that Tom, a student of Jones, takes English lessons from Jones, I can infer the knowledge that Jones is an English teacher. I have not been conditioned by non-verbal stimuli to know the meaning of the sentence 'Jones is an English teacher', but I can grasp its meaning and use it properly after constructing it out of the sentences which I have learned so far by other means. We can go on constructing sentences about abstract objects in a similar fashion. This kind of combinatorial inferential activity gives rise to a set of sentences interconnected with each other.

But notice that all of these sentences which are related to each other in a logical scaffolding rest on some others which are directly conditioned by non-verbal stimuli. This stage of stimulus-response can be regarded as a vantage point from which a philosopher of meaning can take a look at her theory and makes necessary changes. So, in this sense, we can talk of a theory of meaning as a set of sentences some of which are linked to non-verbal stimuli, while others are related to each other by some logical connections. Since we are concerned with a theory of meaning for a natural language, sentences of our theory happen to be the sentences that we learn and use in the course of our linguistic behavior. The way I have described the extensional view of language does not lead to the absurd result which Chomsky thought it would. This extensionalism is perfectly compatible with Chomskian 'creativity' of human language.

Quine's acceptance of "quality space", according to Chomsky, implies accepting the doctrine of innate ideas, which is a departure from empiricism. Earlier we have seen that a child starts learning a language by verbally responding to stimuli, which is corrected or reinforced by society. This is true whatever the cause of the child's ability of verbal response might be. Now Quine thinks that we must ascribe to the child the ability to grasp more resemblance between some stimuli than others. If we do not assume this, then the child, after being reinforced a dozen times to say 'red' in front of red things, would no more be encouraged to make the same response to a thirteenth red thing than to a blue thing. So Quine credits the child with a 'pre-linguistic quality space', where certain stimuli are placed nearer to each other than others. If the child, after being reinforced to say 'red' in the presence of crimson things and being discouraged to say 'red' in the presence of yellow things, says 'red' in front of pink things and not in front of orange things, then we might assume that, in the 'quality space' of the child, crimson and pink stimuli are placed closer to each other than crimson and orange. I am not concerned with the question whether Chomsky's doctrine of innate ideas is really a revival of the old Cartesian theory, nor do I want to enter into the debate whether Chomsky's evidence substantiates his claim that the theory of innate ideas is to be accepted. My present aim is to show how much of the notion of innate ideas can be accommodated within an extensional view of language. If talking of innate ideas is necessary to explain linguistic behavior and if extensionalism cannot tolerate innate ideas, then extensionalism— as a theory of linguistic meaning falls short of its task.

Chomsky's 'innateness hypothesis' is the view that the human mind is born with a faculty of language. This faculty helps in analyzing the linguistic data giving rise to a schematism which we call grammar. Each grammar is a theory of a language that specifies the formal and semantic properties of the sentences of that language. The language faculty, being appropriately stimulated by a linguistic environment, will construct a grammar. The person knows the language generated by such a grammar.

The evidence Chomsky gives in support of the innateness hypothesis can be divided into three groups:[19] i) those related to language learning, ii) those related to human language versus non-human communication system, and iii) those related to the universal features of generative grammar. The first kind of evidence centres round the fact that when a child hears other people talking, those speech acts are fragmentary and full of imperfections. But the child learns the language in a relatively short span of time and performs this remarkable feat by constructing (subconsciously) a theory of that language. Moreover, different individuals in the same speech community learn essentially the same language. From these observations Chomsky concludes that language learning is explicable only on the assumption that these individuals use certain principles which guide their "internalization" of the grammar.

An extensionalist will agree with Chomsky concerning the general conditions of language learning. If Chomsky's problem is to explain a child's language acquisition, then it is the same problem I am dealing with. But our approaches are different. Chomsky's approach is empirical and inductive. My approach is philosophical. Like Chomsky, I am trying to give an answer to the question that what it is the knowledge of which enables one to know a language. So the fact that a child internalizes the grammar of the language she is learning does not by itself imply any innateness hypothesis, for one can also claim that one's language acquisition can be explained by ascribing a truth conditional semantics to her, which does not seem to require postulating the innateness hypothesis.

The second group of evidence relates to the

unique feature of human language, viz., language is a discrete system and that it goes beyond the mechanism of stimulus control. Knowing a language, for Chomsky, is mastering a set of rules that will determine an infinite number of sentences, each having a fixed meaning.

Once again, an extensionalist agrees with these two features of human language. I have shown earlier that an extensional semantics can adequately explain the "creativity" of human language and its ability to go beyond the mechanism of stimulus control. *Solely* on the basis of these evidences we cannot justify the innateness hypothesis.

The third source for innateness hypothesis is what Chomsky calls "linguistic universals". Chomsky believes that there are some features of generative grammar which are universal and it is the knowledge of these universals which constitutes the child's innate language acquisition. Chomsky classifies these linguistic universals into three groups: i) Substantive universals, ii) Formal universals, and iii) Universal constraints. If we can find out that there are certain syntactic categories like noun, verb, etc.—which can be found in the syntactic representation of any language—those syntactic categories will be the examples of substantive universals. Formal universals are rules of grammar that might be present in the grammar of any language. Transformation rule might be an example of formal universal. If certain kind of grammatical rule is never found in human languages, then one can say that there are universal constraints on that form of grammatical rule. For example, in English, we cannot remove 'old men' from the conjunction 'old men and women' so as to derive 'old men are loved by my father and women' from 'my father loves old men and women'. What this shows is that there is a constraint over moving words in or out of a conjunction. If this were true of all languages, this would be an example of a universal constraint.

I am not objecting to the existence of linguistic universals, as such. Whether such linguistic universals do really exist is a matter of further empirical investigation into the grammar of different languages. What I am claiming is that we cannot rest our semantics on such linguistic universals. If we try to come up with a theory of interpretation for L, we cannot use our knowledge of the expressions of the language, their compositional structure. A theory of interpretation is supposed to explain this very knowledge, knowledge that enables one to know the meanings of the expressions of the language. If our theory of interpretation wants to further our understanding of meaning, we cannot use our knowledge of the language to develop a theory of interpretation for that language. This does not imply that linguistic universals do not exist. This suggests that linguistic universals do not have an explanatory role in a theory of interpretation.

The expression 'innate ideas' is open to different interpretations. We have seen earlier that Frege rejects equating sense or meaning with mental ideas. It goes against inter-subjectivity of linguistic behavior and fails to explain the mechanism of language acquisition. It might happen to be the case that we often entertain an idea or image whenever we utter a sentence, but a philosophical conception of meaning cannot rest itself on such ideas or images. So innate ideas— in the sense of a speaker's innate mental construction allegedly attached to every uttered sentence cannot be entertained in an extensional framework.

But if by 'innate ideas' we mean an innate capability or predilection to learn a language, I do not have any reservations. In fact, if we do not assume any prior capacity on the speaker's part, we cannot explain habit-formation, conditioning, etc. And, I imagine that this innate aptitude can be explained by principles of genetics. But language acquisition, where this innate ability becomes manifest, is entirely dependent on inter-subjectively available cues. When we learn a language, we have to make sense of whatever goes on in that procedure on the basis of, behavioural data. And since to learn a language is to know the meanings of the expressions in that language, any attempt to explicate the notion of meaning must fall back on these behavioral data. Thus if we interpret Quine's 'quality space' as an innate ability to partake in combinatorial activity of language, this does not pose any threat to the form of extensionalism which I have been explaining.

Chomsky writes "It is, first of all, not at all obvious that the potential concepts of ordinary language are characterizable in terms of simple physical dimensions....".[20] Chomsky claims that Quine is being dogmatic in differentiating learning by direct conditioning from analogic synthesis on qualitative grounds. And this dogmatic thinking is based on the assumption that learning by direct conditioning is somehow "simpler" than learning by analogic synthesis. Chomsky doubts this assumption. Chomsky argues that even the most elementary notion of 'physical object'— which plays an important role in learning by direct conditioning— is quite complex. It involves some notion of function, some notion of human agency, some Gestalt property, all of which are rather complex notions.

Firstly, it is not true to suggest that Quine's conception of learning by conditioning excludes the notions of functions, Gestalt properties, etc. In *The Roots of Reference,* while explaining the learning of the observation sentence 'Mama', Quine writes that "... it is apparently a sort of similarity that we are innately predisposed to appreciate. The well-known Gestalt effect is basic .[21] Quine also talks about "A similar readiness to recognize the persistence of an object in uniform motion, despite temporal interruption."[22] From these passages it is clear that Chomsky's allegation that Quine's theory of learning by direct conditioning is simplistic does not hold.

Secondly, when Chomsky argues that even the most 'elementary' notion of 'physical object', which plays an import role in learning by direct conditioning, is rather a complex notion, he is conflating the task of semantics with that of ontology. The thesis that the notion of 'physical object' is more complex than what we normally think of in our everyday life is evident in none other than Quine's own works on ontology. It is Quine's theory of ontological relativity that has compelled us to critically analyze our notion of 'physical object' (whether ontological relativity is a valid doctrine or not is a different issue). But in semantics we do not call our notion of 'physical object' into question. Here we call into question our knowledge of the meaning of a sentence. It is true that since in a distal theory a sentence is directly related to an external object or event, a theory of external object or event remains at the background. Since a distal theory exploits a theory of truth to generate a theory of meaning and, since, in a theory of truth, a sentence is tied to its truth condition, a theory of external object is presupposed here. So the notion of a 'physical object' is not the subject matter of semantics. In a way the notion of 'physical object' can be regarded as a simple given in semantics, especially the kind of semantics I am defending here, because the external objects give the interpreter and the interpretee a common ground on the basis of which interpretation can start. These external objects are the inter-subjective cues. So, in this qualified manner, we can say that in a semantics for natural language we can take the notion of 'physical object' as simple or given.

Another important point that has been overlooked by Chomsky is that for Quine "the denizens of quality space are expressly stimulations".[23] Quine posits 'quality space' the way a physicist posits elementary particles. So the motive behind positing 'quality space' is not indulging in mentalistic talk, rather giving an explanatory model. Since the subject matter of this explanatory model is natural language and since language is primarily a social phenomenon, where we learn a language by social emulation, the explanatory model must rest on the behavior of the speakers.

It is true that when we are engaged in a philosophical theory of meaning, we are not talking of philosophy of meaning of particular natural languages like English, German, etc. We are talking of a general notion of meaning that is present in all languages. But this does not mean that we are talking of specific meanings that exist independent of all languages. We cannot talk of meaning without talking of verbal behaviour of the speakers. For this is where meaning starts to play its role in the inter-subjective communicatory process. This is why my extensionalism requires of a theory of meaning to be inalienably related to a speaker's behaviour, which, in its turn, is related to the external world. Innate properties of mind do not determine the nature of experience, but they help us in permuting and combining different experiences to give expression to new complex experiences.

Chomsky goes to say that when we learn a language, we are not learning sentences or piling up a "behavioral repertoire", but "we somehow develop certain principles (unconscious, of course) that determine the form and meaning of indefinitely many sentences."[24] Notice that Chomsky now uses the expression 'develop certain principles.' So these principles are not innate, but we acquire them. How do we acquire them? Chomsky does not specify it other than by saying 'somehow.' I think that we acquire them through constant behavioural interaction with the world. When we learn a language, we do learn sentences and we also learn how to make new sentences out of old ones. And the principles by which we come to create new sentences gain their substance from behavioral data. We acquire them as we proceed through different stages of language acquisition.

Let me mention one more point where, I think, Chomsky fails to appreciate the extensional viewpoint. Chomsky distinguishes Quine's views in 1960 from Quine's views expressed in the late 1960s and thinks that later Quine abandons his own earlier suggestions.[25] It is not my aim to go into details in interpreting Quine's writings. Nonetheless, I do not think that the two sets of doctrines ascribed to earlier Quine and later Quine are inconsistent. And the reason is as follows.

We have seen earlier that extensionalism views language as a set of sentences where some are directly related to external stimuli while some others are interconnected with each other. Accordingly, I have also touched on the mechanisms of language acquisition. After acknowledging this, if I say that the method of conditioning cannot carry us far in language acquisition, Chomsky thinks I would be contradicting my earlier views. But notice, I have already said that in a language some sentences are related to each other by means of inferential connections. We do not learn these sentences by direct conditioning. We learn some sentences by direct conditioning to external world, and then come to grasp new sentences by analogy. From the very beginning an extensionalist is aware of the limitation of the method of conditioning. But, at the same time, an extensionalist is also aware of the immense potential power of this method, for herein lies our ultimate checkpoint.

When we talked about the mechanism of language acquisition, we already acknowledged the fact that at one level we become free from the restraint of direct conditioning to external stimuli and come to create new sentences. But the higher level sentences are ultimately founded on some basal sentences which we learn by direct conditioning. And the principles by which we create new sentences originate from behavioural pattern which speakers exhibit during their interaction with the world. The ability to extract these principles and to apply them properly may be innate in the sense in which I have described earlier. So, contrary to Chomsky, it seems to me that the observation that direct conditioning is not sufficient to explain language learning is perfectly compatible with the observation that language is a set of sentences related to each other and to external stimuli.

Chomsky attributes three methods of learning sentences to Quine.[26] The first method is the association of sentences with sentences, the second one is association of sentences with stimuli. And the third one is analogic synthesis, where we learn new sentences out of the already known ones by virtue of analogies. Chomsky claims that after acknowledging the first two methods of learning— viz., associating sentences with sentences and associating sentences with non-verbal stimuli— if we accept the third method of analogic synthesis, then that "would be to deprive the notion of "conditioned response" of its strict meaning,"[27] — for the responses and the stimuli need not appear together. So, either we have to give up the, notion of conditioned response if we take it in its strict sense, or, if we take the expression 'conditioned response' in some unspecified sense, then the thesis that language is characterizable by the mechanism of conditioned response becomes vacuously true.

But, as Roger Gibson[28] has ably shown, Quine does not propose *three* methods of learning sentences in his *Word and Object* to which Chomsky is particularly referring. There are two methods: i) Direct conditioning, and ii) Analogic synthesis. Contrary to what Chomsky thinks, analogic synthesis is not the 'third' method, it *is* the method of association of sentences with other sentences that Chomsky mentions as the first method while discussing Quine's views. After explaining the methods of direct conditioning and analogic synthesis, Quine acknowledges that "speech thus confined would be strikingly like bare reporting of sense data". So he thinks "further inter-verbal associations are required".

But these "further inter-verbal associations" do not constitute a third method; this suggests enlarging the scope of analogic synthesis. When from 'This is my foot', 'This is my hand' and 'My foot hurts' we come to learn another sentence 'My hand hurts', this is an example of 'analogical substitution', where we learn sentences by substitutional transformation of already known sentences. There are other formation rules as well by which we can learn to relate old sentences with the new ones which have been described by Quine in his *The Roots of Reference*. The generic name of all those different ways of relating sentences with one another (in the case of learning new sentences) is 'analogic synthesis'. So all cases of analogic substitution are the cases of analogic synthesis, but not vice versa. In any case, "further inter-verbal associations" do not refer to the 'third' method. It only suggests that there are various modes of association among sentences other than analogical substitution.

Chomsky's misinterpretation of Quine further led him (Chomsky) to suggest that, according to Quine, analogic synthesis is theoretically dispensable. But analogic synthesis is not a 'third' method, it is identical with the first method which Chomsky mentions. If this is true, then analogic synthesis is *not* theoretically dispensable according to Quine. I am afraid Chomsky's differentiation of the 'first' method of the association of sentences from his 'third' method of analogic synthesis (which is also association of sentences) raises some serious doubt about his use of the expression "association of sentences with sentences".

In the above discussion I have tried to show that the alleged inconsistency between Quine-I and Quine-II is due to Chomsky's misinterpretation of Quine. Quine-I's thesis that language can be described as a fabric of sentences learned by direct conditioning and by analogic synthesis is not at variance with Quine-II's thesis that direct conditioning is incapable of carrying us far in language. In fact, from the above discussion, it is clear that Quine-II is contained in Quine-I. The fact that the Quine-II's thesis is compatible with the overall philosophy of language of Quine is evident when Quine says that the recognition that direct conditioning is insufficient to explain language learning is of a piece with his doctrine of indeterminacy of translation.

2.3 Does extensional semantics lead to absurd results? — A reply to Jerrold Katz

Let me pass on to another critic of extensionalism. Jerrold J. Katz has argued against many versions of extensionalism. For my present purpose, I will take a look at Katz's comments on the Quine-Davidson version of extensionalism and I will show how far I can agree with Katz and why.

Katz defends a version of intensionalism that says that the logical form of a sentence and its meaning are the same. So a theory of the one is a theory of the other. Logical laws apply to senses of the sentences; it uncovers the laws of valid inference by stating the regularities in the behavior of the semantic objects. I presume that by 'semantic objects' Katz means the objects which have semantic value— which are the sentences in a language. Semantic theory describes the structure of senses with such detail so as to provide an account of every feature which logic requires for a complete statement of its laws. According to Katz, intensionalists claim that it is only at the level where the sense of a sentence is represented, that we can provide an adequate account of the semantic structure which, in its turn, will provide an adequate account of the concept of a valid argument. Extensionalism, on the other hand, claims that adequate explanations of linguistic structure, that makes laws of logic applicable to them, can be given without information about semantic representation (sense) of sentences.

At the beginning of his paper "Logic and Language : An Examination of Recent Criticisms of Intensionalism,"[29] Katz gives a description of the tussle between extensionalism and intensionalism. From his own description of intensionalism, it is clear that this approach rests on postulating an entity known as 'sense' which we allegedly attach to every meaningful segment of our language. Indeed, he even thinks it quite plausible to identify the sense of a sentence with the proposition expressed by that sentence. And logical laws of inference apply to this sense or proposition.

Earlier I have expressed my reservation about Frege's notion of "sense" to explain meaning. If Katz tries to rehabilitate that notion, then, I am afraid, Katzian intensionalism rests on a very shaky ground for the reasons explained earlier. This attempt to explain meaning by taking refuge in entities like sense or proposition arises from an unanalyzed and uncritical acceptance of a reified notion of meaning. Meaning is not a mental entity with which we are born and then keep on sticking the stamps of meaning in the course of learning a language. Meaning is not something that a sentence carries with it independent of a speaker's use of it. Meaning is whatever we can extract from observing a speaker's verbal behaviour. Meaning is the point of commonality on the basis of which two speakers can communicate. If, as Katz puts it, "Intensionalism holds that there is an independent level of semantic representation"[30], then intensionalism is heading in a wrong direction, because the notion of sentence-independent meaning is a myth whose origin can be traced back to older empiricists.

To know the meaning (at least in the sense in which we are using the term 'meaning' here) is to know the meaning of a sentence. And, to know the meaning of a sentence, is to be able to place it properly within a fabric of other related sentences. This network of inter-connected sentences constitutes a language. Whatever a sentence means or whatever a speaker means by uttering a sentence, this meaning is determined by the contribution the sentence makes to the fabric of related sentences.

Katz says, "The extensionalist position claims that the theory of meaning is reducible to the theory of reference....".[31] We have to be careful about this talk in reductionist terms. I am not claiming that thinking or meaning is nothing but a set of neuro-muscular movements. Nor do I claim that meaning is a set of neuro-muscular movements as well as a set of senses or proposition that we attach to those physiological movements. We should avoid both 'nothing-but' and 'as well as' attitudes. Katzian intensionalism seems to entertain an 'as well as' attitude. By opposing Katz, I am not advocating a 'nothing-but' theory of meaning.

Mastery of a language consists in the ability to use sentences in appropriate situations. Since some sentences are directly conditioned by external stimuli, the 'appropriate situation' is to be determined by observing the state-of-affairs in the external world. But where sentences are not so directly conditioned, rather related to each other in a network, the 'appropriate situation' is to be determined by observing inferential links among the sentences of that network as used by the native speakers of a language. Since even these sentences ultimately rest on the basal sentences whose meaning is determined by external stimuli, a theory of reference gains most importance in an extensional view of language. Hence, in order to explain the mastery of a language, we have to focus our attention on the referential apparatus of that language. And, to know a language is to know the meanings of the expressions of that language. Attempts to have a theory of meaning, as such, is illusory, for there are no such meaning entities.

But, then, how can we explain the mastery of a language that is said to consist in grasping the meanings of the expression of that language? We can do this by having a theory of reference, for to know the meaning of an expression is to be able to use this in appropriate circumstances. So a theory of reference explains everything for which the notion of meaning was invoked, without talking of those fuzzy entities like sense, proposition, etc. Extensionalism takes into account all the linguistic phenomena that the notion of meaning was called for and then tries to explain those phenomena by means of a referential apparatus. It is only in this qualified sense that the theory of meaning is reducible to the theory of reference in an extensional framework.

According to Katz, the central assumption of Quinean extensionalism is that meaning "is somehow suspect as occult or unscientific, and that we are better off not depending on it in philosophical or linguistic inquiry."[32] I think that this statement is phrased in a simplistic manner. As I have shown earlier, sense or proposition lacks any explanatory power. Our aim is to explain the fact of knowing the meaning of an expression. This whole phenomenon of knowing the meaning is situated in the context of a linguistic community where speakers know the meanings of sentences uttered by fellow speakers. Meaning is central to this on-going communicative process. A theory of meaning, in this context, also explains mastery of a language, for to know a language is to know the meanings of the expressions of that language. This is important, especially in view of the fact that we are interested in a philosophically adequate notion of meaning for a natural language. In that case, our theory of meaning must be empirically verifiable. To do that, we have to keep the linguistic behaviour of a speaker constant and assign meaning to the utterances in the way that gives us a coherent picture of the speaker's behavior.

Katz thinks that meaning is a set of rules governing the underlying grammatical structure and these rules are internalized by a speaker while acquiring the knowledge of a language. Here Katz seems to suffer from the same confusion that Chomsky did regarding the notion of innate ideas. As I have argued earlier, an extensionalist is very much willing to accept the knowledge of the underlying grammatical structure internalized by a speaker. As philosophers of language our task is to make that internalized knowledge explicit— explain it with all necessary details. And the only way to achieve this task is to observe overt verbal behavior along with the present stimuli. If we talk of underlying grammatical rules in any significant sense, these rules must be manifest in speech behaviour, for this is where we talk of linguistic meaning in full-blooded sense of the term. Katz talks of statements of meanings as 'hypothetical postulations.' To me, this hypothesis is an expensive one and without any big gain.

Katz objects to Quine's attempt to reduce the problem of meaning to two notions, i) significance, and ii) synonymy. Katz thinks that there are many other concepts that semantics should deal with, for example, ambiguity, contradictoriness, antinomy, etc. I agree with Katz at this point. All these are important semantic concepts which any theory of meaning for a natural language should address. But it seems to me that the concept of significance or having a meaning is logically prior to all other concepts. We cannot talk of ambiguity or contradiction unless we presume that expressions concerned possess significance or meaning. And, once an extensionalist shows that notions like significance or synonymy can be explained without talking about sense or propositions, it is a short step to see that the other semantic concepts that Katz mentions can also be accounted for in a similar fashion.

According to Katz, semantics answers the question 'What is meaning?'. This question is misleading. This kind of phrasing encourages people to think of meaning as a reified entity— neither mental ideas nor material objects— belonging to some twilight zone. For me the question which semantics asks is : 'What is it to know when a speaker knows that a certain expression in her language means something?' If we can produce a picture of the speaker's knowledge that enables her to know the meaning of the expressions of her language, this amounts to a description of one's mastery of language. And this is what a semantics of natural language aims at.

Even if we concentrate just on these two notions— significance and synonymy, Katz finds problems with the way a Quinean extensionalist explains these concepts. An extensionalist defines the notion of significance (of an expression) with reference to the reaction of the nativespeaker. If the sequence of morphemes uttered does not provoke any bizarre reaction on the part of the nativespeaker, the sequence of morphemes can be regarded having significance. Katz thinks, "this explication for 'having a meaning' is question-begging".[33]

I admit that this notion of the bizarreness of the reaction of a native–speaker is not a clear-cut one. It is to be noted here that now we are talking about a radical theory of meaning, where we do not have any previous information about the linguistic community whose language we are trying to interpret, nor can we take any help from the dictionary for there exists no such dictionary at all (Whether we can meaningfully talk of this kind of radical theory is a matter of dispute that I will discuss later in the fourth chapter.) In that case we have to depend entirely on the behaviour (both verbal and non-verbal) of the native speaker.

Katz makes a distinction of 'homogeneous' and 'heterogeneous' reaction of native–speakers. 'Homogeneous' reaction is aimed at just one kind of linguistic malady and 'heterogeneous' reactions may be due to a violation of syntactic rules or conceptual incoherence of word concatenations, etc. I am not questioning this distinction, as such. This difference of 'homogeneous' and 'heterogeneous' reaction, by itself, may be valid. But, at the radical level where we are trying to interpret a native's utterance just by observing her behavioural pattern along with external stimuli, we are not in a position to make that 'homogeneous-heterogeneous' distinction of native speaker's reaction. There is no way we can detect whether native speaker is reacting to syntactic violations or to conceptual incoherence, for we do not have any idea of the conceptual framework of that community. Katz thinks since 'heterogeneous' reaction involves 'semantic commitment,' explaining the concept of significance with reference to bizarreness of reaction of the native– speaker is question-begging. But this 'homogeneous-heterogeneous' distinction does not make any sense at that radical level. And it is only in this radical situation we try to explain significance with reference to a native–speaker's reaction. So an attempt to explain significance with reference to native–speaker's reaction does not beg the question.

In a recent paper[34] Katz renews his attack on extensionalism. While criticizing Quine's claim that any attempt to explain semantic notions like synonymy or analyticity would turn out to be circular, Katz claims that "there is nothing viciously circular in defining concepts in the theory of meaning in terms of other concepts in the theory of meaning...."[35] This non-vicious nature of circularity involved in defining concepts may be true in certain branches, for example, in developing a system of formal language. But the situation is different when we are concerned with natural languages. Our aim is to explain a speaker's mastery of her native language. I have rejected any 'innate ideas' by saying that nobody is born with a mental idea of meaning. So, to explain a speaker's mastery, all we have as our data is speech and other kinds of behaviour of the speaker and appropriate conditions which trigger that behaviour. We have also to explain the creative aspect of the speaker's use of language. Now if we explicate a speaker's mastery with reference to concepts that are circular in nature, we would never be able to explain a speaker's creative power by means of which she can produce infinite number of sentences. To do justice to this creativity, our theory of meaning needs to impose a recursive structure on the language concerned. Extensionalism, as a theory of natural language, takes into account this recursivity of language.

Katz raises his salvo against many other forms of extensionalism including that of Davidson. We have seen earlier that Davidson has all along stressed the point that introducing Fregean sense or meaning will not help us to solve the problems that a theory of meaning faces. According to Davidson, if we want to explain the meaning of the sentence 'Theaetetus flies', a Fregean analysis will run like this: given the meaning of 'Theaetetus' as argument, the meaning of 'flies' generates the meaning of 'Theaetatus flies' as value. But this does not explain the meaning of 'Theaetetus flies', for the explanation itself involves the notion of meaning which it is supposed to explain. We require of a theory of meaning to provide us with an effective method of explaining meaning non-trivially of an arbitrary sentence in a language. It is no explanation to say that the meaning of 'Theaetetus' and the meaning of 'flies' yield the meaning of 'Theaetetus flies'.

Katz accepts the vacuity of this explanation but thinks that this does not necessarily mean that intensionalism, if applied to more complex sentences, will also turn out to be vacuous. But if we have to account for the meanings of sentences compositionally, which Katz himself recognizes, then it is hard to imagine that a theory, which does not work for simple sentences, will work for more complex ones. How can a theory, which cannot explain the meaning of 'Theaetetus flies' in a significant manner, be expected to explain the meaning of 'Theaetetus flies and Theaetetus is afraid of danger?' The applicability of a theory to simple sentences is most important. If our theory succeeds at this basic level, then, by means of certain patterns, our theory can be made to apply to more and more complex structures.

I agree with Katz that we cannot take it for granted that in 'Theaetetus flies' 'Theaetetus' is an argument and 'flies' occupies the place of a function. There is a whole lot of semantic structure that needs to be explained. I have shown earlier that Davidson's theory of meaning à la Tarski's truth theory can show us that underlying semantic structure.

Davidson's central insight is that meaning, truth and states of affairs (described by a sentence) are inalienably related to each other. Giving any two of these ends up in producing the third one. Since our aim is to grasp meaning, let us start with truth and states of affairs. If we have a theory which specifies truth condition of every sentence of a language (relating truth of a sentence to the corresponding state of affair), then this theory gives us everything we want from a theory of meaning. Here Davidson has taken recourse to Tarski's semantic theory of truth. So, instead of saying 's means that p', we will have a theory which will produce a theorem for every sentence s of language L such that 's is true if, and only if, p.' Here 's' is to be substituted by the name or description of the sentence whose meaning we are trying to explain and 'p' is to be substituted by specifying the truth condition of that sentence. If the object-language and meta-language happen to be identical, then 's' and 'p' happen to be the same sentence, only in case of 's' it is used and in case of 'p' it is mentioned. Thus we get a theorem like :

> 'Snow is white' is true if, and only if, snow is white.

But what if our theory entails a theorem like

> 'Snow is white' is true if ,and only if, grass is green?

Katz thinks "that the mere fact that a theory that says that each sentence" like 'snow is white' "is part of the semantic analysis of the other" like 'Grass is green' "is sufficient to establish that the theory is missing something essential to the idea of meaning, namely an adequate account of synonymy."[36]

Katz misses an important point here. So Katz's point is that, if in order to explain meaning all we need is a theory of truth, then we can have a T-sentence of the form '"Snow is white" is true if, and only if, grass is green' where it is obvious enough that the T-sentence does not tell us the meaning of 'Snow is white'. Thus, if a speaker knows the theory of truth, she is not in a position to explain the meaning of the sentences and consequently such a theory of meaning fails to be a theory of interpretation in the sense explained earlier.

I want to raise two points here with regard to Katz. First, I do not think that there is anything wrong with the T-sentence, by itself. For it is, in principle, possible to have a language (different from English) where 'Snow is white' is true under the condition of grass being green, where 'snow' means grass and 'white' means green. Since the meta-language being used here is English, 'snow' in that hypothetical language refers to what wc call 'grass' in English—and similar with 'white'.

Secondly, if we want to come up with a theory

of meaning for English and if we find out that our theory has a T-sentence of the form just mentioned, then it is clear that the theory of meaning does not explain the meaning of 'Snow is white'. Fortunately, we can block the possibility of such bizzare T-sentence by thinking of the theory as having a holistic structure. The above, mentioned T-sentence is related to other T-sentences like ' "This is snow" is true if, and only if, this is snow', '"This is white" is true if, and only if, this is white' and a whole group of other T-sentences containing the words 'snow' and 'white'. Since the same word plays the same semantic role (meaning) in all these different contexts (sentences), given the interpretation of 'snow' and 'white' in those sentences, we cannot have a theorem like '"Snow is white" is true if and only if grass is green'. For then this T-sentence will conflict with other T-sentences containing the words 'snow', 'white', etc. Of course, we can change all those T-sentences as well, but in that case we have altered the English language, and then we are talking of a different language, where, as I have mentioned earlier, there is nothing wrong in having a T-sentence of the form '"Snow is white" is true if, and only if, grass is green'. This T-sentence does not explain the meaning of 'Snow is white' only because we take the object language to be English. This T-sentence sounds bizzare to us, where 'us' refers to the English speakers and given the interpretation of 'snow', 'white', 'grass' and 'green' in English we cannot accept the T-sentence as explaining the meaning of 'Snow is white'.

Katz thinks that 'Snow is white' is true if, and only if, snow is white does not explain anything. He even lays the charge of vacuity against Davidson that Davidson himself laid against Frege. Part of Katz's confusion arises from the fact that, in this example, our object language and meta-language happen to be identical. Is it vacuous to say 'Schnee ist weiss' is true if, and only if, snow is white? It conveys a significant amount of knowledge to an English–speaker who does not know German. Similarly, how would one explain the meaning of 'Snow is white' to a child brought up in English–speaking community, or how one would one come to know that a speaker knows the meaning of 'snow is white'? To a child we have to show the corresponding state of affairs and inform her that 'snow is white' is true if, and only if, she utters that sentence under appropriate condition. To utter 'snow is white' when, in fact, snow is white, is not a tautology, rather it is an important advancement in the mechanism of language acquisition.

Gradually Katz[37] came to realize that the Fregean intensionalism has its problems. He tries to come up with a revised version of intensionalism which he claims to be free from defects plaguing Frege's theory. He summarizes the fundamental tenets of intensionalism as :

i) Sentences have a sense

ii) Senses are compositional

iii) Sense of a sentence determines its logical structure, and

iv) Sense is essential to reference.

Extensionalism, which I have been pursuing, denies the very first premise. Whatever sense or meaning a sentence is supposed to have must be made explicit by its referenial function. A sentential meaning is whatever a speaker uses the sentence to refer to. Consequently, extensionalism rejects the other three premises too.

It has been said earlier that Frege defines sense as a mode of presentation of the referent. Realising the problems arising out of this definition, Katz "characterizes sense as directly as the aspect of sentence structure on which such grammatical properties and relations as meaningfulness, ambiguity, synonymy, antonymy, redundancy, etc. depend".[38] As a result, for Katz, whether proper names have a sense or not "is a matter of which hypothesis best accounts for the facts about their semantic properties and relations."[39] Notice how Katzian intensionalism is becoming more and more liberal toward extensional view-point. As I have argued earlier, grammatical properties like ambiguity, synonymy, etc. logically rest on the notion of meaningfulness or significance. And,

I have also shown that this notion of meaningfulness (better to use the expression 'sentential meaning', for terms with '-ness' smacks of Platonic universals) can very well be explained without invoking any notion of "sense". Even then, if Katz wants to use the term 'sense', that amounts to a dispute over terminology without any philosophical significance.

Katz realizes the problem Frege's theory gives rise to in respect of substitutional inference to opaque contexts, as has been shown by Benson Mates.[40] Katz tries to block this problem by introducing the notion of "hyperopacity."[41] A sentence like (1) 'Gretel realizes that she is an adult human female who never married' does not entail the sentence (2) 'Gretel realizes that she is a spinster.' If we hold on to Frege's principle that we can substitute in an opaque context if the substituted expression is synonymous with the expression substituted for, and since 'spinster' is synonymous with 'adult human female who never married,' we should be able to infer (2) from (1). But (1) might be true while (2) being false at the same time.

Recognizing this loophole, Katz claims that opaque verbs like 'realize,' 'believe' etc. contain elements of hyperopacity. An opaque verb is hyperopaque "when, and only when, the sense of the verb operates to change the sense of the compliment clause in the process of determining the sense of the higher verb phrase."[42] In other words 'realize' is a hyperopaque verb since, when we apply 'realize' to the compliment clause (object of the propositional attitude), the sense expressed by the whole sentence (applying the verb 'realize' and including the compliment clause) is different from the sense expressed by the compliment clause in itself. The sense of 'Gretel is an adult human female who never married' is different from the sense of 'Gretel realizes that she is an adult human female who never married.' Since 'realize' is a hyperopaque verb, it makes this difference. This is why the substitutional inference from (1) to (2) does not hold.

I suspect that this whole move involves circularity. First, Katz finds out that we cannot infer (2) from (1). Why does this substitutional inference fail? Katz replies because 'realize' is a hyperopaque verb. A hyperopaque verb changes the sense of the compliment clause when applied to it. But why does a hyperopaque verb behave in this manner? There are two possible answers : i) By definition it follows that a hyperopaque verb behaves in this manner which is totally an arbitrary definition, or ii) Otherwise we would be able to perform substitutional inference from (1) to (2), which we cannot and in which case, we are trapped in a circularity. Thus I fail to share Katz's optimism about his version of intensionalism.

2.4 Does extensional semantics ignore expressive dimension of language? — A reply to Charles Taylor

Now I would like to discuss another critic who claims to threaten the very assumptions of an extensional theory of meaning. Charles Taylor wants to argue against a family of theories in the sciences of man, and the guiding idea of this family is to study man in the model of natural sciences. And, according to Taylor, theories of this kind either end up in elaborating the obvious, or fail to address the interesting questions or end up spending a long time to show that, after all, they can recapture the insights of ordinary life in their reductive explanatory languages. Naturalism of any sort fails to recognize the notion of a person or self. One way of getting at this feature, according to Taylor, is in terms of the notion of self-interpretation.

Taylor views the extensional view of language as a variety of naturalism where language is used to depict the world. By contrast, in a hermeneutical view (where Taylor's sympathy lies) language also helps to constitute our lives. Part of what we are is constituted by self-interpretation and this self-interpretation can vary according to our linguistic background. So, Taylor concludes, language not only depicts, it helps shape our form of life.

Charles Taylor discovers two important features of an extensional view of language : i) "their stress on representations", and ii) "their assumption of the observer's stance."[43] Language, according to extensionalists, is primarily representative in nature. It describes or depicts the reality to us. Even a request or wish depicts a state of affairs which we are asking to be brought about or which we are wishing to be brought about. Extensionalism gains its substance from observing the behavior (linguistic and other) of the foreign tribe. Extensionalist does not 'participate in' the foreigner's world. Both these assumptions, according to Taylor, can be challenged by another conception of meaning, which he names 'triple-H theory.' This theory has taken its shape in the hands of Herder, Humboldt and Heidegger.[44]

Taylor mentions three important aspects of our speech activity.[45] First, through language we formulate things. We bring them to the focus of our consciousness and we also delineate a particular object from others by constructing proper boundaries. Second, language helps us to come out of solipsism to put things in 'public space' which all speakers can share. Third, language serves a medium through which we express some of our 'characteristically human concerns.' Taylor gives the example of the contrast of anger and indignation which, he thinks, cannot be ascribed to a non-linguistic animal.

From these three aspects of language, three points emerge.[46] If we look at the last two functions, we find that language not only articulates or describe things, it also expresses, it brings things out in a 'public space' which all language users can share. Language helps to establish a 'rapport' among different speakers. Second, all the three functions of language involve 'different ways of disclosure.' Language brings an object to the focus of our consciousness, it brings an object out in 'public space.' Third, language not only describes things, but it constitutes certain phenomena, some essentially human feelings, inter-personal relations, etc.

So far, I do not seem to find any fundamental rift between my extensionalism and Taylor's views on the functions of language. I accept most of Taylor's observations, though I might use a different terminology. Taylor's main point against extensionalism seems to be that it fails to explain the meanings of statements expressing emotions, aspirations, goals, social relations and practices, etc. In order to know the meanings of such statements, we have to participate in the native speaker's daily life, their social relations and practices, etc. Taking an observer's stance and the mere stating of truth conditions would not help in grasping the meanings of the native speaker's sentences.

I agree with Taylor's suggestion. As a

philosopher of natural language, our theory must explain meanings of statements expressing emotions, goals, etc. But how can we participate in native speaker's life that Taylor thinks is necessary? I suggest, it is only by working within an extensional view of language, that we can participate in native speaker's life. First we have to know what 'Gavagai' means in the native speaker's language, what purpose Gavagai serves in the native speaker's life, etc. Only then can we attempt to determine the meaning of a native statement expressing a prayer to God for success in hunting a Gavagai. It is only by employing an extensional view, we can make sense of native speaker's aspirations, goals, emotions, etc. It is true that while working in this way, we have to impose our conceptual framework, to some extent, on the native speaker's way of thinking, but this is unavoidable for there is no vantage point from where we can grasp native speaker's thought structure in its pristine purity. All we can do is to act on the principal of charity and to come up with an interpretation of native speaker's behaviour as coherent as possible. Extensionalism serves as foundation of all of these.

If we deny the role of extensionalism, we would be trapped in a vicious circularity. In order to know native speaker's language, we have to participate in the native speaker's life. In order to participate in the native speaker's life, we have to know the native speaker's language. Extensionalism breaks this circle and shows how, on the basis of minimal interpretation, we can succeed in interpreting the whole of nativespeaker's linguistic behaviour.

I am not denying the expressive dimension of language. But we can make sense of this expressive act only on the basis of extensional theory of language. Unlike Taylor, I do not think that an expressive act can exist without a representative act. To take Taylor's own example, when just in order to establish a rapport with my neighbour in the train I say "Whew, it is hot in here!" it is true that representative act is not the main focus here. But the sentence has its independent representative nature in that condition, and only on the basis this representative nature can we focus our attention on its expressive value. Otherwise, any and every sentence could have established that rapport— which clearly is not the case. Taylor says, to understand native's language, "you have to understand what it would be like to be a participant."[47] He also talks of 'fusion of horizons' among the interpreter and the native. But I do not find any way to make sense of these claims without resting our theory on some form of extensionalism. We have to start as a detached observer and the more we get along with interpreting a native's behaviour, the more we can participate in the native's world and, at one point, we can transcend the representative aspect and grasp the expressive dimension of native's language.

This kind of argument leads to the bipartite division of literal and metaphysical meanings ending up in establishing the primacy of literal meaning. Taylor mentions some contexts (specifically religious ones) where invocative use, and not literal use, sounds primary. He also gives examples of certain cultures where invocative use of language is the primary one. Taylor observes, "The assumption that there is such a thing as the strict and literal meaning of an expression turns out to be ethnocentric assumption."[48] Since at present we are not concerned with the issue of cultural-relativism, I refrain from making further comments on these points.

NOTES

[1] Quine, W. V., "Five Milestones of Empiricism" in his *Theories and Things*, Cambridge, Mass., Harvard University Press, 1981, p. 68.

[2] Frege, G., "On Sense and Nominatun" in *Readings in Philosophical Analysis*, Ed. by H.Feigel and W. Sellars, New York, Appleton-Century-Crofts, 1949, p. 85.

[3] Ibid., p. 86.

[4] Ibid, p. 89.

[5] Frege, G., "The Thought: A Logical Inquiry" in *Philosophical Logic*, Ed. by P. F. Strawson, Oxford, Oxford University Press, 1976, p. 20.

[6] Ibid, p. 28.

[7] Ibid., p. 29.
[8] Quine, W. V., *From A Logical Point of View*, Cambridge, Mass., Harvard University Press, 1980,
p. 52.
[9] Quine, W. V., "Mind and Verbal Dispositions" in *Mind and Language*, Ed. by S. Guttenplan, Oxford, Clarendon Press, 1975, p. 87.
[10] Ibid, p. 88.
[11] Lepore, E. and Loewer, B., "Dual Aspect Semantics" in *New Directions in Semantics*, Ed. by Ernest Lepore, London, Academic Press, 1987, p. 84.
[12] Grice, P., *Studies in the Way of Words,* Cambridge, Mass.: Harvard University Press, 1989, p. 214
[13] Ibid., p. 220.
[14] Ibid.
[15] Ibid., p. 137.
[16] Chomsky, Noam, "Quine's Empirical Assumptions" in *Words and Objections: Essays On the Work of W. V. Quine*, Ed. by Donald Davidson and Jaakko Hintikka, Dordrecht, Holland, D. Reidel, 1969, 53-68.[17] Ibid., p. 53.
[18] Ibid., p. 55.
[19] Chomsky, N., "Recent Contributions to the Theory of Innate Ideas" in *The Philosophy of Language*, Ed. by J. Searle, Oxford, Oxford University Press, pp. 121-129.
[20] Chomsky, N., "Quine's Empirical Assumptions," p. 63.
[21] Quine, W. V., *The Roots of Reference*, La Salle, ILL., Open Court, 1973, p. 54.
[22] Ibid., p.54.
[23] Quine, W. V., "Reply to Chomsky" in *Words and Objections: Essays On the Work of W. V. Quine*, p. 306.
[24] Chomsky, N. "Quine's Empirical Assumptions" in

Words and Objections: Essays On the Work of W. V. Quine ,p. 64.
[25] Chomsky, N., *Reflections on Language*, New York, Pantheon Books, 1975, p. 198.
[26] Chomsky, N., "Knowledge of Language," *The London Times Literary Supplement*, 1968, pp. 523-24.
[27] Ibid., 524.
[28] Gibson, R., *The Philosophy of W. V. Quine*, Tampa, University Presses of Florida, 1982, p.187.
[29] Katz, Jerrold, J. "Logic and Language: An Examination of Recent Criticisms of Intensionalism" in *Language, Mind and Knowledge,* Minnesota Studies in the Philosophy of Science, Vol. VII, Minneapolis, University of Minnesota Press, 1975, p. 39.
[30] Ibid., p. 39.
[31] Ibid., p. 40.
[32] Ibid., p. 43.
[33] Ibid., p. 53.
[34] Katz, Jerrold, J., "The Domino Theory" in *Philosophical Studies*, Vol. 58, 1990, pp. 3-39.
[35] Ibid., p. 5
[36] Katz, Jerrold, J., "Logic and Language: An Examination of Recent Criticisms Intensionalism," p. 69.
[37] Katz, Jerrold, J., "Intenstionalists Ought Not Be Fregeans" in *Truth and Interpretation*, Ed. by Ernest Lepore, Oxford, Basil Blackwell, 1989, pp. 59-91.
[38] Ibid., p. 63.
[39] Ibid., p. 63.
[40] Mates, Benson, "Synonymity" in *Semantics and the Philosophical Language*, Ed. by Linsky, Urbana, University of Illinois Press, pp. 118-125.

[41] Katz, Jerrold J., "Intensionalists ought not to be Fregeans," p. 69
[42] Ibid., p. 69.
[43] Taylor, Charles, *Human Agency and Language*, Cambridge, Cambridge University Press, 1985, p. 255.
[44] I do not want to discuss the theories of these three philosophers in detail, for that would take me beyond the scope of my present purpose. I trust Taylor's interpretation of those philosophers and I will evaluate Taylor's claims accordingly.
[45] Taylor, Charles, *Human Agency and Language*, 1985, p. 257.
[46] Ibid., p. 263.
[47] Ibid., p. 280.
[48] Ibid.

CHAPTER 3
SEMANTIC HOLISM

This chapter is devoted to the issue of semantic holism, i.e., the thesis that the unit of meaning is a sufficiently large group of sentences. I shall start by explaining the arguments given by Quine and Davidson in support of semantic holism. I will distinguish extreme holism from moderate holism and I will justify my sympathy for moderate holism. Then I will discuss and evaluate the arguments put forward by the critics of holism.

I will start with Michael Dummett. I will show that Dummett's molecularism is similar to what I will call 'moderate holism'. Dummett mentions two premises in support of his contention that holism is not a version of a theory of meaning, rather the denial that a theory of meaning is possible. I reject both of these premises and show that if a theory of meaning is a theory of understanding, in the sense explained earlier, then a theory of meaning should possess a holistic structure. I will also show that Dummett's molecularism leads him to contradiction. Dummett is worried about how holism can explain the inclusion of a new sentence in the network. I explain that this inclusion can happen at two levels and I will show that this inclusion only justifies the claim of the holism thesis. I reject both of Dummett's premises that holism makes meaning ineffable and that holism fails in giving an account of our linguistic communication. I argue, on the contrary, that if a theory of meaning is used to explain the speaker's mastery of a language, then we should ascribe a holistic theory of meaning to the speaker.

Hilary Putnam does not oppose holism as such, but he talks of sophisticated mentalism (Chomsky's theory) as a plausible option for a theory of meaning. Then Putnam mentions three requirements that any theory of meaning should satisfy. I will explain those requirements and I will show that a holistic theory of meaning satisfies all those requirements, thereby weakening the plausibility of a mentalistic theory of meaning.

Contrary to what Jerry Fodor thinks, the fact that people can differ in their estimates of the relevance of what Fodor calls 'epistemic liaison' in order to determine the meaning of a sentence does not in any way show the absence of a holistic structure in a theory of meaning. We can make sense of a disagreement among two people only if there is a shared area among them and that shared linguistic knowledge has to be explained by a holistic conception of meaning. Fodor thinks that we need some form of verificationism in order to establish holism, and verificationism, according to Fodor, is wrong. Here I will clarify the issue of verificationism versus extensionalism and then I will argue that extensionalism puts the issue of a theory of meaning in a different perspective which, in my opinion, helps us to formulate the problem clearly; where the problem is to develop a theory of meaning that is adequate to explains one's knowledge of a language.

In opposition to Jerry Fodor and Ernest Lepore, I will give a transcendental argument for the impossibility of a non-compositional language. By explaining their thought experiment with two children speaking two different languages, I will show that if we want to come up with a theory which will enable us to interpret the sentences of those two children, compositionality is a necessary prerequisite. I offer an analysis of what it means to say that T-sentences are law-like and then I argue for the nomological nature of the T-sentences.

I will end this chapter by making some comments on the scope of holism. I will show that neither Quine nor Davidson advocates extreme holism, and, also, the difference between extreme and moderate holism should not be overplayed.

3.1 Quine's arguments for holism

In the previous chapter, I argued that it is preferable to uphold an extensional view of meaning. In the course of that discussion I have shown that some of the claims made by intensionalists can be included in an extensional theory, while some others are misleading.

According to Quine, chronologically speaking, our language learning starts with sentences that are directly conditioned to external stimuli. This is the foundation of a larger edifice. After this foundation is laid down, we permute and combine already known sentences to create new ones by means of analogy. Thus, language is a system of closely interconnected sentences. Any semantic change in any part of the system affects a large part of the network. Earlier, we shifted our attention from word meaning to sentence meaning. Now it seems we have to move further. It is not an individual sentence, but a set or system of interconnected sentences that is to be regarded as the vehicle or unit of meaning. This kind of view is known as meaning holism in the philosophical literature.

Both Quine and Davidson subscribe to

meaning holism. Quine suggests that "our statements about the external world face the tribunal of sense experience not individually but only as a corporate body."[1] We can view a natural language as a body of infinitely many sentences, some of which are observation sentences while some others are theoretical sentences. In Quine's image, observation sentences lie in the periphery because of their direct relation to experience. And theoretical sentences belong to the interior of the linguistic network. By 'linguistic network' I mean a group of sentences whose constituent parts recur in many sentences with identical roles assigned to them. Take, for example, these three sentences: 'This is a dog', 'Fido is a dog' and 'Fido is a dog which wags its tail'. All these three sentences have the word 'dog' as their parts that carries the same meaning. So these three sentences constitute a network where its meaning–bearing units occur in many different contexts carrying the same semantic significance. In Quine's theory, 'This is a dog' is an observation sentence which is directly keyed to observation in the sense that its truth value varies with the surrounding environment prevailing at the time of its utterance. Learning proper names and predication as involved in 'Fido is a dog' is a step beyond observation sentences. Notice that the truth of 'Fido is a dog' does not depend on the circumstance present at the time of its utterance. Nor is it directly keyed to observation, for even in the absence of a dog in front of us it makes perfect sense to say 'Fido is a dog'. But we cannot say the same thing with the observation sentence 'This is a dog'. Even then it remains true that after learning 'This is a dog' we carry on the meaning of 'dog' to non-occasion sentences like 'Fido is a dog', etc.

If this is a true picture, then it is not correct to say that an individual sentence has its own meaning independent of others, especially if that sentence belongs to the interior of the linguistic network. For, changing the meaning of such a sentence necessitates a change in meaning of other related sentences. So the unit of meaning does not seem to be an individual sentence but a network of sentences. The fact that observation sentences do not depend on other sentences for their meaning does not go against the holistic thesis. It still remains true that meaning of a basal sentence may affect the meaning of higher level sentences.

Following Roger Gibson Jr.,[2] I will present Quine's three arguments in support of holism which I will defend in the course of this chapter. These three are 'the scientific practices argument', the 'language learning argument' and the 'reductio argument.' The last two arguments are important for my present purpose. The scientific practices argument says that, as a matter of fact, when a scientist tests an hypothesis, she can always save the hypothesis by making adjustments in the truth values of auxiliary assumptions which she made before starting testing the hypothesis.[3] When a scientist makes an experiment with a hypothesis, she already has a backlog of accepted theory and she is trying to incorporate the hypothesis in question into that theory. The theory tells her that if the hypothesis under consideration is true, then under a certain observable situation a certain effect should take place. Thus the test of the hypothesis rests on a logical relation of implication, implication which holds between the backlog of theory including the hypothesis in question and the observational effect. A general form of this implication is 'Whenever this, that', which is called an 'observation categorical' by Quine.

When we deduce an observation categorical, we may have to call on the (theoretical sentences of) backlog of the accepted theory, and our knowledge of mathematics as well. Now, if the observation categorical turns out to be false, it does not conclusively refute the hypothesis. Rather it refutes the antecedent of the observation categorical, i.e., the conjunction of the sentences that was thought to imply the observation categorical. We can save the hypothesis by retracting some of the sentences in that conjunction. If, for example, we have a set S of sentences which implies the false observation categorical, one or more of the sentences of the set S can be rescinded. A scientist normally tries to avoid changing the logico-mathematical truths at the beginning. She ignores the sentences changing which will not make the observation categorical true. Of the remaining members of S, sentences that seem most suspect or crucial for the observation categorical will have to be repealed. We keep on repealing until we neutralise the negative implication of the observation categorical. We must also rescind the sentences implied by the newly repealed sentences. We keep on doing this until we restore consistency in the theory.

Adolf Grunbaum has been one of the leading critics of this argument.[4] According to Grunbaum, if we construct this scientific practice argument (which is also called Quine-Duhem thesis) in its restricted sense disallowing the revisions of the theory which changes the meaning of the terms of that theory, then it is false. Let us suppose that we have a theory composed of hypothesis H and a set of auxiliary assumptions A and this theory has observational consequences O. According to the restricted version of Quine-Duhem thesis, the failure of O (say O_1) is not sufficient to refute it, for there always exists another set of auxiliary assumption A_1 which, in conjunction with H, entails O_1. In other words, we can save the hypothesis without changing the meanings of the terms of the theory, since there always exists another set of auxiliary assumptions. According to Grunbaum, there is no logical guarantee that there exists such an alternative set of assumptions. The existence of such an alternative set of assumptions needs separate demonstration for each particular hypothesis. But Quine does not give any such empirical support. Also, Grunbaum suggests that in the history of physics there are instances where no such alternative set of assumptions exists. And if we read the argument in an unrestricted sense, i.e., allowing revisions of a theory by changing the meanings of some of its terms, then the thesis is true but trivial. For if we take a false empirical hypothesis (to take Grunbaum's own example) that "Ordinary buttermilk is highly toxic to humans", we can save this hypothesis in the face of observed wholesomeness of ordinary buttermilk by making 'drastic enough' (Quine's expression) adjustment in our system, by changing the English usage of the terms involved viz., by 'ordinary buttermilk' we might mean 'arsenic' in its ordinary usage. We can do this with any hypothesis whatsoever. But then, in this unrestricted version, Quine-Duhem thesis is true but trivial.

It is interesting to note the way Quine responds to Grumbaum. Quine acknowledges that his thesis "is probably trivial."[5] But Quine does not hesitate to advocate this trivially true thesis, for he wants to question our uncritical acceptance of the mentalistic notion of meaning where understanding meaning can be segregated from the collateral information of the relevant object.

It is important to notice the difference between Duhem's application of holism and that of Quine. Duhem applies his holism just to theoretical physics as opposed to mathematics or natural history. Quine's holism does not maintain these boundaries. His notion of 'science' is a broad one, for Quine views common sense as a primitive scientific theory. And a scientific theory is a group of sentences some of which are related to inter-subjective observational situations, while some others are not so but rest on the former group of sentences for their meaning. So Quine's holism applies to knowledge in general. Of course, Quine is primarily interested in our knowledge of the world and this is where his stress on physics comes in for, according to Quine, it is only theoretical physics that engages itself in the task of describing the catalogue of the furniture in the world which is adequate to justify our knowledge of the world.

Grünbaum argued, as we have seen a little earlier, that if we take Quine's holism in its unrestricted version, then the thesis is trivially true. Recall that Quine introduces holism in order to undercut the analytic/synthetic distinction. To achieve this aim it is enough if Quine can show that *many* so-called synthetic sentences can be held true— come whatever may, and *many* so-called analytic sentences can be declared false— if a theory can be adjusted to recalcitrant experience.

The second argument for holism can be drawn from our language learning mechanism.[6] I have mentioned earlier that there are some sentences that we learn by being conditioned by external stimuli. These are the so-called observation sentences. But much of our language goes beyond the limit of observable external stimuli. Such parts of language are mastered by what Quine calls 'analogic synthesis.' Thus the language consists of sentences that are keyed to external stimuli and there are other sentences which are learned by looking at the analogous role the words play in the observation sentences. This shows that observation sentences, together with theoretical sentences, constitute a whole, where the meaning of each sentence is related to the meaning of others. If one of our linguistic predictions fails to occur, then we have to revise that sentence to avoid the false prediction. For example, I interpret a sentence S uttered by you in such a way that confirming S implies confirming another sentence T as well. And later, if I find that you confirm not-T, then I will look back at my interpretation of S and, perhaps, I will amend the interpretation. But since the meanings of the sentences are connected with each other, revision in one sentence will affect other parts as well. We will want to keep this revision as localized as possible. We normally act on the maxim of 'minimum mutilation'.[7] What this means is that if we find that one of our linguistic predictions fails, then we have to change the interpretation of some of the sentences in our already accepted theory, because the prediction was related to the sentences of that backlog theory in a causal chain. Here we have to make a choice of which sentences we will alter. We might exempt those sentences whose interpretation— even if changed– does not affect the failed prediction. We might also exempt purely logical truths, for one thing, even in a newly interpreted system of sentences, we will need some logical laws to see the implications among different sentences and, secondly, changing logical truths would reverberate intolerably through the network of sentences. The sentences that will be in our hit list are the ones that seem most suspect for the failure of the prediction and ones which are least crucial to our overall theory. So here our guiding idea is to minimize the change of interpretation in the sentences of our theory while trying to neutralize the false prediction. Here we have a choice as to which sentences to revise to minimize the change. That there is a choice as to which sentences to revise in the face of a false prediction is due to the fact that our language goes beyond observation sentences to contain theoretical sentences whose meanings are learnt by means of analogy from observation sentences. All these confirm the holistic thesis.

Quine's third argument is a kind of *reductio* argument. If holism was false, then we would be able to distinguish absolutely the analytic sentences from the synthetic ones. And Quine has shown that there are serious problems in drawing an absolute line between analytic and synthetic sentences.[8] There are questions as to whether Quine is guilty of arguing in a vicious circle here. Quine seems to be using the rejection of analytic-synthetic distinction to prove holism, and, also, he seems to be using holism to establish the rejection of analytic-synthetic distinction. This is a matter of exegesis into which I need not enter. However, I will interpret Quine as establishing holism from the rejection of an absolute analytic-synthetic distinction. And, to me, rejection of analytic-synthetic distinction is, at bottom, rejection of a mentalistic theory of meaning.

Synthetic sentences are thought to have an empirical content, while analytic sentences are considered true by virtue of their meaning. This compartmentalisation of meaning and empirical content is what fosters mentalism and, consequently, has been questioned by Quine. The moment we start thinking of language in terms of its dual aspect, meaning on the one hand and empirical content on the other, we have to explain what this 'meaning' is. Faced with this question, we tend to reduce meaning to some subjective ideas or, as Frege did, to the sense of an expression. And neither of these is satisfactory. If we start from the assumption that language is a social phenomenon of inter-subjective communication (which I take as given), then the only way to explain meaning is by referring to the speaker's utterance and the external object or event described by that sentence. And earlier, with reference to language learning, we have shown how meaning ultimately rests on empirical evidence. So, if rejection of the analytic-synthetic distinction is based on a rejection of the mentalistic theory of meaning, then the resulting vindication of extensionalism paves the way for the holism thesis. And in the previous chapter I have shown why a theory of meaning is best developed on the basis of extensionalism. If extensionalism is true, then, along with the language learning mechanism (briefly sketched earlier), semantic holism follows. We can construct the meaning of observation sentences by directly relating them to external stimuli and then we carry on this observational part of language to generate the meaning of theoretical sentences as well. Some lexical parts of a sentence (in a language) occur in many other sentences and we carry our knowledge of those components to the newly built sentences. So the unit of meaning is not a single sentence, but a group of sentences which contain the same components but in different syntactic order. Thus, if a theory of meaning is taken to represent a speaker's linguistic knowledge, then it must be under the constraint of holism, for the speaker's knowledge of a language is compositional in structure. The Holism thesis might sound trivial (as it did to Grunbaum), but the fact that it is not trivial can be shown from people's observations made against holism which I will discuss shortly.

3.2 Davidson's holism

Davidson introduces holism in his theory to block the possibility of bizarre T-sentences and thus to make the theory a theory of interpretation (in the sense explained earlier). We have already seen that Jerrold Katz, while arguing against Davidsonian extensionalism, thinks that if all we need is a T-sentence of the form 'S is true if, and only if, P', in order to explain the meaning of s, then we can also have a T-sentence of the form '"Snow is white" is true if, and only if, grass is green' which clearly does not give the meaning of 'snow is white'. One might go further and claim that even if in a T-sentence the sentence of the meta-language is a translation of the sentence in object language, we cannot be sure of the validity of this translation in a radical interpretation. In radical interpretation, since we do not have any previous knowledge of the object language, there is always a great possibility that we can come up with a T-sentence which fails to interpret the sentence of the object language. How can we ensure the interpretative nature of T-sentences?

Here Davidson advocates a holistic structure of T-sentences. Taken individually, a T-sentence states the truth condition of a sentence in the object language. But this is not enough. T-sentences should be generated by a theory that will show how truth conditions of the sentences are built of the words of which those sentences are composed. Now the same words occur in very many different sentences. So T-sentences are related to each other because they share the same components. The theory which generates T-sentences like '"Snow is white" is true if, and only if, snow is white', will also generate T-sentences like '"It is snowing" is true if, and only if, it is snowing' etc. What is important is not only the material equivalence of a single T-sentence, but rather the fact that this equivalence holds in the context of many other equivalences which together constitute a single network. Davidson talks of a theory where each T-sentence will be a proof of that bi-conditional and the proof demonstrates "how the truth-value of the sentence depends upon a recursively given structure".[9] And to give a theory a recursive structure is to show how the theory generates its proofs drawn from a finite stock of elements by means of formation rules.

Since our theory is a theory of truth for a natural language, corresponding to infinitely many sentences of the language, there will be infinitely many proofs in the form of T-sentences. But that infinite number of T-sentences will share their component parts which are words in the language. Thus a theory of truth for a language will generate T-sentences for the sentences of the object language and these T-sentences constitute a fabric where each one is connected with each other in so far as their semantic elements are concerned. If we view an individual T-sentence as a part of that larger network, then that would block the possibility of bizarre T-sentence like '"Snow is white" is true if, and only if, grass is green'. For if this T-sentence is a proof of the theory, then this would affect other T-sentences as well. Of course, we can make drastic changes in the whole network to accommodate this T-sentence. But then the object language of such a theory would be quite different from English.

From the holistic structure of a language, Davidson talks of the holistic structure of one's beliefs. He thinks that to ascribe a belief to a creature is to ascribe many other related beliefs. "The system of such beliefs identifies a thought by locating it in a logical and epistemic space."[10] We can identify one's particular belief only if we know that person's other related beliefs. So beliefs are individuated only by relating them with other beliefs. In order to ascribe the belief 'Whales are mammals' to a person, we have to ascribe many other related beliefs to that person, for example, 'Whales are animals' etc. Davidson does not think it possible to specify the exact number of beliefs we have to ascribe to the person in order to ascribe any particular belief to that person. "But it is necessary that there be endless interlocked beliefs."[11] Since, for Davidson, a belief is a sentence held true, the holistic structure of a language leads to holistic structure of one's belief system.

3.3 Extreme and moderate holism

Following Jane Heal, I shall make a distinction between two versions of holism.[12] According to one formulation, meaning, in its primary sense, belongs only to entire theories. We can talk of the meaning of individual sentences only in a derivative sense and this derivation must be explained in terms of the contribution a sentence makes to the entire fabric of sentences. The second formulation of holism states that meaning can be, quite properly, ascribed to words or sentences. But having a meaning requires the presence of other meaning-bearing units that together constitute a network and it also requires the absence of certain undesirable items from that network. In this second formulation, both sentences and the whole theory are dependent on each other for possessing a meaning. Neither of them is conceptually prior to the other. We might call the former version extreme holism and the latter version moderate holism.

According to the extreme holist (some philosophers have taken Quine and Davidson to be extreme holists. I think that they are wrong which I will discuss in 3.7), it is only the whole theory which displays its meaning, bearing function by isolating the whole range of corresponding experience, and it does so by considering the connections which they have as wholes with what is meant, quite apart from the meanings of smaller parts. In moderate holism, even though the possession of meaning requires the presence of other meaning–bearing units, the dependence of smaller units and the total theory is mutual. In the history of language acquisition, the meaning of the sentence 'Fido is a dog' depends on the prior knowledge of the meaning of the observation sentence 'This is a dog'. Also, the meaning of 'This is a dog' depends on the meaning of 'Fido is a dog' in the sense that one's knowledge of the meaning of 'dog' in 'This is a dog' gets clarified in one's knowledge of the meaning of 'Fido is a dog'. For our initial interpretation of 'dog' in 'This is a dog' might conflict with our interpretation of some theoretical sentences containing the word 'dog'. In that case, we might have to change some of our interpretation. So, the more we can carry through our interpretation consistently from the observational part to the non-observational part of the language, the better our interpretation will work. The meaning of the whole is not prior to that of the parts in any significant way. So the slogan 'the fundamental unit of meaning is the whole' is misleading as a summary of moderate holism. The central idea, however, remains the same and that is : meaning involves a complex structure of sentences.

In extreme holism, meaning does not divide evenly over any set of sentences, i.e., individual components do not have any meaning. Individual words play the same role as 'ant' plays in the name 'Kant'. Hence to utter a sentence is not to give expression to an individual experience, but it is a mere step toward the working of the whole theory. It is as totally inappropriate to talk of a sentence having a meaning as it is nonsense to talk of phonemes of a word having their own meanings.

It seems to me that extreme holism rests on a faulty analogy of 'word' with 'sentence'. A sentence possesses a meaning of its own in the way words do not. Since we are concerned with meaning in a natural language, we must pay maximum attention to the communicative process, for this is where meaning starts playing its crucial role. And we cannot communicate with others by uttering a single word, unless it is embedded in a sentence or *is* a sentence.

In extreme holism, the only way to describe the semantic import (meaning) of a sentence is by describing the function of the whole theory and then describing the contribution that sentence makes toward the total function. One way of describing an individual sentence's contribution is to contrast it with other sentences having different contributions. But this presupposes that we already, in some sense, know the meanings of a large number of sentences.

Another way to explain the semantic import of a particular sentence is to show how this sentence has the same import as another already known sentence. This is another way of saying that the sentence to be explained means the same as another sentence already known does. Here we seem to presuppose the very notion of meaning that we are supposed to explain.

As I have said earlier, according to moderate holism, possession of meaning requires the presence/absence of certain elements in the network. Let me give an example to illustrate my point. In a picture of a face, a certain line represents the nose, etc. But the circle by itself cannot represent the eye, it represents the eye only in the background of some other suitable elements like nose, mouth, etc. The assemblage of the circle, line, etc., constitutes the whole picture of a face and the circle represents the eye only in the context of the other items that together constitute the picture. But it would be misleading to say that it is the whole picture that is the primary vehicle of representation, for the whole represents a face only because the parts have their representational roles. So far I have talked about the necessity of the presence of certain elements to enable the circle to represent an eye. Equally,we can see that the absence of certain elements is also required. The very same lines and circles, occurring in the context of some further lines and circles, may not suggest a face at all, perhaps the wheels of a machine or whatever one's interpretation might devise.

Following this analogy, I want to suggest that moderate holism claims that an individual sentence can be said to be the unit of meaning and is also such that it has the meaning for a person only if it occurs in a certain context, which contains sentences to which suitable related meanings can be assigned and which does not contain sentences inappropriate to that meaning. But here one is tempted to ask: How can we say which items are required and which are not required to explain the meaning of a particular utterance? Let us imagine the situation where I am engaged in interpreting a native's utterance (assume, for time being, that this is a radical interpretation). My starting point would be the behavior (linguistic and otherwise) of the native. I will try to figure out the circumstances under which a native utters her sentences. First I make a hypothesis about the meaning of the uttered sentence. If, at the next moment, I find the native behaving in a certain way that, for me, is contradictory to the meaning which I assigned, I will start doubting my hypothesis. Since I am acting under the constraint of holism, I should be able to predict the native's linguistic behavior from my hypothetical meaning ascribed to the native's utterance. For example, I might assume that the two native sentences I have heard mean, in English,'Snow is white' and 'This is a dog'. On the basis of this knowledge I will expect the native to say something which in English would mean 'The dog is white' in front of a white dog. If my prediction fails to obtain, my hypothesis becomes weaker.

Two important points emerge from this picture. First, since I revoke my hypothesis that ascribes a contradictory behavior to the native, I presume that the native possesses, at least, minimal rationality. By 'minimal rationality' I mean exhibiting a behavioual pattern that recurs in the native's life. This pattern might be very different from my life-world. But in so far as there is a recurring behavioral pattern in the native's life, and if my hypothetical meaning cannot do justice to that pattern, there is every reason to change my hypothetical meaning.

Secondly, the candidate for interpretation will be intelligible to us only if we can see her to be thinking, at least partly, of the world we share with her. This does not rule out the fact that the native might be aware of the things that we cannot detect. The point is that if the native was always talking of the things that are totally inaccessible to us, then we could never make sense of the native's utterances.

If we act on these two assumptions, this might act as our guide to determine the structure of the linguistic network which holism seems to ascribe to the native. The nature of minimal rationality and the shareability of a common world will discount items from the network which will violate either of these two assumptions. Consequently, we will have an assigned network of meanings which is consistent with the native's overall behaviour and which also ascribes meaning to all individual sentences uttered by her.

And all these follow from moderate holism. We can very well assign a meaning to an individual sentence of a native. But this requires that we put that sentence in a broader network, free from disruptive elements, and which will tally with the totality of behavior exhibited by the native. The distinction between extreme and moderate holism can be seen to be important when I discuss some of the critics of the holism thesis.

Acceptance of this moderate holism does not

imply that, whenever we consider a particular utterance, we have to bring the whole set of interconnected sentences in focus. This is conspicuous when we engage in interpreting an utterance within a language. When I, as an English–speaker, interpret another English speaker, large numbers of beliefs are taken for granted. This does not threaten holism. The holistic theory of meaning makes us aware of those intricate details of how language works, which we normally need not to pay attention to in our everyday discourse. One lesson of radical theory of meaning is to make us see what a great deal is taken for granted during day-to-day parlance.

3.4 Dummett's confusion about holism

In the preceding pages I have shown why an adequate theory of meaning should act under the constraint of holism. Though I accept the basic insights of extreme holism, it seems that an extreme holist has stretched her position too far and it is based on a faulty analogy between word and sentence. This led me to be sympathetic to moderate holism. People have confused this distinction and put forward their arguments against holism which, I think, are primarily directed to extreme holism.

Michael Dummett is one of the most

formidable opponents of the holistic view of language. He contrasts holism with what he calls the 'molecular conception of language.'[13] After giving a brief description of holism, Dummett asks whether introducing a new rule of inference would alter the meaning of existing sentences (recall the structure of language consisting of sentences having inferential relations among them). The answer depends on the nature of the new rule of inference. Here we have to act on the principle of 'minimum mutilation.' We will try to change the truth-values of sentences as little as possible, keeping the vast majority of other sentences— including the observation sentences— intact. If we have to modify some of the observation sentences, that would require a radical change in the whole of linguistic framework.

Dummett's molecularism says that each sentence has its own semantic import that can be understood independently of the entire language. Each sentence retains its separate content, even if it belongs to an extremely small part of the language which contains only that sentence and other expressions of the same or lower levels, whose understanding is necessary for the understanding of that particular expression. It seems that this sort of molecularism comes close to my moderate holism for, according to moderate holism, an individual sentence can be said to be a unit of meaning and the sentence has the meaning in the context of other related sentences. I agree with Dummett that we can understand the meaning of a sentence without knowing the entire language. But even Dummett himself admits that understanding a sentence requires putting the sentence in a proper setting of related beliefs on the part of a speaker.

Dummett's notion of "fragmentary language" (which contains expressions of the equal logical complexity) can very well be viewed as the set of observation sentences that we learn by direct conditioning. Then, throughout the language–learning procedure, we can extend the scope of that fragmentary language, finally including the whole of the actual language. It is true that in order to grasp the fragmentary language, we do not have to understand the whole of the actual language. But our understanding the fragmentary language determines our understanding the whole of the actual language.

After conceding that molecularism requires assuming an interconnected network of a fragment of language, Dummett thinks it necessary for a molecular view to hold that we can distinguish some sentences whose representation of meaning does not involve representation of the meanings of sentences of greater complexity. Probably Dummett is thinking of the observation sentences which come first in the course of language acquisition and which are atomic in nature.

I agree with Dummett's molecularism here, but I must qualify it.

Let us imagine the situation where I am trying to interpret a native's utterance. It is true that to know what 'gavagai' in the native's language means, I do not have to know the entire language of the native. But the situation is more complex than it seems. To know what 'gavagai' means is also to know what beliefs and interests the native possesses. And the native's belief and interests etc. involve a large complexity. It is not only a question of what a particular word means, rather how consistently we can ascribe that meaning to the total behavioral pattern exhibited by the native.

If we ignore this holistic underpinning, we will never be able to interpret the native's utterance in full-blooded sense of the term. Interpreting a language is not just a random assignment of meaning. Interpretation involves our seeing how the native could have come to the meaning of her utterances and this requires us to see some kind of defensibility in the structure of the native's language. And our theory of meaning for a foreign language should be empirically testable by the behavior of the native speakers. To achieve these, we must be sensitive to the holistic structure of that language. So even if, in order to interpret 'gavagai', I do not have to possess the literal knowledge of the whole of the native's language, still

I am imposing a network of belief structure which will act as a limit to my future interpretation of the native's utterances.

Dummett does not think of holism as a theory of meaning. "It is the denial that a theory of meaning is possible."[14] He makes this observation on the basis of two premises that he ascribes to holism. First, a theory of meaning explains the workings of a language "by giving a model for the content of a sentence" and holism denies any such content for an individual sentence. I do not agree with this. Sentences, according to moderate holism, can very well be ascribed their semantic contents. If explaining mastery of a language (as described in the first chapter), is our aim, then we can never deny the semantic value of sentences. For it is through sentences that we communicate with each other and this is where mastery of a language is manifest. So moderate holism does not deny individual semantic content (meaning) of a sentence, rather, it focuses on sentential meaning and explains it in a broader perspective.

Second, even if we succeed in grasping the whole of the linguistic network, it can never "give us a clear view of the contribution of any particular part of the apparatus."[15] This, it seems to me, is a misrepresentation of holism. My moderate holism aims at explaining the notion of meaning for a natural language. It is only through sentences that we engage in the linguistic behaviour of asserting, questioning, commanding, etc. A theory of meaning should be able to state meanings of every sentence of the language for which the theory is prescribed. Since a language consists of a potentially infinite number of sentences, our theory of meaning should be able to generate the meanings of those infinitely many sentences. One way of noticing this infinitude of the members of a linguistic framework is to see how each of the elements of that fabric is related to others. Since we create infinitely many sentences out of a finite stock of words, our theory of meaning has to be recursive in nature. We permute and combine the same words in very many different ways to create new sentences. But all these different sentences are related to each other in a single framework. Because of this concatenation, alteration in the semantic content of a single sentence may necessitate changes in other parts of the fabric.

This does not mean that individual sentences do not have their own semantic contents. Rather, it stresses the point that the semantic content of each sentence is closely related to the semantic content of other sentences. A theory of meaning which fails to take note of this holistic element cannot properly describe a speaker's mastery of her language. Only by working within this holistic framework can we determine the contribution a particular sentence makes toward the whole system. Our aim is to explain the meaning of every sentence of a language and we can achieve this aim only by putting all the sentences in an interconnected network.

It appears that Dummett himself is not clear about the status of his molecularism because he seems to contradict himself. We have seen just now that Dummett thinks that holism denies the possibility of a theory of meaning. A little later he says "it is at best very misleading to describe Quine's view as involving the rejection of the notion of meaning."[16] Also, Dummett ascribes a holistic thesis to Quine.[17] Now, if Quine subscribes to holism and if holism denies the possibility of a theory of meaning, then the conclusion follows that Quine rejects any notion of meaning. But Dummett draws an opposite conclusion.

In order to avoid this undesirable situation, we have to focus on the term 'holism' used in Dummett's premises. It seems to me that the only way to save Dummett from this is to follow the distinction of extreme holism and moderate holism that I drew earlier. Moderate holism does not deny a theory of meaning. Nor does it deny semantic import of an individual sentence. Moderate holism is a model of meaning among other possible ones. And it is the correct model, to my mind. Moderate holism aims at explicating the notion of meaning of a natural language. It does so by viewing a language as a set of sentences interconnected with each other in various ways and where every sentence contributes its semantic import to the construction of a consistent system. By doing so, moderate holism explains the mastery of a language (i.e. ability to use) which is all we require of a theory of meaning.

Dummett seems to have trouble in explaining how a holistic theory would explain the inclusion of a new sentence in the network. For this new sentence will affect the whole network and, consequently, a holistic theory of meaning alone will fail to explain a speaker's linguistic behavior at future dates. This inclusion may be at two different levels. If the newly included sentence belongs to the category of observation sentences that lie on the foundational level of language, then that would necessitate a massive change in the network. If, for example, we come to discover that what we call 'rain' today is not actually water, rather some kind of extraterrestrial being, then we would have to change the truth condition of the sentence 'It is raining'. But then this would affect many sentences in which the word 'rain' occurs. A large group of sentences in geography and meteorology have to be reinterpreted. Fortunately, this does not happen often. It is true, of course, that this new sentence might very well get along with other observation sentences not requiring any change in the network.

But what happens if this newly included sentence belongs to the theoretical part of the language where sentences are not directly related to external stimuli, but related to each other in various inferential connections? Here, as I said earlier, we have to act on the principle of 'minimum mutilation.' First we will revoke sentences which seem most suspect by the new sentence and which are also least crucial to the entire network. But this change will affect other related sentences. So we have to keep on doing this until consistency is restored. Consistency can be restored in more than one way (the elements of indeterminacy, which I will discuss in the next chapter). We will accept the one which maximizes 'minimum mutilation' and which has the best predictive power. Dummett thinks that inclusion of a new sentence might change a speaker's disposition to assent to or dissent from other related sentences, but "a change in these dispositions is no indication of any change in the meanings of the words."[18] I do not know what Dummett means by 'meaning' here. Meaning is whatever a speaker conveys by uttering a sentence in terms of its truth-condition. As I have said earlier, meaning is not something that exists independently of a speaker's linguistic behaviour. We can extract meaning only by looking at the linguistic dispositions of a native speaker.

Dummett argues that since speakers cannot

foresee what kind of change would occur in a future situation, the meaning of words cannot determine that change. But we need to remember that we are concerned with a natural language that is not a static and closed system, but an ongoing communicative system susceptible to change. Hence the content of our theory of meaning of such a language will also be open to change. We might revoke some so far accepted sentences and instead introduce new sentences to give expression to new experiences, to accommodate those experiences within our framework. It is true that our theory of meaning can not always predict such changes. But, instead of being a vice, this is a virtue of our theory. For such a theory is true to the speaker's experience (linguistic and otherwise). Since our theory acts under the constraint of holism, it can very well accommodate those new experiences, giving us a faithful picture of a speaker's mastery of a language. So the content of a theory of meaning will keep on changing along with changing human experience.

Dummett's failure to see the importance of moderate holism has led him to make some other observations that are, to my mind, inappropriate. Recall that we described language as a set of sentences directly related to external stimuli (which lie at the periphery) while some others are related to each other via inferential links (which lie at the interior of language). Now Dummett argues, "If the system confronts experience only as a whole, then there is no periphery and no interior."[19]

The trouble lies with the expression "the system confronts experience only as a whole." This does not mean, at least on my idea of moderate holism, that no sentence has a significance on its own. Since inclusion of a hitherto recalcitrant experience within our network can be made possible by making sufficient adjustments in the inferential connections of the sentences of that network, it is evident how a change in a part of the system affects the whole of it. This phenomenon would have been impossible, had our system not been holistic in nature. Our system confronts experience as a whole, only because if we want to include a new experience that would affect a large part of the system. And this might happen to peripheral sentences or to sentences lying in the interior of the system. In any case, we will act on 'minimum mutilation.'

Dummett levels the charge against holism of turning meaning into "something essentially ineffable."[20] Since whatever we do to include a new experience by making sufficient adjustments in the system also forms part of the system itself, this little part can- not convey anything on its own for it is only the system as a whole which conveys significance.

Here we must distinguish two levels of language. Firstly, we can talk of language as such.

Secondly, we can talk of the experience of the world to which language gives expression. We tend to ignore this distinction especially when we theorize about natural language, where object language and meta-language happen to be identical. When we are talking about our system, theory or network, we are talking about the language itself and not about the world which language describes. Now, when we want to include a new experience into our system, that new experience has already been shaped by our background system, for every perception is conceptually laden. There is no such vantage point that lies outside all systems, from where we can look at the experiences in their pristine purity. It is only due to the fact that the new experience has already been interpreted by our background theory that we are able to see that the inclusion of the new experience will necessitate semantic changes in our network. If we link this observation with my moderate holism, we can see— unlike Dummett— that what we say about including the new experience in our network— though it forms another sentence in the network— does convey significance on its own. In order to know this new experience, we do not have to know the entire theory, but we have to know how that new experience is going to affect our existing theory. Meaning does not become ineffable, but gains a holistic structure.

A holistic model of language, according to

Dummett, "fails to use language as an instrument of communication, or how we acquire a mastery of language."[21] As opposed to Dummett, I think these are the two points taken care of with utmost importance by an extensional-holistic view of language. I am not claiming that when I talk to someone, I have to know my interlocutor's entire system of beliefs in order to have a successful communication. But it is also true that in a communication there are a large number of beliefs shared by speakers that often go unnoticed. The scope of this shared area of beliefs is greater than we think. Holistic elements come to be noticed when, in the course of communication, I am led to ascribe contradictory beliefs (or at least beliefs radically different from mine) to my interlocutor. Since I act on charity, I will try to avoid any such ascription, otherwise our communication would collapse. The reason for this breakdown is that I ascribe such a network of beliefs to my interlocutor where individual members cannot get along with each other. So, to succeed in communication, I have to change that ascribed system by re-interpreting the interlocutor's words. This is not an uncommon experience in our everyday life. So, instead of acting as an impediment, holism enables us to have a successful communication.

Similar comments hold about mastery of a language. While learning a native's language, if I end up in ascribing inconsistent beliefs to the native, I will have to change bits of my interpretation to produce a consistent picture of the native's behavior. If I fail to do so, my mastery of the native's language would certainly be considered incomplete and haphazard.

I am not denying that while we learn a language we first master a fragment of it and then on the basis of that we grasp another fragment, and so on. These are well-recognized facts. A moderate holist only says that "in learning an initial fragment one has not *fully* mastered it, and one will only learn it fully if one learns others."[22] For during the course of learning a language if we end up in attributing inconsistent beliefs, then we might have to revise our knowledge of the initial fragment.

3.5 Holism and Putnam's theory of meaning

Hilary Putnam[23] thinks that holism retains a verifiability theory of meaning. Earlier in the introduction I talked about two 'unassailable tenets of empiricism.' And one of them is that meaning must ultimately be explained in terms of empirical evidence. Quine adds holism to this and argues that the unit of empirical significance is the chunk of a theory. So Quine sticks to verifiability theory but puts a holistic interpretation on it. And, according to Putnam, the verifiability theory of all versions is wrong. This led him to consider what he calls 'Sophisticated

Mentalism' as a viable option. It is not my intention to enter into a discussion of the verifiability theory here. For my present purpose, I will accept three constraints put by Putnam on any theory of meaning. I will show that a holistic conception of meaning satisfies all those requirements. If it does, then I do not find any reason why we should opt for mentalistic theory of meaning— be it 'naive' or 'sophisticated.'

First, according to Putnam, meaning "must have the right powers of *disambiguation*."[24] We are trying to arrive at a philosophically cogent conception of meaning. Our theory of meaning represents the knowledge a speaker possesses when she knows a language. This does not mean that we have to learn a theory of meaning before starting to learn a language. Obviously a child cannot be taught such a theory of meaning before she learns a language. We learn a language by various methods described by linguists and philosophers of language. What a philosopher of meaning does is to explain a speaker's ability to engage in linguistic behavior with necessary details, sometimes referring to mechanisms of language acquisition and then tries to develop certain general principles about language and the speaker's knowledge of it. This shows that our theory of meaning, to be a true picture of a speaker's knowledge, must assign identical meanings to expressions which a speaker uses synonymously, and it must also assign different meanings to expressions which a speaker supposes to have different meanings.

I think that my extensional-holist view of language achieves this purpose quite ably. When I try to interpret a native's language, I observe the native's behavior on the one hand, and look at the surrounding world on the other. In the course of interpretation, if I find myself attributing inconsistent meanings to her utterance, I start revising my interpretation. The revision is required since we have to represent the speaker's linguistic knowledge and we assume that speaker's knowledge cannot be inconsistent within itself. Only holism provides us with an insight into speaker's knowledge of language as a set of interconnected sentences.

The second constraint is referred to as "invariance of meanings under normal process of belief fixation."[25] Let us take Putnam's own example. Normally we use the word 'tiger' in such a way that it is not analytic that tigers have stripes, i.e., 'having stripes' is not considered as a definition of 'being tiger'. But if someone doubts whether there are any stripeless tigers, we might decide to use the word 'tiger' irrespective of having stripes or not. Though the stimulus meaning (Quine's terminology) of 'tiger' has changed as a result of our decision, we do not think that the word 'tiger' has changed its meaning. Though our process of belief fixation has changed, for we now use the word 'tiger' to mean tigers having stripes as well as tigers not having stripes, our linguistic intuition does not consider it to be a change in meaning.

It seems that holism can show why meaning remains unchanged. We are now interpreting the speaker's use of 'tiger' to mean tigers both having and not having stripes. In the course of interpretation we can find out whether our speaker is using the word 'tiger' consistently to mean both kinds of tigers. This can be found out by observing whether the predicates the speaker is applying to tigers having stripes are also being applied to tigers not having stripes. We also have to figure out whether those predicates are consistently used in other cases too. If we can extract a systematic pattern in the native's behavior, we have to admit that the word 'tiger' has not changed its meaning though it is being used to mean both striped and stripeless tigers. This is possible only because holism teaches us to view language as a set of interrelated sentences having inferential connections among them. This puts pressure on us to interpret the speaker's utterances within a consistent holistic framework.

The last constraint mentioned by Putnam is that meanings must be known by "*every speaker who counts as fully competent in the use of the language.*"[26] Since we are developing a theory of meaning for a natural language, knowledge of a competent speaker is our ultimate court of appeal. For a theory of meaning explains what it is to know when one knows a language. Our theory of meaning must be empirically testable against the linguistic practice of competent speakers.

This point has been well taken care of by extensional-holist view of language. As I said earlier, a theory of meaning is a theoretical presentation of the practical ability of a speaker to engage in linguistic behavior. So a theory of meaning is not just a detailed description of the mechanism of language acquisition, though such a theory should be able to account for that mechanism. A theory of meaning describes the knowledge that enables a speaker to utter and interpret infinite number of sentences. This is possible only if we assume that a competent user of language knows all the meanings of different expressions of her language. And this assumption is not only a hypothetical one but is born out of facts.

3.6 Fodor's misunderstanding about semantic holism

Let me wind up my analysis by discussing Jerry Fodor's[27] comments on holism. Fodor defines meaning holism in terms of what he calls 'epistemic liaison.' If the semantic value (meaning) of a sentence P is relevant to the semantic value of a sentence Q, then P is an 'epistemic liaison' of Q. So meaning holism says that the semantic value of a sentence is to be determined by the totality of its "epistemic liaisons."[28] Now people can differ in their estimates of the relevance of "epistemic liaisons." Someone might think that P is relevant to determining the semantic value of Q, while others might think R is relevant to Q. Since we can determine the semantic value of a sentence only with reference to a set of "epistemic liaisons," then "it's going to turn out de facto that no two people (for that matter, no two time slices of the *same* person) ever *are* in the same intentional state (except, maybe by accident).[29] So no two persons can be brought under the same intentional generalization. So we cannot have intentional generalization, hence there is no chance of intentional psychology.

I am not in a position to make any comment on the status of intentional psychology, nor does that concern me directly. What I am claiming is that meaning holism does not reject the possibility of disagreement among two people, nor does it follow that no two people are ever in the same intentional state. With reference to Chomsky, I argued earlier that disagreement can occur at two levels. We can disagree at the level of observation sentence. But this is very unlikely, for disagreement at this level suggests that we are using words in different ways. What is more common is disagreement at the level of theoretical sentences, where sentences are related to each other by different inferential connections. Here disagreement occurs due to the differences in views as to what inferential connections hold among which sentences. This leads to different assessments of the relevance of 'epistemic liaisons.' Our linguistic network is such that we can ascribe different relations to the same set of sentences without destabilizing the total outcome. Once again we have to act on 'minimum mutilation.'

I cannot see how from meaning holism it follows that no two people are in the same intentional states. By 'intentional states' I take Fodor to mean entertaining beliefs. We often tend to ignore the fact that even in a case of disagreement there is a massive area of beliefs which is shared by both parties. Disagreement makes sense only in the background of a commonality. So even if two persons are not in the same intentional state with reference to a particular belief, there is a vast area where they are in the same intentional states.

Fodor might ask : What would happen if there is a radical disagreement? Radical disagreement could occur only at the level of observation sentences. If I say 'It is raining' and if you say 'It is sunny' at the same time, then we are involved in a dispute where we are virtually using different languages. So people involved in this dispute are virtually using different languages. Only then are they in radically different intentional states. But still meaning holism does not become irrelevant. For if I radically disagree with you, the only way to interpret your utterance is to put that utterance in a proper setting of 'epistemic liaisons.' Determining which epistemic liaisons are relevant might be a difficult task. I have to observe your behaviour (linguistic and otherwise). I have to make a hypothesis and explain a fragment of your speech. Then, on the basis of that, I have to keep on interpreting larger and larger fragments with the aim of ascribing a consistent pattern to your behaviour. So, even in the case of radical disagreement, the only way to make sense of that disagreement is to ascribe a consistent set of 'epistemic liaisons' to the interlocutor. And this is what meaning holism says.

Fodor thinks that though meaning holism demands choosing a set of 'epistemic liaisons,' "it gives us no idea of how are we to do so."[30] It seems to me that the notion of truth can help us here. Let us think, for example, that I am trying to interpret a belief B_1 expressed by you. Holism requires that, in order to interpret it, I have to fit B_1 in the background of a set of other beliefs. The problem is : How am I going to identify this set? B_1 might be expressed by an observation sentence. In that case, I have to figure out what other higher level sentences you hold true, whose truth-values rest on the truth-value of B_1. If I can find out that there are sentences P, Q and R which directly rest on B_1 for their truth values and which you hold true, I would accept the set of P, Q and R as the proper set of 'epistemic liaisons' in order to understand the semantic value of B_1.

But B_1 might be expressed through a higher level sentence. At this level disagreement about the choice of 'epistemic liaisons' mainly arises from attributing different kinds of inferential connections to varieties of sentences. Here again the notion of truth can help me. I will find out other higher level sentences that are directly affected by B_1's truth value. I will find out what you think of truth-values of those sentences. While doing all these, I have to keep on trying to ascribe a systematic pattern to your belief system. So, truth can guide us in making a choice about an appropriate set of 'epistemic liaisons.'

The problem here is that there seems to be more than one way of ascribing truth-values to different sets of 'epistemic liaisons.' By making systematic adjustments in truth-values of different sentences, we can come up with two or more sets of 'epistemic liaisons', all of which appear to be relevant to the truth-value of B_1. In that case, we have to act on 'minimum mutilation.' We will accept that particular set which necessitates least change in the entire, network, which is simpler and which has also better predictive power.

Fodor mentions three ways that philosophers have tried to establish meaning holism :[31] i) From epistemology via confirmation holism, ii) From philosophy of mind via psycho-functionalism, and iii) From philosophy of language via functional role theory of meaning. Fodor criticises each of these attempts. I will focus on the first method of establishing meaning holism, because this is the one I mentioned before while explaining Quine's reasons for holism. The latter two attempts to prove meaning holism fall outside the scope of the present work.

Fodor's confirmation holism is what I earlier called the 'scientific practice argument'. It says that different sentences in a scientific theory are related to each other in significant ways. If we add a sentence or abandon any of those sentences, this has effects throughout the theory, resulting in distributing the strain through the network. The distribution of effects shows, according to confirmation holism, that the unit of significance is not an individual sentence but the whole system or theory.

Now Fodor thinks that if we give confirmation holism as the reason for semantic holism, then we will run into problems. First, to get semantic holism from confirmation holism we need the support of verificationism, and verificationism, according to Fodor, "is the doctrine that the content of a belief is identical to the means of its confirmation."[32] Fodor thinks that verificationism is false (although he does not give any arguments). So the move from confirmation holism to semantic holism is problematic.

I agree with Fodor in saying that we need some form of verificationism in order to get semantic holism from confirmation holism. If the meanings of sentences are tied to empirical verification, and if it is the theory as a whole which is the unit of significance, then it is no step at all to get to semantic holism from confirmation holism. It seems to me that extensionalism that I have defended earlier retains basic elements of verificationism where meaning is ultimately explained in terms of sensory evidence. Here we have to be careful when we say that Davidsonian distal theory retains the elements of verificationism. Earlier I defended Davidson's attempt to generate a theory of meaning out of a theory of truth. Dummett, on the other hand, advocates a theory of meaning where not truth, but verification is the central notion. So here Davidsonian theory of meaning is non-verificationist. But Davidson subscribes to verificationism in so far as he holds that whatever meaning a sentence has must be explicable in terms of empirical evidence. It is important to remember that Davidson is not concerned about *how* we acquire a language. A Davidsonian theory of meaning is descriptive of our knowledge of language, it is not a genetic study of our knowledge of meaning. Since the kind of evidence on which a theory of meaning rests is the speaker's holding a sentence true and since truth relates a sentence to what the sentence is about, Davidsonian theory of meaning rests on a version of verificationism, especially if we think of radical interpretation. So, in one way, Davidson is a verificationist and, in another way, he isn't. In order to avoid this apparent contradiction of espousing and rejecting verificationism, I have used the word 'extensionalism'. And, whether or not we should have an extensional theory of meaning is a debate as to on what kind of evidence we should have to rest our theory of meaning. And espousal of a truth conditional semantics amounts to defending a version of extensionalism. If this is true and if I succeed in vindicating extensionalism, then I don't see any problem in giving confirmation holism as the reason for semantic holism.

Secondly, Fodor thinks that semantic holism is actually presupposed by the arguments for confirmation holism. Hence, to argue for semantic holism from confirmation holism, is circular.[33] He analyzes the structure of Quine's arguments in the latter's "Two dogmas of Empiricism" and shows that Quine infers confirmation holism from the refutation of semantic localism (assertion of semantic holism).

I want to raise two points in response. Firstly, even if we concede that to argue semantic holism from confirmation holism involves circularity, this does not diminish the hope for semantic holism. As mentioned earlier, Quine has two more arguments in support of semantic holism, viz., the language learning argument and a reductio argument. Secondly, Davidson, as explained earlier, talks about a theory of meaning having a holistic structure so that it can be an interpretative theory, and also to account for the compositional structure of language. So there are many other arguments to infer semantic holism. Of course, one can say that all these arguments are related to each other. But, then, this is a virtue of an integrated philosophical theory.

Fodor would probably ascribe the doctrine that he calls 'meaning nihilism' to me. 'Meaning nihilism' is his name for the theory that rejects a mentalistic theory of meaning by questioning the analytic-synthetic distinction along with rejecting any notion of 'sense' or 'proposition.' I am a meaning nihilist in the sense that I do not believe in meaning as certain psychological entities which speakers attach to every word. Nor do I believe in meaning where 'meaning' stands for sense or proposition that is present across different languages. I am not a meaning nihilist in the sense that I believe that it is meaning which differentiates language from just emitting sounds. Mastery of a language consists in knowing the meanings of the expressions contained in a language. So if we can develop a satisfactory theory of meaning, that would enable us to know what a speaker knows when she knows a language. For knowing a language implies the ability to use it with fellow– speakers. Meaning holism implies meaning nihilism by denying mentalistic notion of meaning. Meaning holism explains meaning in the sense of explicating one's mastery of language.

3.6.1 A transcendental argument for holism

As I have argued earlier, we can block the possibility of bizarre T-sentences like '"Snow is white" is true if, and only if, grass is green' if we ascribe a holistic structure to our theory of truth. 'Snow is white' possesses the truth condition it does only because it is a member of a network of sentences that has sentences 'This is snow' and many other sentences containing the expressions 'is white' and 'is snow' as its members. A theory of truth which exhibits the 'logical form of a sentence', i.e., how the complex sentence is composed of its smaller units, is capable of being a theory of interpretation. In other words, a theory of interpretation must show the compositional structure of a language.

Not all critics are convinced that ascription of a compositional structure can solve the problem of bizarre T-sentences. Jerry Fodor and Ernest Lepore[34] have argued that if it is because of the structural similarity between 'Snow is white' and 'This is snow' that 'Snow is white' means that snow is white and not that grass is green, then there should be an a priori argument against the possibility of a non-compositional language. Fodor and Lepore opine that "we doubt that there could be such an argument".[35] They make a thought experiment to justify their conclusion. I will briefly describe the thought experiment and show why it fails to make any point about the possibility of a non-compositional language. Then I will give a transcendental argument in support of a compositional language.

Fodor and Lepore have asked us to imagine a child who has mastered a part of English that is non-recursive. So the child knows the sentences like 'This is snow', 'Snow is white', 'Everybody hates me', 'I hate spinach', etc., but the child does not know 'Snow is white and grass is green', 'Everybody hates frozen spinach', etc. So far the compositionality thesis is not violated, for, in the child's dialect, there are sentences like 'Snow is white', 'This is snow', etc.

But now let us imagine another child who is "just like" this one except when child 1 uses 'Snow is white' to say that snow is white, child 2 uses the expression 'Alfred'; when the child 1 uses 'This is snow' to say that this is snow, child 2 uses the expression 'Sam' and so on. Fodor and Lepore insist that the environment which prompts the child 1 to say 'This is snow', (exactly the same environment) also prompts child 2 to say 'Sam'. Next, Fodor and Lepore make the crucial statement: "... if compositionality is a necessary condition for content, then there is an a priori argument that child 2 couldn't mean anything determinate by what he utters. We take it that it is just obvious that such an argument couldn't be sound".[36] For what child 2 means depends on his intentions and there is no a priori argument to show that child 2 couldn't utter 'Sam' to mean that snow is white.

I do not agree with Fodor's and Lepore's assessment of the compositionality thesis. The fact that language has a compositional structure does not imply that child 2 couldn't mean anything determinate by his utterances. Let us skip the problem of meaning indeterminacy for time being (I will discuss this issue in the fourth chapter). If by compositionality we mean, as Fodor and Lepore do, that the same expression can occur with the same meaning in indefinitely many sentences, then it does not follow that we cannot make sense of the content of the utterances of child 2 simply because child 2 says 'Sam' where the child 1 says 'Snow is white'. We can very well imagine child 2 having mastered a more complex linguistic knowledge, where we can pair each utterance of child 2 with another of the child 1, where both the utterances are prompted by exactly the same environment. The fact that Fodor and Lepore think that there cannot be an a priori argument to show that child 2 couldn't utter 'Sam' to mean that snow is white suggests that we can imagine two children speaking two different languages where one is saying 'Snow is white' and the other is saying 'Alfred' and so on. But if we try to give a theory of interpretation for the language of child 2, our theory must ascribe a compositional structure to the language of child 2. Otherwise, the theory will give rise to the bizarre T-sentences and, consequently, such a theory will fail to be an interpretative theory.

I think that there is a transcendental argument as well for the compositionality thesis. It is perhaps trivial to claim that in our everyday life we, as adult speakers of English, successfully communicate with each other using our knowledge of language (in most of the cases). Now imagine English as having a non-compositional structure. In that case the word 'snow' will have a different meaning in 'This is snow' and 'Snow is white'. In fact, it will convey different meanings in each and every sentence where it occurs. We can universalize this feature. We can extend this to all the expressions in English. Then each expression will have a different meaning each time it is used in a different sentence. Since there are an infinitely large number of sentences in English, we will end up having an infinite varieties of meaning for an infinite number of expressions. Consequently, we can never claim to learn English, for there will always be expressions in English which we will never know (I am not referring to the accidental phenomenon of not knowing the meaning of some expressions of English). Even compiling a dictionary for English would be impossible. If there is no constancy in meaning, that would seriously hamper our linguistic communication. If we compare the situation where people are communicating using a language which has a non-compositional structure with the ordinary situation where we use language having a compositional structure, it is obvious that the former is infinitely more complex than the latter. And our pre-philosophical linguistic knowledge will certainly opt for the latter picture not only because it is less complex, but also because it is closer to reality.

Since our aim is to generate a theory of meaning out of a theory of truth, I have been trying to put enough constraints on the theory of truth so that it exhibits a speaker's knowledge of a language. Earlier I said that if a person knows the truth condition of a sentence and also knows that the particular T-sentence is part of a general truth theory of the language, she can claim to interpret that sentence. In other words, a T-sentence is entailed by a theory of truth for the language to which the sentence whose truth condition is being stated belongs. This is what Davidson means when he says that T-sentences are law-like. Fodor and Lepore think that the nomological nature of T-sentences goes contrary to the conventional nature of language. That language is conventional means that it cannot be a law that a sentence means what it does. If a T-sentence is law-like (as Davidson holds), then that T-sentence must hold in all the nearby worlds. If '"Snow is white" is true if, and only if, snow is white' is law-like, then all the worlds in which 'Snow is white' is true are the worlds in which snow is white. "But there is no reason to believe that this *is* the case"[37], think Fodor and Lepore. There might be a world where snow is not white but 'Snow is white' means something true, for in that world 'Snow is white' means that grass is green. So T-sentences cannot be law-like.

I interpret the expression 'law-like' as follows: We can interpret a T-sentence properly only against the background of other related T-sentences. We can think of a law only on the basis of certain observations, some hypothesis and some empirical consequences of that hypothesis. A law is, in some sense, implied by a host of other statements. So is the case with the T-sentence. If a T-sentence is to be interpretative in nature, it is not enough for a speaker just to know a T-sentence, she must also realize that the T-sentence is entailed by a truth theory.

But how are we going to understand 'entailed by'? How do we know that which T-sentence is/is not entailed by a truth theory. Obviously, we cannot use the notions like 'correct meaning theory', for that would be question begging. We are trying to develop a correct meaning theory. Also, the notion of entailment seems to get us involved in using intentional notions, for the context of entailment does not guarantee to preserve truth in the case of the substitution of co-extensive terms.

Two points are worth mentioning here. First, we should make a distinction between the thesis that language is extensional and that a theory of meaning can be given by an extensional theory of truth. I (following Davidson) do not accept the former while I do accept the latter. Our theory does not require that we should get rid of all intentional idioms in a language. What our theory requires is that in giving this theory we should not exploit any intentional notion for the reasons explained earlier. One might ask: Since 'a theory entails that ...' is part of the vocabulary of the meta-language, isn't our theory exploiting intentional notion to give a theory of meaning? Perhaps it does, but this is not philosophically damaging, for this apparently intentional notion is explained within the corpus of a theory of truth meeting the constraints that we are discussing now.

Second, if a T-sentence is a law and since a law is what it is only with reference to a body of truths, the nomologicality of T-sentence does not clash with the conventional character of a language. For, if we have a different body of truths, i.e., if we have different reports of observation and different sets of hypotheses and different sets of empirical consequences, we will end up with different laws. So the fact that T-sentences are law-like suggests that language is conventional, i.e., that a sentence means what it does only against the background of a set of other related postulates. If we change those postulates, we will end up having a different set of T-sentences. This is a step toward indeterminacy of meaning which will be discussed in the fourth chapter. So, I agree with Fodor and Lepore in claiming that there might be a world where snow is not white but 'snow is white' means something true. But this is because in that world there is a different set of postulates working. The nomological nature of T-sentences remains unchanged.

I do not agree with Fodor and Lepore when they say that "the nomologicity approach ... is not holistic".[38] If my interpretation of the notion of 'lawlike' is a plausible one, and if T-sentences are law-like in that sense, then we can conclude that we can talk of a T-sentence only in the background of a group of related T-sentences. We ascribe nomologicity to the T-sentences in order to make T-sentences interpretative, i.e., if one knows those T-sentences, she will be able to interpret (or give meaning to) those sentences, whose truth conditions are being given. It is not enough to employ, as Fodor and Lepore call, "the method of difference", i.e., to manipulate the environment and see whether, for example, Kurt holds 'Snow is white' true. For our theory is supposed to exhibit what one's knowledge of a language consists in, and since a language consists of an infinitely large number of sentences, the theory must show how to build those large number of sentences out of a finite stock. This is possible if we ascribe a holistic structure to our theory. Since our theory takes the form of a theory of truth, we must think of T-sentences as 'law-like'.

3.7 The scope of holism

Steven J. Wagner distinguishes between weak and strong versions of holism.[39] In the weak version, we can talk of the verification conditions of an individual sentence even though verification of each sentence presupposes its connection with other sentences. Here "a given observation may still confirm H (an hypothesis) to a certain degree without equally confirming sentences in the surrounding theory"[40]. Notice the expression 'to a certain degree'. We have seen earlier that Akeel Bilgrami also mentions degrees of knowledge of one's language. And, in the stronger version of holism, testing an individual hypothesis means testing the whole theory which contains that hypothesis. Wagner thinks that it is this stronger version of holism which we need to justify for extensional view of language.

There are a number of occasions where Quine tells us not to be over–enthusiastic about the scope of holism. Quine urges, "Still I must caution against over-stating my holism."[41] He sees stronger version of holism as "pure legalism." The difference between weaker version and stronger version of holism is not a matter of tremendous philosophical significance. The fact is that the semantic content of each sentence is related to semantic content of many other sentences and talking about the meaning of one sentence involves talking about the meaning of other related sentences. And any change in one part will necessitate change in other parts as well. Quine clearly sides with what he calls "holism in this moderate sense."[42] And, unlike Wagner, I do not think, as I have shown earlier, that it is necessary to uphold an extreme version of holism in order to advocate an extensional theory of meaning.

It is interesting to note that Quine acknowledges the possibility of a non-holistic language, but that language would be restricted to observation sentences only. Observation sentences do have their empirical contents individually. But observation sentences cannot take us far in our knowledge of language. Introducing non-observational part brings holism with it.

Alan Weir's paper shows how people have overestimated the dichotomy between extreme and moderate holism.[43] Weir quotes Davidson saying "we can give the meaning of any sentence (or word) only by giving the meaning of every sentence (and word) in the language".[44] Weir remarks that it is absurd to say that one does not understand the meaning of 'red' unless one understands the whole of English language. And I agree with Weir. But Weir goes on to argue that if we want to say that one needs to understand a substantial portion of English in order to understand the meaning of 'red', then we need to specify "lower bounds on the size of linguistic systems, if they are properly to be termed 'languages'".[45] Weir finds this specification project to be problematic, for even if we succeed in specifying the lower bounds on the size of language, Davidsonian holism is wrong, according to Weir. Suppose that a child knows only a fragment of English that contains the word 'red' with its ordinary meaning. According to Weir, it is evident that there will be words in that fragment of which the speaker could be totally ignorant of while displaying perfect mastery of 'red'.

I am not sure how far Weir's observation is correct. According to Davidson, to know the meaning of 'red' we should have a T-sentence involving the word 'red'. But, as we have seen earlier, an individual

T-sentence is not interpretative in nature. If a single T-sentence is enough to give the meaning of the sentence of the object language, then there is no way to block the possibility of T-sentences like '"Snow is white" is true if, and only if, grass is green'. So knowing a T-sentence involving the word 'red' is not enough to know the meaning of 'red'. We have to know a host of other related T-sentences that together constitute a coherent network. It is only when we know that the T-sentence involving the use of the word 'red' is a part of that network, we can claim to know the meaning of 'red'. And thus we can reject the possibility of above-mentioned bizarre T-sentences.

For an English speaker, to be able to know a T-sentence involving the word 'red' is not enough to know the meaning of 'red'. It might be a happy coincidence that the speaker utters 'red' in an appropriate circumstance. It is logically conceivable that a speaker utters an English sentence in an appropriate situation without knowing the meaning of that sentence. If what Weir says is correct, then we have to accept that the speaker knows English. In order to explain one's mastery of a word it is not enough to ascribe to her an individual T-sentence. So I do not agree with Weir in claiming that one understands the meaning of 'red' without knowing any other words of the fragment of that language.

It might be the case that by learning a small fragment of a language we come to learn the 'fully-formed language.' But, Weir asks, how can we define a 'fully-formed language?' New words are continually entering into our vocabulary due to scientific and social progress. I agree with Weir in saying that it is hardly possible to specify the exact scope of a 'fully-formed language.' Nor do I aim at such project. It goes without saying that natural languages are open to change by way of inclusion of new words. But I think that this inclusion of new words affirms the holistic thesis that when we talk of meaning of a sentence we should talk of the meaning of the whole network of sentences which contains that particular sentence. When we include a new word, we have to see whether sentences containing that word are consistent with other sentences of that fabric. We might have to adjust the relation between several sentences to include this new word. If a language lacks internal consistency, then we will not be able to communicate with each other using that language.

NOTES

[1]Quine, W. V., "Two Dogmas of Empiricism" in *From a Logical Point of View*, Cambridge, Mass., Harvard University Press, 1980, p. 41.

[2]Gibson, Roger, Jr., *Enlightened Empiricism*, Tampa, University of South Florida Press, 1988, p. 33.

[3]Quine, W. V., *Pursuit of Truth*, Cambridge, Mass., Harvard University Press, 1990, pp.13-16.

[4]Grunbaum, A., "The Falsifiability of Theories. Total or Partial? A Contemporary Evaluation of the Duhem - Quine Thesis." *Synthese*, Vol. 14, 1962, pp. 17-34.

[5]Quine, W. V., "A Comment on Grunbaum's Claim" in *Can theories be refuted? Essays on the Duhem-Quine Thesis*, Ed. by S. Harding, Dordrecht, Holland, D. Reidel Publishing Company, 1976, p. 122.

[6]Quine discusses this in many of his works. A brief exposition can be found in "The Nature of Natural Knowledge" in *Mind and Language*, Ed. by S. Guttenplan, Oxford, Clarendon Press, 1975, pp. 72-77.

[7]Quine, W. V., *Pursuit of Truth*, p. 14.

[8]Quine, W. V., "Two Dogmas of Empiricism", pp. 20-37.

[9]Davidson, D., "Semantics for Natural Languages" in *Inquiries into Truth and Interpretation,* Oxford: Clarendon Press, 1986, p. 61.

[10]Davidson, D. "Thought and Talk" in *Inquiries into Truth and Interpretation*, p. 157.

[11]Ibid., p. 158.

[12]Heal, Jane, *Fact and Meaning*, Oxford: Basil Blackwell, 1989, pp. 86-87.

[13]Dummett, Michael, "The Justification of Deduction" in *Truth and Other Enigmas*, Cambridge, Mass, Harvard University Press, 1978, p. 302.
[14]Ibid., p. 309.
[15]Ibid., p. 309.
[16]Dummett, Michael, "The Significance of Quine's Indeterminacy Thesis" in *Truth and Other Enigmas*, p. 378.
[17]Dummett, Michael, "Frege's Distinction between Sense and Reference" in *Truth and Other Enigmas*, p. 134.
[18]Ibid., p. 137.
[19]Dummett, Michael, "Original Sin" in *Frege Philosophy of Language*, London, Duckworth, 1973, p. 495.
[20] Ibid., p. 596
[21] Ibid., p. 598.
[22]Bilgrami, Akeel, "Meaning, Holism and Use" in *Truth and Interpretation,* Ed. by Ernest Lepore, Oxford, Basil Blackwell, 1989, . 117.
[23]Putnam, Hilary, "Meaning Holism" in *The Philosophy of W. V. Quine*, Ed. by L. E. Hahn and P. A. Schilpp, La Salle, Illinois, Open Court, 1986, p. 409.
[24]Ibid., p. 410.
[25]Ibid., p. 411.
[26]Ibid., p. 412.
[27]Fodor, Jerry, *Psychosemantics*, Cambridge, Mass., The MIT Press, 1988, pp. 55-95.
[28]Fodor has defined meaning holism using intentional terms that I have avoided.
[29]Fodor, Jerry, *Psychosemantics*, p. 57.
[30]Ibid., p. 58.
[31]Ibid., p. 62.

[32]Ibid., p. 32.
[33]Ibid.
[34]Fodor, J. and E. Lepore, *Holism: A Shopper's Guide*, Oxford: Basil Blackwell, 1992, p. 65.
[35]Ibid., p. 65.
[36]Ibid., p. 66.
[37]Ibid., p. 85.
[38]Ibid., p. 90.
[39]Wagner, Steven J. "Quine's Holism", *Analysis*, Vol. 46, 1986, p. 2.
[40]Ibid., p. 2.
[41]Quine, W. V. "Reply to Hilary Putnam" in *The Philosophy of W. V. Quine*, edited by L. Hahn and P. Schilpp, La Salle, Ill.: Open Court, 1986, p. 16.
[42]Quine, W. V., *Pursuit of Truth*, p. 16.
[43]Weir, Alan. "Against Holism" in *The Philosophical Quarterly*, Vol. 35, 1985, pp. 225-244.
[44] Ibid., p. 225. This quotation is taken from Davidson's "Truth and Meaning" in his *Inquiries into Truth and Interpretation*, Oxford, Clarendon Press, 1986, p. 22.
[45] Weir, Alan, "Against Holism", p. 226.

CHAPTER 4
SEMANTIC INDETERMINACY

In this chapter I will explain and defend the thesis of indeterminacy of meaning. First I shall briefly present the Quine-Davidson position with regard to indeterminacy. This will take me to the evaluation of some of the important criticisms of indeterminacy. Acknowledging, with J. Katz, that radical translation/interpretation is different from "actual translation/interpretation", I will argue that indeterminacy does not lead to meaning nihilism, but it leads to meaning relativism. I accept that indeterminacy follows only if we start from radical interpretation, but then I will argue that radical interpretation is possible, i.e. radical interpretation is adequate for giving us a theory of interpretation for the object language. The fact that radical translation/interpretation rests on the 'nothing is hidden' principle does not lead to the absurd consequences, which critics like J. Fodor and E. Lepore allege. I will also show, by opposing J. Wallace's views, that deciphering and interpreting are different. Interpretation, in a way, presupposes decipherment.

I will try to establish that indeterminacy does not imply that there is no difference between the two sets of interpretations of the object language as J. Searle tends to think. Interpretation is relative to the theory of truth that works as a background theory. I will also show that extensionalism in the form of a theory of truth does not deny a speaker's intentions, or beliefs, it only denies their foundational role in a theory of interpretation. Here I introduce, following J. Van Cleve, the notion of 'semantic supervenience', the thesis that non-semantic facts determine semantic facts. If developing a theory of meaning is our aim, then both the advocates of indeterminacy and the people who oppose it would accept semantic supervenience. The debate is about what to include in the range of non-semantic facts. Proponents of indeterminacy claim that a translation manual (for Quine) or a theory of truth (for Davidson) is what constitutes non-semantic facts. People opposed to indeterminacy claim that this is not enough, we should include something more, preferably the speaker's intentions etc.. I argue why such a move is futile.

I will argue that the indeterminacy thesis is not to be conflated with the fact that two speakers disagree over the truth-value of a sentence as M.

Dummett seems to do. The claim of indeterminacy is more radical than two speakers disagreeing about a particular belief. The disagreement between two people can be resolved if both of them have a better understanding of what the other person is talking about. But this does not remove indeterminacy, for understanding others' utterances is exactly the place where indeterminacy arises. I exploit the 'just more theory' objection which H. Putnam gives against metaphysical realism and show that Dummett's attempt to eradicate indeterminacy is not successful for it suffers from the 'just more theory' objection.

4.1 Quine on indeterminacy and Underdetermination

So far I have tried to show that a theory of meaning of a natural language is better explained extensionally and by ascribing a holistic structure. By 'extensional' I meant that a theory of meaning could be developed by giving a theory of truth. And, by 'holistic structure' I meant that the meaning of a sentence is inextricably related to meanings of other sentences that together constitute a consistent network. Accepting these two theses will lead us to what is known as indeterminacy of meaning in Quine. According to extensionalism, to discover the meaning of the native's sentence we have to observe both the native's verbal behaviour and the surrounding world. And if the meaning of a sentence is linked with the meaning of a group of sentences, then we give up the assurance of determinate meaning and recognize that there is no meaning beyond that which is implicit in a speaker's verbal dispositions.

While defending a distal theory of meaning, I have supported explaining meaning in terms of truth. Truth links up a sentence with what it describes in the external world. So, in order to explain meaning we will listen to the speaker's utterance on the one hand and we will take note of the surrounding circumstance on the other. If we think of this project of discovering meaning in the case of what Quine calls "radical translation" where we are translating the object language without any pre-existing aid, we will end up having indeterminacy of meaning. The essence of Quine's doctrine of indeterminacy of translation is the claim that we can set up more than one set of translation manual for the object language, each of which is compatible with the totality of the speech dispositions of the speaker of the object language, yet incompatible with each other. So what we will have is more than one translation for the sentences of the object language. Since, on extensionalism, to discover meaning all we can do is to observe the speaker's behavior and the surrounding world, and, since by doing this we end up having more than one translation manual, indeterminacy of translation leads to indeterminacy of meaning. As a consequence, we will have more than one interpretation of the object language.

Let me state briefly the way Quine arrives at the indeterminacy thesis.[1] Let us imagine, for example, that the speaker whose language I am trying to interpret and I are standing in a field where cows are eating grass and the speaker utters 'Gou'. As a first step I will translate 'Gou' as cow. But this is a very rough approximation. For 'Gou' might mean 'field with grass', 'cows eating grass in the field,' 'cows have four legs,' and so on. The problem is that I cannot even ask which one of these is meant by 'Gou,' for I do not possess the vocabulary to communicate with him.

Though I have started with an observation sentence uttered by a native–speaker, my aim is to understand the totality of the sentences of the language and not just the sentences that the native speaker happens to utter. In other words, to understand a language we have to understand the speech dispositions of the native speakers of that language, so that in any given situation we can predict and understand a native speaker's utterance. To achieve this aim, I have to manipulate external circumstances, to put the native speaker in those different circumstances and to follow her assent/dissent behaviour. But I do not know what the native speaker's assent/dissent behaviour consists in.

Once I have the knowledge of assent/dissent behaviour of the speaker, it becomes easier for me to discount certain possible candidates of the meaning of 'Gou'. For example, if the native speaker assents to 'Gou?' in the cases of cow eating grass in the field and a farmer ploughing his field with cows, I can assume that 'eating grass in field' is not necessary for something to be a 'Gou'. Notice how important the external stimulus condition is in ascertaining the meaning of an observation sentence like 'Gou'. Since I do not have any information about the speaker's language, culture, beliefs, etc., stimulus condition is the only thing that we share with each other. This gives me a common ground on which I can start interpreting the speaker's utterances. I can figure out whether the speaker assents to or dissents from the query 'Gou?' under exactly the same condition where I would assent to or dissent from 'Cow?'

In any case, I can construe certain expressions of the speaker as corresponding to certain expressions in my language. I want to call these statements mapping one language to another 'semantic postulates'. They are semantic since they are concerned with the meaning of the expressions of two languages. They are postulates, for we have not yet applied these pairs of expressions to the whole of our linguistic practice and we are not sure how far they turn out to be valid.

But we need to take a closer look at these semantic postulates. A semantic postulate says, for example, " 'Gou' is translated as 'Cow'." This means that the speaker utters 'Gou' in exactly the same situation where I would utter 'Cow'. The picture is more complex than it seems. For in exactly the same situation 'Gou' might be translated as 'cow part' or 'cow stage' or even the universal 'cowness'. From the behavioural data of the speaker, it is hardly possible to uniquely determine any one of these translations. Obviously I cannot ask the speaker, for I do not yet possess the vocabulary needed to phrase that question. The difference in these different possible translational candidates consists in individuation, in how we slice the reality. And there is no evidence on the basis of which I can say that the speaker and I slice the reality in the same way. So simple stimulus conditions (and this is the only common element between me and the speaker) allow me to translate 'Gou' in more than one way. As a result, we have more than one semantic postulate for translating 'Gou'. And, in so far as behavioral evidence is concerned, it does not enable me to prefer one translation to another.

One might argue that by observing the assent/dissent behavior of the speaker, I can determine a unique translation. But the problem remains the same, for in the presence of a cow when the speaker is assenting to my query 'Cow?' she might be assenting to something which can be translated as 'Cow-part' or 'cowness', etc. Pointing to a cow also involves pointing to a 'cow-part' or 'cowness'. Ostension does not help to restore determinacy.

The upshot is that different interpreters can arrive at different semantic postulates while interpreting the same utterance. Thus, all the semantic postulates involve indeterminacy. It is not merely the case that due to some kind of human ignorance we are unable to settle on a semantic postulate. We are not talking of inductive indeterminacy. The point is that even after considering exhaustive evidence, there remains the possibility of a rival set of semantic postulates. But all these different semantic postulates, resulting in different linguistic networks, correspond to the totality of speech dispositions of the speaker being interpreted. Though they are consistent with speech dispositions, they generate different translations for the same expression. Meaning is whatever we can (potentially) extract from a speaker's behaviour. And a speaker's linguistic behavior is amenable to more than one translation manual. Hence, meaning loses its uniqueness and becomes indeterminate. The same expression means different things in different systems of semantic postulates, though all of them agree with the totality of speech dispositions of a speaker.

When this indeterminacy occurs with respect to a theory what happens is known as underdetermination of a theory. What this means is that our theory of the world transcends our observations of the world in the sense that different competing theories can be developed from the same set of observations.[2]

This underdetermination of a theory can occur in three different ways. A theory can be underdetermined by past observations because some future observations could conflict with the theory. A theory can be underdetermined by past and future observations because some conflicting observation might have gone unnoticed. In these two cases a theory can, in fact, be underdetermined. There is another kind of underdetermination where all observations are fixed and we have two theories that are compatible with the observational data but are at odds with each other. In this sense, any theory is underdetermined in principle. In other words, theories can be logically incompatible but empirically equivalent.

Let us clarify this point a further. Recall that observation sentences are direct reports of a person's sensory experience. The truth of the observation sentences depends on the condition prevailing at the time of their utterance. Since science (theory of the world) aims at universal truths, the sentences implied by science cannot be occasion sentences. They have to be standing sentences whose truth-values are fixed, and do not depend on the condition of the time of their utterance. Of course, we can convert occasion sentences into standing sentences by assigning a spatio-temporal coordinate to each of them.

Now we can explain what Quine means by 'empirical content' of a theory. Typically a theory predicts some phenomena from some other already established phenomena. In other words, a theory will imply some observation conditionals whose antecedents would be a conjunction of already verified standing sentences and whose consequence would be another standing sentence. The class of observation conditionals said to be implied by a theory is the empirical content of the theory.

But how can two theories, having the same empirical content, be logically incompatible? By 'logically incompatible' it is meant that the truths of each of those theories would differ. Each theory will make certain claims that the other would deny. Since the observational criteria of the terms employed in the theories are rather indeterminate, each theory will make conflicting claims even though the observation conditionals implied by each theory are said to be identical.

At this point we can compare indeterminacy with underdetermination. In radical translation, the field linguist translates the native's observation sentences on the basis of stimulus meaning. Then the linguist starts making "semantic postulates" in order to go further in translating theoretical sentences. But these semantic postulates are underdetermined by the foreigner's theory of the world. Consequently, the linguist could come up with more than one translation manual. As a result, we can have more than one theory in our language into which the native's theory can be translated. And each of our theories will have the same empirical content the way each translation manual will correspond to the totality of the verbal behavior of the native speaker. But these theories will be logically incompatible with each other, for each will assert truths that the other will deny. As a result, meaning becomes relative to the system of semantic postulates. In one system of semantic postulates 'Gou' is translated as 'Cow', while in another system of semantic postulates 'Gou' is translated as 'Cow parts'. No behavioural data enables us to make a choice between these two systems.

One might concede indeterminacy in translating a foreign language, but she might deny any element of indeterminacy while understanding one's own language. Two points are worth mentioning here. First, when a child is learning her native language, she is very much in the same position as when a field linguist tries to interpret a foreign language. Neither of them has any previous knowledge of the community (whose language they are trying to learn), nor can they take any help from bilingual persons. Both of them have to start from observation sentences, figure out assent/dissent behaviour of the native speaker and then both have to construct semantic postulates. The only difference in these two situations is that the linguist already possesses the knowledge of at least one language while the child does not. But, as I have shown earlier, possession of the knowledge of a language does not help to translate the newly learned language in a unique way.

Secondly, part of the reason why the presence of indeterminacy in two adult speakers talking to each other in the same language seems to be counterintuitive is that those two speakers have more or less the same belief structure (they might disagree with regard to particular beliefs) interests, etc. Since they are brought up in the same communal environment, they, interpret and organize their surrounding world in largely the same way. But we can extend the picture of a foreign language translation to our home language? I can interpret my fellow English–speaker's utterance of 'Cow' meaning 'cow part'. Of course this would lead to some adjustments in the total network of sentences ascribed to that speaker. This is, nevertheless, possible. I can come up with more than one system of semantic postulates that would translate the speaker's utterance in very many different ways, but each of those systems would correspond to the totality of the speech dispositions of the speaker. So, instead of 'cow' I can take the speaker's utterance to mean 'cow parts' and then I can systematically change the meanings of other observations and resulting theoretical sentences. This whole system would give us a completely different translation of the speaker's utterances and we cannot reject it, for it corresponds to the speaker's speech dispositions. There is nothing sacrosanct in the speaker's utterance of 'cow' meaning 'cow' and not 'cow part'. By adopting a different system of semantic postulates, we can interpret 'cow' as meaning 'cow part' which will be totally consistent with the speaker's verbal dispositions. And all that is required to interpret one's utterances is to be able to understand her verbal dispositions.

Interpreting a speaker's utterance of 'cow as 'cow part' sounds awkward to English–speakers. But this does not nullify its candidacy as a possible translation of 'cow'. We cannot say that translating 'cow' as 'cow parts' is *wrong,* for this corresponds to the speaker's speech dispositions. The only objective criteria on the basis of which we have to decide meaning are the relevant stimulus conditions. And those stimulus conditions approve of translating 'cow' as both 'cow' and 'cow parts'.

4.2 Davidson on indeterminacy

Donald Davidson[3] also acknowledges the presence of indeterminacy, though the way he arrives at indeterminacy is different from Quine's. Davidson arrives at indeterminacy of meaning via truth theory. He concedes that there can be different ways of formulating truth conditions for sentences of the object language. In other words, there can be sentences in the meta-language which are non-equivalent to each other and which are true if, and only if, a sentence in the object language is true. And these different bi-conditionals will give rise to different theories of truth for the object language, all of which satisfy the empirical and formal constraints and, hence, are interpretative in nature. Indeterminacy arises because the evidential basis of our theory of interpretation consists in facts about circumstances under which the speaker holds a sentence to be true.[4] A little earlier we have seen how such evidence is amenable to more than one interpretation. As a result of which we will have different theories of truth assigning different truth conditions to the same sentence.

To illustrate this point, we can take Quine's example of 'Gavagai' and put it in a Davidsonian theory of interpretation. Then we will have two different bi-conditionals for the native sentence 'Gavagai' such as: '"Gavagai" is true if, and only if, there is a rabbit', and '"Gavagai" is true if and only if there is a rabbit-part'. Davidson does not aim at arriving at a unique interpretation of a sentence. "The meaning (interpretation) of a sentence is given by assigning the sentence a semantic location in the pattern of sentences that comprise the language."[5] And each theory of truth performs this task in its own way. Different theories differ in assigning truth conditions to the same sentence. But within each theory the sentence has been interpreted in such a way that situates it in the background of other related sentences in that theory.

But are we not heading in the wrong direction if we find two different theories of interpretation of the same language, each of which sounds plausible in the face of available evidence? Davidson thinks not. "Indeterminacy of meaning or translation does not represent a failure to capture significant distinctions; it marks the fact that certain apparent distinctions are not significant."[6] If taking into consideration all the evidence we have for interpreting one's utterance leads to indeterminacy of meaning, then it is the logical consequence of the nature of theories of meaning. It only shows that there are alternative ways of stating the same fact.

Is it not a contradiction to say that both theories of truth are acceptable where one assigns a truth condition to a particular sentence and the other does not? According to Davidson, "it is not a contradiction if the theories are relativized to a language, as all theories of truth are."[7] The same sentence, without any contradiction, can belong to two different languages. Since two different languages possess two different theories of truth, two theories assign two different truth-values to a single sentence. We can consider that sentence as belonging to one language and not to the other provided we make sufficient adjustments in the other parts of that language. The intrasentential relations in the two theories designed for two languages are different. Whichever theory we work with, we must ensure the holistic nature of the sentences of that theory.

The thesis of indeterminacy of translation has provoked a vast amount of literature both for and against it. It seems to me that many critics have failed to grasp the true significance of this doctrine because of their failure to place the thesis in its proper perspective. As a result, they have misinterpreted the thesis, exaggerated its claims, and even, sometimes, trivialized it. In the following pages, I will discuss certain recent criticisms of the indeterminacy thesis with the hope of allaying some misapprehensions about it. In the course of this discussion I will try to make clear what exactly indeterminacy claims and how it affects the notion of meaning of a natural language.

4.3 Does Indeterminacy occur in actual translation? — A reply to Jerrold Katz

Notice that we have been talking of translating a native language from scratch. We are presupposing that we do not have any previous information about that native culture. There is no dictionary from which we can take help while translating. So the only data we have which we can start with is the behavior of a native speaker. This is known as radical translation in philosophy. People have conceded that indeterminacy results if we stick to radical translation where we translate on the basis of meagre evidence. Jerrold J. Katz argues that in order to establish indeterminacy one would have to show how indeterminacy results in what he calls 'actual translation.'[8] And Katz has doubts about how far this 'actual translation' would generate indeterminacy.

I presume, by 'actual translation' Katz means cases where, for example, we English–speakers translate German to English or cases where one English–speaker is translating another English speaker. It goes without saying that cases of 'actual translation' are more frequent than that of radical translation. But it seems to me that the philosophical point raised by Quine holds true of 'actual translation' too. When, for example, a German speaker says "Das Kaninchen", I immediately understand that she is referring to a rabbit and not to rabbit part or rabbit stage. But how did I come to know that 'Kaninchen' in German refers to rabbit? Perhaps I took a course on German or I looked at the German-English dictionary. But the same question can be raised about my German teacher or a lexicographer who has compiled the dictionary. At some point in history, we had to start by doing radical translation. This was definitely a long and laborious process. The exact history of that process is vague and not completely available to us. But the importance of radical translation can hardly be denied.

But does this not show that, starting from radical translation, once we come up with a complete dictionary, translation becomes determinate, so that I can say 'Kaninchen' is translated as 'rabbit' and not 'rabbit part' or 'rabbit stage'? Here we have to be careful about the exact claim of the indeterminacy thesis. The indeterminacy thesis does not claim that translating 'Kaninchen' as 'rabbit' is wrong. What it says is that, from the same evidence, we can come up with a dictionary that will translate 'Kaninchen' as 'rabbit part'. Notice that it is not just a matter of translating a simple word 'Kaninchen' to 'rabbit part'. Due to the holistic structure of language, we will have to make necessary adjustments in other parts of the language in order to accommodate 'rabbit part' as a translation of 'Kaninchen'. This might be very complex; nonetheless it is possible in principle. So now we have more than one rival dictionary with rival semantic postulates, all of which are supported by evidence. The fact that in 'actual translation' we translate 'Kaninchen' as 'rabbit' does not in any way prove other translations to be wrong, for they are also supported by the same set of evidence.

It is true that radical translation is not identical with 'actual translation'. In 'actual translation', both the speaker and the hearer assume that they are using the same sets of semantic postulates. Otherwise there would be no communication at all. This choice of a particular set of semantic postulates is not based on any objective evidence but on simplicity and elegance of that particular set which other sets might lack. And the indeterminacy thesis does not have anything against it. What we should be aware of is that, philosophically speaking there is no such thing as *the* correct translation. This is true even in 'actual translation'. It is always possible, in principle, to come up with a rival translation manual. Normally, in 'actual translation', we do not do this in order to facilitate communication. But this does not have any bearing on the philosophical point of the indeterminacy thesis.

One reason why people are disinclined to accept indeterminacy is that they think that the meaning of 'Kaninchen' as 'rabbit' is already determined even before it starts getting used in language. It sounds like there is a group of entities called 'meaning' that we attach to corresponding words. Since this meaning is language–transcendent, we can attach these meanings to different words belonging to different languages.

Earlier I have shown why this view of language–transcendent meaning is wrong and misleading. Moreover, it lacks any explanatory power. It only shifts the problem from the level of language to a special realm of entities called 'meanings'. If our aim is to explain the mastery of a language that consists in knowing the meanings of the expressions of that language, then reference to a language–independent special realm of meaning does not help in any way.

4.4 Is radical interpretation possible? —A reply to Fodor and Lepore

One way of attacking the indeterminacy thesis is by attacking the notion of radical interpretation itself, for once we start from radical interpretation, indeterminacy follows. Fodor and Lepore question the plausibility of radical interpretation. They hold that the Quine-Davidson approach rests on the assumption that nothing can be a language unless its radical interpretation is possible.[9] Fodor and Lepore think that it is not reasonable to endorse this principle. By 'radical interpretation' we mean choosing a theory of truth for the object language on the basis of observations available to the interpreter.

Foder and Lepore argue that when a field linguist starts interpreting a foreign language, she does not *solely* rely on her observations of the informant's behavior plus the general canons of theory construction, etc. The field linguist is already armed with some powerful theoretical assumptions such as her assumptions about cognitive psychology, laws of linguistic change, information about how language learning works, etc. Thus the field linguist knows a lot more than what Quine-Davidson would allow her to know. So *mere* observation of the informant's behavior of holding sentences as true does not enable a field linguist to interpret a language. Consequently, radical interpretation is not possible. In other words, Fodor and Lepore argue that even if it is plausible to assume that the field linguist does choose a truth theory for the object language on the basis of the observational evidence, it does not follow that this evidence is adequate to choose a truth theory.[10] So it does not follow that radical interpretation is possible.

It seems to me that Fodor and Lepore are not denying that the field linguist can arrive at a truth theory on the basis of the evidence which radical interpretation allows; what they are denying is that such a truth theory is a theory of interpretation, i.e., that the knowledge of such a theory will enable one to understand and use the language for which the theory of truth is given. But, earlier in the second chapter, I have argued that a theory of truth— working under certain constraints— can act as a theory of interpretation. It shows that from the evidence radical interpretation allows, we can arrive at an adequate truth theory, knowledge of which enables one to know the meanings of the expressions of the language. Consequently, it follows that radical interpretation is possible.

Another principle, according to Fodor and Lepore, on which radical interpretation is supposed to rest is 'Nothing is hidden' principle.[11] This implies that the evidence on which a theory of meaning rests in order to give rise to a theory of interpretation must, in principle, be publicly accessible data. Fodor and Lepore offer two interpretations of this 'Nothing is hidden' principle, one metaphysical and the other epistemological. On the metaphysical interpretation, if we take 'Nothing is hidden' to imply the supervenience of the semantic on the public, then Fodor and Lepore think that it would be difficult to choose between extensionally equivalent T theories, theories that contain T-sentences like '"Snow is white" is true, if, and only if, snow is white' and theories that contain T-sentence like '"Snow is white" is true if and only if grass is green'. And the reason for this is that if all we have are the T sentences (which rest on public evidence) as the evidence of our theory of interpretation, then it would not be possible to block the possibility of the bizarre T- sentences. If, on the other hand, we take the epistemological interpretation of the "Nothing is hidden" principle, then that would suggest that nothing relevant to developing a T-theory is hidden from the radical interpreter. But to say this is to beg the question. For, if one says that one would not allow anything other than what is publicly available to both the speaker and the interpreter as evidence in order to develop a theory of radical interpretation, and then uses it as a justification for the 'Nothing is hidden' principle, one is assuming the principle itself—instead of giving a justification for it. Thus, in both the metaphysical and epistemological reading of the 'Nothing is hidden' principle, it is difficult to explain radical interpretation.

I do not think that Fodor and Lepore succeed in showing that radical interpretation is impossible. Accepting the metaphysical reading of 'Nothing is hidden', according to Fodor and Lepore, will lead to the possibility of bizarre T-sentences. But, earlier in the third chapter, I have shown that such an apprehension is not well-grounded, provided we make our theory holistic in nature. So 'Nothing is hidden', in its metaphysical reading, does not lead to any problem.

Nor does it beg the question if we take 'Nothing is hidden' in its epistemological reading. Earlier in the third chapter, while arguing for an extensional semantics, I have shown why we cannot rest our semantics on a theory of a speaker's intension or on other semantic notions like 'sense', etc. If this is valid, then it is justified to say that we must not rest our theory of interpretation on something that is hidden from the interpreter. This is not question begging, for I have not argued for extensionalism from a 'Nothing is hidden' principle. I have defended extensionalism first by setting the task of a theory of meaning, showing how the intensional semantics fails in this task, and then by showing that extensional semantics fulfils the task in a better way. So none of the arguments which Fodor and Lepore give succeed in proving that radical interpretation is impossible.

4.5 Has radical interpretation actually been done in practice? – A reply to John Wallace

Critics have argued that the Quine-Davidson picture of radical translation or interpretation is totally unreal. Neither the child, nor the field linguist, nor, indeed, any ordinary adult speaker, really goes through this process of radical interpretation in their real lives. However, I don't think that the viability of a philosophical theory based the notion of radical interpretation depends on whether we really face radical interpretation in our everyday lives. I think of radical interpretation as an idealized situation, very much the way a scientist conducts her experiment in an idealized environment in the laboratory.

Nevertheless, John Wallace[12] claims to find a historical case where archeologists found some inscribed clay tablets in the ruins of Knossos, the site of ancient civilization. One group of tablets is called 'Linear B'. These tablets consist of ideograms, phonetic signs and numerals. By working through various methods and on the basis of certain assumptions, archeologists were able to decipher the script as Greek.

Wallace views the Quine-Davidson program as answering three basic questions :

i) What is the evidence on which interpretation is based?

ii) What are the principles for sorting the evidence to speak for or against competing schemes of interpretation?

iii) In what forms are interpretation stated? Wallace thinks that the answers given by the archaologists to these three questions are very different from those given by Quine and Davidson. So the Quine-Davidson project fails to pass the test of the decipherment of Linear B.

There is a prima facie objection to Wallace's strategy. As Bruce Vermazen has asked, "How can a theory about translation or interpretation be tested by bringing it to a case of successful decipherment"?[13]

Deciphering a text and translating (interpreting) a text are different. By deciphering we figure out the values of the alphabets, syllables or ideograms as inscribed in the text. It is only after one succeeds in deciphering that one goes on interpreting the text, for, ultimately, one wants to know the meaning of the text. A text could be deciphered, but its interpretation might remain unknown. So conceptually decipherment is different from translation, even though they might be intertwined in practice. This difference is reinforced by the fact that, as Vermazen mentions, the great part of the translation of Linear B was performed only after decipherment was complete and people were sure that the language they were dealing with was Greek. But then it was not a radical translation any more, for one could take help from a standard Greek-English dictionary— probably with some exception— for the Greek language might have changed through the course of time.

I do not intend to describe in full details the strategy followed by the archeologists for deciphering Linear B. Both Wallace and Vermazen have done that. I would like to make some comments on what Wallace said about the possible replies of Quine and Davidson to the questions raised by Wallace with regard to the decipherment of Linear B.

Remember the first question concerning the nature of evidence for interpretation. Now, according to Wallace, the evidence which archeologists used for the decipherment is our historical knowledge about the palaces and central administrations of those civilizations, its population, its geography and much more. And surely this is more than what Quine or Davidson would allow an interpreter to rest his evidence on.

I agree with Wallace's claim that the archeologists use all sorts of evidence for deciphering the ancient texts. But does this affect the Quine-Davidson project? I don't think so. For the same questions of evidence can be raised for our interpretations of what those ancient people used to believe, their hopes, their life-style, etc. I am not saying that, at a particular point in history, radical interpretation started. But, conceptually, it is coherent to think of radical interpretation, where interpretation starts from meagre evidence. The criticism that radical interpretation is far removed from anything that ever happens in our conscious experience is not justified, because a theory of meaning— at least the way I am defending it— does not aim at giving a language manual to the students.

Wallace's second question was concerning the way the evidence is marshalled. Wallace thinks that if we try to interpret the Linear B on the basis of one's assent to current stimulation, it does not make any sense because the clerks and administrators who recorded those inscriptions were given considerable training and their ability to write those inscriptions depends on the training they got as much as on current stimulation. Nor does charity help, according to Wallace. For, to maximize the agreement, the interpreter must first grasp what the ancient clerk's place is like. Also, one needs some insights and interpretative moves which make it possible to read the tablets.

Contrary to Wallace, I think that the Davidsonian principle of charity will help us in marshalling our evidence of interpretation. We start by attributing our beliefs to the interpretee. Then if we see her doing things irrational given those beliefs, we change a few of those previously ascribed beliefs. Here we will be guided by Quine's principle of 'minimum mutilation'. We might end up with two sets of belief attributions, which involve some amount of disagreement between me and my interpretee. I suppose Davidson would say that both sets are equally defensible. And the denial of this possibility assumes that there are fixed Greek–English equivalences (in the example of Linear B) which can be discovered by some way other than truth conditional semantics. And this is a mistake that I have tried to deal with earlier in the third chapter.

Wallace's third question was about the form in which the interpretation will be given. Wallace thinks that the decipherment of Linear B shows that the form of the interpretation will be in the way Quine and Davidson have advocated *plus* a gloss. As an example, Wallace mentions that the way Myceneans (an ancient civilization) measured their land is by the amount of wheat that could be sown in the land if it were planted in wheat. Archeologists cannot simply interpret the tablets word by word or sentence by sentence. They have to put a gloss as well.

I think that Davidson's truth theory will give us the kind of gloss that Wallace wants. For, in this theory, we are getting for each sentence of the foreign language a statement specifying the truth condition of the foreign sentence. So, for the sentence describing the measurement of the land will be tied through a bi-conditional with the sentence of the language which will describe the truth condition of the foreign sentence and, while doing this, the measurement will be explained by referring it to the measurement of wheat, etc. This is especially evident if there is some belief or practice referred to in the foreign sentence that does not have a corresponding word in the language of the theory.

4.6 Is semantic indeterminacy counterintuitive? — A reply to John Searle

John Searle[14] starts by describing the behaviourist assumptions from which Quine's indeterminacy thesis follows. According to behaviourist empiricism, meaning is explained in terms of external stimuli and disposition to verbal behaviour. The objective reality of meaning is simply a matter of disposition to make utterances in response to external stimuli. And the external stimuli are defined in terms of the patterns of stimulation of the nerve ending and the verbal response is defined in terms of the sound patterns the speaker is disposed to emit. There are no internal 'meanings', i.e., entities connecting the stimuli and the verbal response. So mastery of a language, in this view, consists in making the right sounds in response to the right stimuli.

Now, if we start from the behaviorist assumption of linguistic meaning, then we end up with indeterminacy. For, while translating the native utterance 'Gavagai' in front of a rabbit scurrying by, we can find two possible and incompatible candidates for translation like 'There is a rabbit' or 'There is an undetached part of a rabbit'. Since meaning is explained in terms of stimulus-response and since stimulus is explained in terms of the patterns of stimulation on nerve endings, the phenomenon of a rabbit scurrying by will permit both the translations mentioned above. So if all what we should consider are the patterns of stimulation, then it is impossible to distinguish between 'There is a rabbit' and 'There is an undetached part of a rabbit'. We cannot tell which one of these is a proper translation of the native's utterance 'Gavagai'. But we, as English–speakers, all know that there is a difference between the native's meaning 'There is a rabbit' and her meaning 'There is an undetached part of a rabbit'. We know, independent of any theory, that there is a difference between the meanings of these two sentences. But, if behaviorist assumptions are correct, then there should be no way of discriminating the meaning of those two sentences, for both the sentences are valid translations of the native sentence 'Gavagai'. We do know that there is a difference between the two translations. So, according to Searle, behaviorism leads us to an absurdity. In the philosophy of language and mind it is necessary that we take a first-person perspective. Since I, as an English–speaker, know that there is a difference in the meaning of 'rabbit' and 'undetached rabbit part', any theory which leads to the conclusion that there is no such difference is mistaken.

Searle describes the indeterminacy thesis saying that insofar as questions of meaning are concerned, there is no such thing as getting it right or wrong, because there is no fact of the matter to be right or wrong about. The indeterminacy thesis also says that there are an indefinite number of valid but incompatible translations of a foreign language. It is to be noted, according to Searle, that Quine rejected any appeal to psychologically real meaning at the very beginning. Quine *assumes*, from the very start, the non-existence of such meanings. So, for Quine, the real issue is, *given* behaviourism, whether we can make sense of the notion of meaning. This is how Quine concludes indeterminacy. But if we reject Quine's assumption about the validity of the behaviourist thesis, then it is hard to see how indeterminacy follows.

Of course, Quine is aware of the supposed absurdities that indeterminacy leads to. If indeterminacy is a valid thesis, then there is no difference between my meaning rabbit and my meaning rabbit part, nor is there any difference between my referring to a rabbit or my referring to a rabbit part. Quine resolves this absurdity by relativizing the reference and ontology. So, the fact that I take 'rabbit' as the proper translation of 'Gavagai' is explicable only by taking English as a background language. Here Quine compares this kind of relativity with our talk of position and velocity of an object only relative to a coordinate system. So we can talk of the reference of an expression only relative to some background language.

But Searle thinks that Quine's attempt of relativizing reference won't help to get the indeterminacy thesis free from its absurd results. For if I assume that my idiolect of English can be explained behavioristically, then any translation of an expression to another in my idiolect is completely arbitrary. There is no way I can tell whether by 'rabbit' I mean rabbit part or rabbit stage. It won't solve the problem by saying that we arbitrarily choose a translation manual, for the arbitrariness of the selection of the translation manual is the very problem we are dealing with. So Quine's relativity of reference does not help us in determining that I mean rabbit and not rabbit part. The absurdity still remains, according to Searle. We cannot simply take our mother tongue at its face value and take that as the background language, for the mother tongue itself, according to Quine, is explained in terms of stimulus-response.

Let us take Henri and Pierre, for example, who are translating the English sentence 'There is a rabbit' into French (assume that they don't know English). Imagine that Henri translates it as '*stade de lapin*' and Pierre translates it as '*parti non-détachée d'un lapin*'. According to Searle, our pre-Quinean common sense will say that both of them are wrong. These are just bad translations. It is plain to me that when I said 'There is a rabbit' I did not mean *stade de lapin* or *parti non-détachée de lapin.* The fact that they are wrong shows that there is a matter of fact to be right or wrong about.

According to Quine, both Henri and Pierre are right relative to the translation manual they are working with. The absurdity cannot be resolved by relativizing the translation to a background language, for— independent of any theory— we know that both of them are wrong. It is true that the meaning a word *possesses* is only relative to a language, but this only presupposes non-relativity of the *meaning* possessed. Some words are meaningful, while some others are meaningless in English. Let us call the feature that all meaningful words share as opposed to meaningless words the *meaning*. From the fact that 'rabbit' means whatever it means only relative to English, it does not follow that its feature called 'meaning' exists only relative to English. In fact, the very attempt of translation is an attempt to find a word which has the same feature like the word being translated. Since indeterminacy makes it impossible to distinguish between the two alternative features called 'meaning' and since this feature is not relative to a background language, referential relativity does not remove the reductio.

Thus Searle claims to show that how behaviouristic assumptions lead Quine to some absurd results. But Davidson is not a behaviourist. Still he subscribes to the indeterminacy thesis. Searle argues that, like Quine, Davidson ignores the first person role in his semantics. According to Searle, from the two premises, viz., that the evidence for radical interpretation is the speaker's holding sentences true, and that there are alternative ways of linking words with objects all of which will explain why a speaker holds a sentence true, it does not automatically follow that meaning is indeterminate unless one assumes that all the semantic facts must be publicly available to the speaker and the interpreter and that those facts must rest on empirical evidence. As we have seen earlier, Davidson, in fact, holds this extra premise to be true. Meaning is an empirical matter and it must be equally accessible to the interpreters.

Searle raises the same objection against Davidson that he did against Quine. Even before any theory came into the picture, I know that when I said 'Wilt is tall' I meant the person Wilt and not the shadow of Wilt. These are just plain facts. Any theory of meaning has to start with these facts. But Davidson's theory makes us believe that I am not in a position to differentiate between my meaning Wilt and my meaning the shadow of Wilt, for in Davidson's truth conditional semantics the same sentence can be related to different truth conditions. The only evidence we have is the speaker holding a sentence true under publicly observable condition. But this seems to threaten the distinction that we observe in pre-Davidsonian life.

Davidson rejects determinate reference, for he starts from the assumption that semantic facts are public features of language and, consequently, they are subject to indeterminacy. But since we know, quite independently, according to Searle, that the conclusion of indeterminacy is false, the original assumption should be doubted. When I said 'Wilt is tall', I know I meant the person Wilt. Since I interpret another's utterances in the light of how I interpret my own utterances, I interpret somebody else's utterance 'Wilt is tall' as meaning that the person Wilt is tall and not that the shadow of Wilt is tall. When I understand myself, I know more than the truth conditions of the utterances I make, I also know what I mean. The same explanation applies to my interpretation of other people's utterances.

In our pre-theoretical life we can figure out, from the totality of the relevant evidence, that by 'Wilt is tall' the speaker means the person Wilt and not his shadow. Searle thinks that understanding the speech of one another is possible in the background of non-representational mental capacities that are shaped culturally and biologically. It is only when we forget our real life and try to build a 'theory' that we get the absurd results exhibited in the indeterminacy thesis.

According to Searle the notion of 'radical translation' or 'radical interpretation', which Quine and Davidson advocate, impresses a third-person point of view upon us. It puts an interpreter or a translator in a situation where she is observing the foreigner verbally responding. And the result is to confuse the epistemic with the semantic. It confuses the question 'How do you know?' with 'What is it that you know when you know?' But the linguistic knowledge of what I know when I know a sentence must be the same as what I know when I know somebody else's utterance.

According to Searle, both Quine and

Davidson adopt an anti-mentalistic and public shareability attitude toward semantics. Hence they are led to the absurd thesis of indeterminacy of meaning. Both these attitudes are more a matter of preference for a certain level of description than some real discovery. Searle thinks that the study of semantics must involve a level of intentionality, for semantics includes the level where we express our beliefs, desires, etc.

Davidson's emphasis on public shareability and empirical evidence makes him adopt a third person perspective. Then he argues that what cannot be grasped in a third person perspective is not actually a feature of semantics. According to Searle, one meaning of the term 'empirical' test is subject-object or third person test. But there is another meaning of 'empirical' that Searle mentions as 'actual' or 'factual'. The argument for the former interpretation, i.e., for the third person perspective, succeeds only if we assume that what is not valid from a third person perspective is not actual, which Searle claims to prove wrong. If, on the other hand, we accept the latter interpretation, i.e., 'actual' or 'factual', then, Searle claims to have shown, there is a distinction between what one has as the empirical evidence for interpreting somebody's utterance and what somebody actually means. In either case, according to Searle, there is no argument left to support indeterminacy.

From the Quine-Davidson standpoint these

objections seem to arise from a misconstrual, by Searle, of the indeterminacy thesis. Indeterminacy does not imply that there is no difference between 'rabbit' and 'rabbit part'. Remember that the indeterminacy thesis claims that there are more than one mutually incompatible translations of the native's language. If the translations are mutually incompatible, then, by definition, it follows that there is a difference between meaning rabbit and meaning rabbit part, because this is what is meant by being incompatible. Indeterminacy thesis seems to presuppose the very claim that we can and do differentiate between the meaning of 'rabbit' and 'rabbit part'. Otherwise, we cannot talk of the indeterminacy of meaning at all.

It is true, as Searle says, that when I confront a native uttering 'Gavagai' I will translate it as 'rabbit' and also I know that translation of 'Gavagai' as 'rabbit part' is wrong. Does it go against indeterminacy thesis? I don't think so. Here 'I' refers to a speaker of English and according to English usage 'rabbit part' is a wrong translation. I can well imagine a speaker, who, after hearing the native sentence 'Gavagai', will translate it as 'rabbit part' in her language. So the 'I' as the speaker of this language is working within a different translation manual. Obviously, it would be foolish to say that I, as an English speaker know that the speaker of the other language is wrong in his translation. For both translations tally with the totality of available empirical evidence.

This brings me to Searle's criticism of Davidson, for Davidson holds that all the semantic facts must be publicly available and rest on empirical evidence. Searle argues that since the assumption of the public and empirical nature of evidence of a semantic theory leads to indeterminacy, which we independently know to be wrong, Davidson's assumption is invalid. Searle talks of including the speaker's intentions within a theory of meaning.

First let me clarify what I mean by 'theory' in a 'theory of meaning', since Searle thinks that it is only when we develop a 'theory' and we diverge from real life that we get into absurdities like indeterminacy. A theory is a systematic presentation of that of which it is a theory. By doing this, a theory is expected to elucidate or explain the phenomenon concerned. We start from certain observations that can be regarded as the axioms of the theory. Then we try to derive certain consequences from those observations that can be regarded as theorems of the theory. Of course, for the derivation we need some auxiliary hypotheses and derivation rules. We can fit our description of a theory with natural language. A natural language contains an infinite number of sentences. But our knowledge of those large number of sentences rests on our knowledge of a finite stock of primitive expressions and their rules of combination. This explains why we understand new sentences on the basis of our knowledge of those already learned. So, if we try to have a theory of meaning for a natural language L, such a theory should have a finite number of axioms that will give the semantic properties of the words of L, and it must also show how by different modes of combination a large number of theorems can be produced that give the semantic properties of all the sentences of L.

Earlier, with respect to extensionalism, I have explained why a theory of meaning is better approached from an extensional viewpoint. Extensionalism is not opposed to a speaker's intention, as such. Extensionalism only claims that we cannot rest our theory of meaning on the speaker's intention. In other words, a theory of intention cannot be the foundation of a theory of meaning. And the reason is that what a person believes and what a person means are interlocked with each other. Knowledge of the one requires the knowledge of the other. It is true that we can guess what a person believes from her non-linguistic behaviour. But we can do this to a very limited extent. If we want to have an account of a person's total belief system involving fine distinctions, we need a theory to interpret her utterances. And we need a theory of the person's belief in order to know what she means (this is the point Searle makes and Davidson agrees with this). The way to break the circle is to have theory of truth that will specify the truth conditions of the utterances made by the speaker. So although Davidson rejects the attempt to explain meaning on the basis of a speaker's mental states, he clearly recognizes the importance of propositional-attitude psychology for a theory of meaning. Thus, Davidson's version of a theory of meaning is not opposed to a theory of speaker's intentions, etc., it only rejects their explanatory role.

This shows what kind of evidence we need to have a theory of meaning. Just now I have shown that we cannot rest our theory of meaning on a theory of intention, etc. Earlier in the chapter on extensionalism I have argued why we cannot use notions like 'sense' etc. to generate a theory of meaning. Sense and other related notions seem to presuppose rather than explain meaning. So if we want to generate a theory of meaning in a non-question-begging manner, then we cannot rest our theory on semantic notions. This is where Davidson finds the notion of truth-condition helpful. So the evidence on which we can rest our theory of meaning consists in our knowledge of the speaker's holding sentences true under certain conditions. We can have this bit of knowledge even before we know the details of the speaker's belief system. At the same time, we are not exploiting the semantic notions like 'sense', etc.

But if we rest our theory on the speaker's holding a sentence true, are we not resting our theory on a speaker's belief system, for holding a sentence true is having a belief about that sentence? Davidson would respond to this question in the affirmative. But this is permissible for two reasons. First, knowledge of the speaker's holding a sentence true does not seem to presuppose the knowledge of the speaker's other intentions, desires, hopes, etc., although all of them are related to each other. And, also, this belief in holding a sentence true is itself explained in the course of developing a theory of truth. Secondly, as mentioned earlier, a theory of the truth condition of a speaker's utterances seems to give us what we want from a theory of meaning of that speaker's language, which is our ultimate aim.

This is where one can see that truth conditional semantics is not reductionist. It is not reducing the notions like thinking or meaning to some physiological processes. Since truth conditional semantics rests itself on the speaker's holding a sentence true, truth conditional semantic denies that meaning can be reduced to something non-mental. It only claims that if we have a theory which will assign truth conditions to a speaker based on the speaker's holding sentences true, it will do the job of a theory of meaning of the speaker's language.

This brings me to Searle's criticism of third-person perspective. According to Searle, the notion of radical translation (or interpretation) implies the third-person perspective where the interpreter is interpreting another person's utterances and, consequently, it conflates the epistemic with the semantic; it confuses the question 'How do you *know* a language'? and 'What is it that *you* know when you know a language'?

One of the motives for drawing the picture of radical interpretation stems from the idea that the primary function of language is communication. The *raison d'etre* of a language is that there exists a community of people who want to express their thoughts, desires, hopes, etc., to each other. It is true that often I talk to myself. Whether this is communication *per se* or not is a philosophical problem. But it is true that even when I talk to myself, I use the language and follow its rules the way as when I talk to my fellow–speakers. So using language is a form of communication. We seem to successfully communicate when we know what we mean by the sentences we utter. This is why, when we talk of meaning, we talk of two speakers trying to interpret each other's utterances. I don't think that the first-person perspective is necessarily opposed to a third-person perspective. The rules *I* follow and the meaning *I* attach to the sentences when *I* know a language are the same rules and the same meaning I attach when I am in the position of an interpreter.

Earlier I mentioned that a theory of meaning

is not the knowledge of 'knowing how', but the knowledge of 'knowing what' (this too, with some qualification). Davidson's truth conditional semantics does not say anything about how we know the truth of the sentences. It only says that *if* one possessed a theory of truth condition for the sentences of L, then one would be in a position to interpret the sentences of L. Thus Davidson's theory gives an answer to the semantic question that what is it that one knows when one knows a language.

One can explain the issue of semantic indeterminacy in terms of 'semantic supervenience' as developed by James Van Cleve.[15] Semantic supervenience is the thesis that the non-semantic facts determine the semantic facts.

Van Cleve gives the general form of the argument for indeterminacy as follows:

i) Supervenience: An A-statement is true or false in virtue of some B-fact.

ii) Underdetermination: The totality of B-facts does not suffice to determine the truth-value of the A-statement.

iii) Indeterminacy : A-statement lacks determinate truth-value.

Van Cleve also argues that Quine needs semantic supervenience in addition to underdetermination to get indeterminacy. Underdetermination alone could not lead to indeterminacy, for someone might argue that there are intentional states of the speaker which are facts of the matter by referring to which we can remove indeterminacy. To rule this assumption out, Quine advocates semantic supervenience by saying that linguistic meaning supervenes on verbal behavior, i.e., verbal behavior determines linguistic meaning.

I think that Van Cleve's analysis of Quine is correct. But the picture is more complex. It is perhaps true that we can take Quine and Davidson as subscribing to the semantic supervenience thesis and Alston, Searle, etc. denying it. But we might think of Searle as accepting semantic supervenience, but supervenience of semantics in a somewhat larger domain. Perhaps this will throw some light upon Searle's differing viewpoint. Recall that semantic supervenience says that non-semantic facts determine semantic facts. I don't think that Searle would be opposed to this premise taken by itself. The problem arises when we try to demarcate the realm of non-semantic facts. What are the non-semantic facts that will determine (explain) meaning? Quine explains the range of non-semantic facts in terms of stimulus-response. Davidson explains it in terms of a theory of truth. Both can be branded as extensional theories of meaning, although my sympathy lies with Davidson. Searle, who opposes extensionalism, thinks that both stimulus-response and theory of truth fail to exhaust non-semantic facts and, consequently, the Quine-Davidson approach is inadequate to explain semantic facts. According to Searle, we should also include intentional states of a speaker within the scope of non-semantic facts to adequately explain semantic facts. Viewed in this manner, the debate between Quine-Davidson and Searle is not a debate as to whether to accept semantic supervenience or not. Rather, it is a debate as to how to explain non-semantic facts, what to include into the range of non-semantic facts. Both the parties in the debate are willing to accept that non-semantic facts determine semantic facts.

In this setting, I can now clarify my objection to Searle's stance. Both the camps, Quine-Davidson on the one hand and Searle, etc. on the other hand, are trying to explain meaning, a notion which we exploit when we claim to know that the sentence 's' means p or that the sentence 's' is synonymous with the sentence 'p', etc. And these are what constitute what Van Cleve refers to as 'semantic facts'. So, explanation of semantic facts is the common goal. How can we attain this goal? One thing, for sure, is that we cannot use any semantic notion in order to explain semantic facts, for that would be question begging. Since semantic notions like Fregean 'sense' or an entitative notion of meaning presuppose our knowl-, edge of what meaning is, we cannot exploit these notions in order to explain semantic facts. So we have to look for some non-semantic facts which will help us in explaining semantic facts.

This is where I find some of the comments made by an anti-extensionalist philosophically non-explanatory. At one point Searle says that, in one's own case, when one understands what she is talking about, one not only knows the truth condition of the sentence she utters, "in addition I know what I mean".[16] But, as a semanticist, my task is to explain this knowledge of what one knows when one knows the meaning of the sentence uttered by a speaker. If our aim is to explain meaning, saying that when a speaker utters 'Snow is white' she *means* snow is white does not explain our understanding of what meaning is, for the question still remains : What is happening when the speaker means that snow is white by the sentence 'Snow is white'? Nor can one exploit other semantic notions like 'sense' or 'proposition' for that seems to involve our knowledge of what meaning is. So if we want to explain Searle etc. advocating a semantics which claims to explain our knowledge of meaning, then we must take them subscribing to the thesis of semantic supervenience, a thesis that says *non-semantic* facts determine semantic facts.

What are the alternatives if we deny semantic supervenience? Van Cleve mentions two possibilities; i) some semantic facts are not made true by any other fact, or ii) those semantic facts are true because of other facts that are always themselves semantic. If my interpretation of the debate between Quine-Davidson and Searle is correct, then nobody would accept the second alternative for that would be question begging as I have explained earlier. Nor is the second alternative acceptable, I suspect, to Quine-Davidson or Searle for all of them agree that semantic facts are explicable in terms of other facts. The constituent of these 'other facts' is what the problem is about.

One might question my interpretation by arguing that embracing semantic supervenience leads Quine-Davidson to indeterminacy while Searle does not accept indeterminacy. So how can both Quine-Davidson and Searle accept semantic supervenience? My answer is that semantic supervenience, as such, does not lead to indeterminacy. It is semantic supervenience *plus* the assumption that 'non-semantic' only includes patterns of stimulation (in Quine) or theory of truth (Davidson) which leads to indeterminacy. This additional assumption is what I have called extensionalism. So it is semantic supervenience in its extensional interpretation which leads to indeterminacy. Since Searle thinks that indeterminacy leads to absurd consequences (I, however, don't agree with Searle), Searle concludes that semantic supervenience, in its extensional interpretation, is inadequate to explain semantic facts. But this does not imply that

Searle is denying semantic supervenience in its totality. Searle accepts semantic supervenience in its intensional interpretation, for, according to Searle, that would avoid indeterminacy. I would imagine that Searle is willing to accept that we can explain meaning by introducing intensional notions— and this is what I refer to as semantic supervenience in its intensional interpretation.

4.7 Indeterminacy and speaker's knowledge of language — A reply to William Alston

Misconceptions about the claims of the indeterminacy thesis are abound in philosophical literature. William P. Alston's[17] discussion of indeterminacy is one such example. Alston describes the common sense view of language as consisting of expressions which have meanings. Simplest meaningful units enter into a complex structure where the meaning of the complex is a function of the meaning of the simpler units. Alston calls this the 'Standard Picture' view of semantics. According to Alston, Quine is the lonely crusader against this standard picture. And one of the arguments Quine puts forward to oppose the standard picture is the argument for indeterminacy. Alston thinks that, at the deepest level, the opposition between Quine and the standard picture is not the opposition between behaviorism and mentalism, but opposition between two methodologies, a participant stance and a spectator stance (remember, Charles Taylor mentioned the same point). As opposed to Quine's 'Explicitism, a get-it-all-out-in-the-open' attitude, Alston suggests that much of our knowledge is acquired by unconscious process which we can never make fully explicit.

Alston thinks that "Semantic indeterminacy has long been recognized in the form of vagueness of degree."[18] He gives the example of 'City', where we do not have any precise answer as to how many inhabitants we need in order to apply the word 'City' as opposed to 'Village'. How long semantic indeterminacy has been recognized by philosophers is a matter of the history of philosophy. But it would be a misinterpretation if one thinks that the indeterminacy thesis claims that certain words of any natural language are vague in their application. The indeterminacy thesis claims that we can, in principle, construct more than one set of semantic postulates while interpreting any given language, which gives rise to more than one translation manual for that language. And there is no objective evidence on the basis of which we can accept one set of semantic postulates and reject others. For all the different sets of semantic postulates match the totality of objective evidence available. The difference between the indeterminacy thesis and the vagueness of certain terms is qualitative in nature. Indeterminacy thesis is not only claiming that all terms of a natural language are to some extent vague. What it claims is that we can always construct rival translation manuals for a language that are mutually incompatible, but all of which are supported by the total available evidence. The reason why we accept one and not the other does not spring from any objective fact, but from certain internal characteristics of a system like elegance, simplicity, etc.

Alston questions the move from non-availability of objectively correct translations to the impossibility of determinate meaning. He thinks that there are other resources to determine what an expression means that we should not ignore. He goes on claiming that "it seems obvious that I know what I mean by 'rabbit' and other words in my language."[19] I know this just by virtue of being a speaker of that language. This semantic knowledge which one possesses just by virtue of being a speaker has been ignored by advocates of the indeterminacy thesis, so claims Alston. Hence the meaning of 'rabbit' does not solely depend on observing the behavior of a speaker and relevant circumstances.

I would like to ask Alston : How have we, as English–speakers, acquired the knowledge of the meaning of 'rabbit'? How have we mastered the language? What is involved in acquiring the ability to be a speaker of a language? It is not enough to say that we possess the semantic knowledge just by virtue of being a speaker of that language. This does not explain anything. Alston seems to take the notion of semantic knowledge for granted without critically analyzing it. As I have explained earlier, if we carefully explain what is involved in the mastery of a language, we can see that indeterminacy crops up (at least in principle).

Moreover, the indeterminacy thesis does not deny that we English–speakers use 'rabbit' to mean the whole of the enduring organism and not rabbit part or rabbit stage. The indeterminacy thesis asserts that one could construct other sets of semantic postulates that will map 'rabbit' onto 'rabbit part' or 'rabbit stage' and one cannot say that these mappings are wrong. All of these mappings correspond to the totality of speech dispositions of a speaker. The fact that we use 'rabbit' to mean a whole organism of such kind does not make this particular meaning sacrosanct. It is always philosophically (if not practically) possible to construct different sets of semantic postulates giving rise to more than one set of meanings for a given language.

Alston thinks that a fluent speaker will be able to choose between alternative meanings. This is true but this does not mean that other alternatives are wrong. This only shows that the speaker is working within a particular set of semantic postulates which maps 'rabbit' on to the whole of the enduring organism and not to 'rabbit part' or 'rabbit stage'. If we work with different sets of semantic postulates, we might have to map 'rabbit' onto 'rabbit part'. There is nothing wrong with this, for the totality of available evidence supports this mapping relation. The choice between alternate meanings depends on the choice between alternative sets of semantic postulates. And the choice among the systems of semantic postulates does not rest on any objective facts, for the totality of available evidence lends support to all of those different sets of semantic postulates. I agree with Alston when he claims that "one who is prepared to accept the existence of intelligible discourse is in no position to deny that speakers frequently know what they mean by the words they use."[20] But the indeterminacy thesis claims that same words can be mapped onto different meanings that are also being supported by the totality of evidence available. Consequently, a speaker's utterance is amenable to more than one interpretation. Normally, for successful communication, the speakers of a community stick to one particular interpretation. But this does not invalidate other interpretations.

The same kind of argument has been used by Alston to show that from the existence of rival translation manuals it does not follow that all of those translations are correct. Alston gives us a solution that is apparently plausible but philosophically naive. He argues that if language L_1 is amenable to rival translation manuals, then a speaker of language L_2 can learn L_1 and then she knows both languages. Consequently, she can tell us which translation of L_1 to L_2 is the correct one. But the important point is that when a speaker of L_2 will start learning L_1, this learning procedure itself comprises indeterminacy. The speaker of L_2 will face the problem of determining the meaning of 'Gavagai', whether as the whole of an enduring organism, or as rabbit part or as rabbit stage. Since she does not yet possess the semantic knowledge (according to Alston himself) of L_1, she is not in a position to settle for *the* correct translation.

4.8 Semantic indeterminacy and disagreements among speakers — A reply to Dummett

Michael Dummett, who acknowledges Quine's great contribution to philosophy of language, is far from convinced that Quinean theory is free of problems. According to Dummett, Quine presents a model of language as an articulated structure where some sentences lie toward the periphery and others at different stages within the interior. Experience impinges directly on the periphery, but since sentences at the periphery are connected with their neighbours in the interior, the impact of experience is transmitted to the interior as well. A model of a language can be viewed as a model of meaning, for a theory of meaning explains what it is that one knows when one knows a language. This is where Quine's picture of radical translation comes in, of which indeterminacy of translation or meaning is the effect. Dummett argues that since indeterminacy of meaning does not give us the picture of what happens when one knows a language, we have to abandon the Quinean model of language because such a model leads us to the indeterminacy thesis.

After formulating different versions of indeterminacy, Dummett says that the thesis "says no more than that two speakers of a language, even though both speak it quite correctly, ... may disagree over the truth value of a sentence even when there is no difference in their present or previous experiences to which this disagreement may be traced."[21] I want to emphasize the expression "even though both speak it quite correctly." Dummett is right in making this observation, but why is it that those two speakers give two different translations that are inconsistent with each other? No English–speaker would consider using 'cow' and 'cow part' interchangeably. But, again, both are correct, each viewed from its own translation scheme, for both these translations correspond to the totality of speech dispositions of the speaker whose language we are going to translate. The only explanation, seems to me, is the fact that those two speakers have derived their translations from different sets of semantic postulates. In one case, the speaker has translated the native sentence to 'cow' in her language and in the other case the sentence has been translated to 'cow part'. Behavioural evidence corroborates more than one set of semantic postulates. Since meaning is whatever we can extract from the behavioral pattern of a speaker, we have more than one meaning for a single expression. By extending this picture to the whole of language, we can say that the interpreted language can have two different translations that are not interchangeable with each other.

If this is the true picture (and I think it is), then it threatens any notion of Fregean "sense" which was invoked to explain meaning. Two sets of semantic postulates gives rise to different 'senses' of the same expression and there is no matter of fact on the basis of which we can say one is right and the other is wrong. There is nothing rigid or immutable about the fact that we attach one particular sense to an expression and not another. It all depends on our choice of semantic postulates. The mode of presentation of an object is amenable to more than one interpretation. In fact, at this level, we can see that the nature of sense or proposition does not serve any useful purpose. Sense gradually shades off to reference, i.e., to the objects of natural kind constituting the environment where I am engaged in interpreting.

The indeterminacy thesis should not be confused with the fact that any two speakers of a language can disagree about the truth of a sentence. This kind of disagreement is a well-recognised fact and nobody is denying this. But the indeterminacy thesis claims that any two speakers can interpret each other's utterances in more than one way that are not compatible with each other. And there is no question of rightness or wrongness of either of them. So the claim of the indeterminacy thesis goes much deeper than mere disagreement about the truth of a sentence.

The indeterminacy thesis is not the claim that disagreement arises because neither speaker has conclusive evidence for assigning truth-values to the sentence in question. The indeterminacy thesis is more radical in nature. The important point is that what constitutes conclusive evidence is open to indeterminacy. We can formulate the concept of conclusive evidence in more than one way. A conclusive demonstration of the truth of a sentence has to be done either by referring to some other basal sentences or some higher level sentences. And, in either case, indeterminacy crops up.

I am not denying that meaning is determined by a conclusive means of establishing a sentence as true. But this conclusive means of establishing a sentence is plagued with indeterminacy. And the conclusive evidence lends support to both interpretations that are incompatible with each other. This does not mean that we cannot have any meaningful disagreement. Any agreement or disagreement is possible only in the background of a system of semantic postulates. Normally, speakers of the same language use the same set of semantic postulates, not because the other sets are wrong, but perhaps because the other sets are more complex and lack elegance. So, within a set of semantic postulates, speakers can quite meaningfully disagree. But one speaker using one set of semantic postulates cannot have meaningful disagreement with another speaker who is using a different set of semantic postulates, for there is no common ground to make sense of that disagreement. Using different sets of semantic postulates implies using the words with different meanings. And if two speakers use the words with different meanings, they are not actually communicating with each other, and, consequently, the question of their disagreement does not arise at all.

Dummett seems to confuse the indeterminacy thesis with the claim that two people disagree over the truth of a sentence. He thinks that in the case of disagreement among A and B, if both come to know that at some point in their debate they have been using the same word in different ways then they "have succeeded in reducing their disagreement to a difference about meaning."[22] Since disagreement is possible only in the background of a commonality, when A differs from B, we can assume that A and B are using the same set of semantic postulates. If they were using radically different semantic postulates, then even they themselves could not make sense of their disagreement. That they are using a particular set of semantic postulates and not others does not invalidate other systems of semantic postulates. The indeterminacy thesis claims that all these different sets of semantic postulates are equally legitimate, for all of them equally correspond to the totality of speech dispositions. There is nothing sacred about one particular set of semantic postulates. So even if A and B come to see the cause of their dispute, this does not undermine indeterminacy. For we can always make use of a different system of semantic postulates which are equally legitimate. Contrary to what Dummett thinks, if A and B succeed in reducing their disagreement, meaning does not become determinate. Their difficulties in acquiring conclusive evidence may be overcome, but this does not threaten indeterminacy of meaning. We can always, in principle, come up with different formulation of semantic postulates.

Dummett thinks that the "Indeterminacy of meaning does not entail indeterminacy of translation."[23] My move is from translation (truth) to meaning and not from meaning to translation. I am engaged in understanding the notion of meaning. My extensional-holistic view of language enables me to understand meaning by observing a speaker's behavioral pattern. This is where translation comes in. Behavioral evidence gives rise to more than one set of semantic postulates. Meaning loses its determinacy. Translation of natural languages are indeterminate— not in the sense of our inability to discover certain empirical possibilities, but— in the sense that natural languages are amenable to more than one translation manual, each of which is equally valid but incompatible with each other.

Dummett fails to see the pervasive nature of indeterminacy. He thinks that even if two speakers adopt two different but empirically equivalent theories, "the resulting dispute between them should lead them to recognize, if they obtain a sufficiently comprehensive grasp of each other's theories, what the situation is, and hence to realize that the disagreement between them is only apparent...."[24] Dummett thinks that both parties can understand each other's theories. But herein lies the indeterminacy. To understand each other's theories, each has to interpret the other's uttered sentences. And these sentences can be understood in more than one way, for they are amenable to two or more semantic postulates. So the phrase "if they obtain a sufficiently comprehensive grasp of each other's theories" seems to be problematic. Both can understand each other's theories in more than one way and there is no objective criterion with reference to which we can say one is right and the other is wrong. If understanding each other's theories is thus plagued with indeterminacy, obtaining a sufficiently comprehensive grasp of each other's theories does not help. There is no objective validity in claiming that this is *the* meaning of a sentence. It is not only a question of using the same term in two different ways.

4.8.1 The 'just more theory' objection to Dummett

In this section I will depart temporarily from Dummett in order to illustrate the 'just more theory' objection which I lodge against him. While doing this I will draw heavily on J. Van Cleve's recent treatment of 'just more theory' by appealing to indeterminacy.

My objection to Dummett is similar to what Van Cleve refers to as the 'just more theory' objection while explaining an argument by Hilary Putnam against Hartry Field.[25] Firstly, I will present Putnam's criticism of a semantic definition given by Field where Putnam argues that Field's definition cannot get rid of semantic indeterminacy. Secondly, I will explain Van Cleve's dispute with Putnam, in terms of his (Putnam's) analysis of indeterminacy. Van Cleve characterizes Putnam's argument as 'just more theory' and rejects it. Next I will critically evaluate Van Cleve's arguments and I will show that Van Cleve's position might be valid in its original epistemological setting but it is not valid when applied to semantics.

Field interprets the reference of a term in terms of a naturalistic relation R that can include causal relations. Then, more precisely, we can say:

x refers to y if, and only if x bears R to y.

Here we are explaining the reference of a term in terms of the causal relation R that the term holds with its referent. This is Field's proposal as introduced by Putnam. Putnam objects to this causal theory of reference by saying that this won't determine reference uniquely— for the reference of the right hand side of the bi-conditional is itself indeterminate. In other words, if an interpretation I was indeterminate before, it will remain indeterminate even after adding Field's account of causal reference to I, for the account of causal reference itself is indeterminate. This is the 'just more theory' objection as Van Cleve characterizes it.

People are not convinced by Putnam's 'just more theory' objection. Van Cleve gives certain arguments to show that Putnam's objection does not hold. First I will discuss those and then show that Van Cleve's arguments have their own problems, beginning with Van Cleve's treatment of epistemology.

Van Cleve talks about two kinds of principles in epistemology.[26] One class includes principles that warrant inference from already justified statements to further statements. There is another class of principles that specify the non-epistemic conditions under which some beliefs come to acquire epistemic status in the first place. These principles are called 'generation principles' by Van Cleve. The generation principles generate the axioms of the epistemology, so to say. The generation principle is a version of epistemic supervenience, i.e., that there be some non-epistemic features that determine epistemic property, which specify the non-epistemic conditions under which some beliefs acquire their epistemic status in the first place. And a corollary of epistemic supervenience is epistemological externalism— the view that there are factors which make knowledge possible regardless of whether they themselves are known.

Van Cleve extends these epistemic principles to semantics. According to Van Cleve, Field's schema, as mentioned earlier, is an example of generation principle in semantics whose right hand side spells out in non-semantic terms the conditions under which certain semantic relations first arise. This generation principle can be viewed as a version of semantic supervenience, i.e., the thesis that there be some non-semantic facts which determine the semantic features. And then as a corollary of semantic supervenience, we will have semantic externalism i.e., the thesis that there are factors which make semantics possible—regardless of whether they themselves are known. Van Cleve utilises this semantic externalism to counter Putnam's objection to Field. Van Cleve thinks that we do not have to 'single out' a partial interpretation as the intended interpretation of 'R' before the theory can do its job. Knowledge of an intended interpretation of 'R' is not a precondition of the successful working of the theory. As Van Cleve comments, "Reference makers need not be referred to".[27] My use of the term 'R' might be related to instances of R by R itself (this is called 'self-subsumption' by Van Cleve) and there is nothing objectionably circular about this.

Putnam objects to this self-subsumption thesis and Van Cleve replies to Putnam. But before going into that I want to evaluate what Van Cleve has said so far. I accept the thesis of semantic supervenience for the reason mentioned with regard to my discussion on Searle. But to view semantic externalism as a necessary corollary of semantic supervenience is to confuse the task of semantics. Semantics gives us a theory which, if one possesses, enables her to interpret a language. So semantics is a description of the knowledge which suffices for one's mastery of a language. This is where semantic supervenience is relevant. We claim that a description of semantics can be given in terms of certain non-semantic facts. In other words, our knowledge of non-semantic facts will shed some light on our knowledge of semantic facts. What precisely our knowledge of non-semantic facts consists in and how to describe our knowledge of those non-semantic facts are the problems we are faced with. If bearing the relation 'R" is supposed to explain the semantic fact of reference (this is Field's formulation which Van Cleve is defending), then we cannot just say that this 'R' is there which makes reference possible regardless of whether 'R' itself is known (this is what semantic externalism holds), for our knowledge of 'R' is supposed to throw light on our knowledge of reference. We should be able to justify why it is the knowledge of 'R' and not something else which explains our knowledge of reference. We should be able to reply to the question : Is our knowledge of 'R' an adequate evidence for our knowledge of reference? If our knowledge of 'R' is supposed to explain our knowledge of reference, then semantic externalism is clearly wrong–headed.

I suspect that the reason why Van Cleve misconstrues the task of semantics is that he pushes the analogy of epistemology and semantics too far while drawing parallels between epistemological and semantic principles. Epistemic principles are principles of justification for believing in a statement, according to Van Cleve. And semantic principles are principles that seek to explain a speaker's knowledge of a language.

Generation principles in epistemology may or may not be known, but generation principles in semantics cannot remain unknown for they are the objects of study in semantics, knowledge of which will throw some light on our knowledge of semantics, provided we believe in semantic supervenience.

Let me get back to how Putnam objects to self-subsumption of 'R' and how Van Cleve replies to it. Putnam argues that if 'R' relates to the instances of R by R itself, then many putative reference relations would be similarly self-subsuming. We can come up with bizarre referential systems where 'table' refers to alligators, etc, and where there will be causation$_1$ which will causally$_1$ relate the use of the word 'table' to alligators. So how can we say that 'table' refers to table and not to alligators, or 'table' is causally related to table and not causally$_1$ related to alligators? So if self-subsumption is all that is required, then causally$_1$ can also be self-subsumed and we can still have referential indeterminacy. Van Cleve responds to Putnam by saying that it is not self-subsumption alone which justifies reference, but self-subsumption plus a true principle of causation which leads one to a true principle of reference.[28] He says that it is a fact that causation has something important to do with reference of the word 'table' and not causation$_1$.

I am afraid, Van Cleve is trapped in a vicious circularity here. First Van Cleve defends Field's schema where reference (semantics) is being explained in terms of a causal relation 'R'. Then, thanks to Putnam, Van Cleve finds out that self-subsumption of 'R' is not adequate enough to rule out indeterminacy. So Van Cleve turns back to the true causal relation which will rule out using 'table' to refer to alligators. Incidentally, the phrase 'true principle' is left unexplained. Here comes in my earlier criticism of Van Cleve as confusing the task of semantics. If non-semantic facts are supposed to explain semantics facts, the aim of semantics is to study critically our knowledge of non-semantic facts. The reason why Van Cleve refers to a 'true principle' of causation is that indeterminacy sounds counter-intuitive. In my discussion of Searle I have shown that indeterminacy is not counter-intuitive. Now I can relate Putnam's 'just more theory' objection to Field with my same objection to Dummett. A "sufficiently comprehensive grasp of each other's theories" won't lead to unique translation, for that 'comprehensive grasp' itself is indeterminate. The theory-cum-comprehensive grasp has interpretations unintended by Dummett and there is no way to rule out those interpretations. Dummett's 'sufficiently comprehensive grasp' only brings in more theory that is fraught with indeterminacy. Thus I conclude that Putnam's 'just more theory' objection to Field and my same objection to Dummett stand in spite of Van Cleve's arguments against indeterminacy.

4.8.2 Indeterminacy and domestic interpretation

Michael Dummett thinks that we cannot make sense of indeterminacy unless we assume that there is a definite relation of compatibility between basal statements and theory. In the absence of any such relation, we cannot even say of two theories that they are empirically equivalent.[29] The indeterminacy thesis does not deny the relation existing between observation statements and theory. What I am saying is that this relation can be construed in very many different ways. And in so far as objective evidence is concerned, all those different constructions are supported by all available evidence. This is what I mean when I say that the two theories are empirically equivalent. In fact, contrary to Dummett, it seems to me that we can talk of two theories being empirically equivalent only if we assume that there is no definite relation of compatibility, rather there are many ways of constructing the relation between basal statements and a theory, each of which are exclusive to each other but each of them tallies with the totality of the available data.

From the above discussion, it is evident that Dummett rests his observations on two assumptions; i) We already have a grasp of the alien theory, and ii) Sentences of the theory are uniquely related to the available evidence. In my radical theory of meaning, I am denying these very two assumptions. Dummett seems to take these two assumptions for granted and then he tries to substantiate these claims. I think, as I have shown earlier, Dummett's arguments fall short of their aims. In the same spirit, Dummett thinks it possible to establish a compatibility relation between observation statements and a theory, and then concludes that we can judge any theory to be true or false independent of semantic postulates. Now, my point is that we can construct this compatibility relation in more than one way and each construction rests on different sets of semantic postulates. Available evidence supports both sets of semantic postulates. So our judgement that a theory is true or false rests much on the set of semantic postulates we are working with. Difference in semantic postulates will lead to difference in theories.

Dummett makes a distinction between a static and dynamic account of language.[30] It is a well-established fact that our natural languages are susceptible to change. In the course of the history of its use, many new words join the old vocabulary, old sentences are re-arranged, truth-values of sentences change, etc. But, in spite of these changes, it seems to me that a general framework of a natural language does not change. And this general framework is made up of extensionalism and holism. It is true that this framework is a theoretical imposition on a natural language. Whether this imposition is correct or not can be judged from its consequences. And we have seen earlier with respect to Davidson's T-sentences that the consequences correspond to the linguistic behavior of the native speakers. If that framework also changed, the language concerned would be unlearnable. No speaker could claim to possess the knowledge of her language, for at any later moment the total linguistic network along with its sentences might change.

My aim is to explain meaning. Meaning is involved both within a language and among different languages. When an English–speaker interprets German, she is engaged in understanding the meanings of the expressions of a foreign language. But when an English–speaker communicates with another English–speaker, she is engaged in understanding the meanings of the expressions of her own language. In any case, the notion of meaning is involved in both foreign and domestic interpretation. So our characterization of meaning must affect both of its occurrences.

Critics have found it difficult to concede the presence of indeterminacy in domestic interpretation. Dummett does not think it to be clear at all that with what right we can extend "the indeterminacy thesis, originally advanced for *radical* translation, to what goes on between two speakers of the same language."[31] This is not clear to Dummett, for he confuses the phenomenon of disagreement in beliefs by two monolingual speakers of the same language with the claim of indeterminacy thesis. The indeterminacy thesis does not in any way deny the obvious fact that two speakers using the same language can disagree with each other about the status of any particular belief. The fact that two speakers can disagree with each other shows that they are working with the same set of semantic postulates. Otherwise there would have been no communication and, consequently, no disagreement among them. Any disagreement is possible only in the background of a shared information. When people disagree whether India should go to war, people know the country which the name 'India' refers to, they have fairly similar conception of what a war is like, etc. Similarly, when people disagree about a particular belief, they start from a common ground and, in the present case, the common ground is the shared linguistic practice—part of which consists in shared semantic postulates.

The indeterminacy thesis, on the other hand, claims that we can construe other sets of semantic postulates, different from that which speakers are using, which also correspond to the totality of speech dispositions of those two speakers. All these different sets of semantic postulates give rise to different interpretations of the same expressions, but none of those semantic postulates can be regarded as wrong, for all of them agree with the totality of evidence available. So, while indeterminacy thesis acknowledges more than one possible set of semantic postulates, disagreement in belief is possible only within a single set of semantic postulates.

This confusion further led Dummett to accuse protagonists of the indeterminacy thesis of ignoring what he calls 'social character of language.'[32] I fully endorse Dummett's observation on the social character of language. I agree that, while using a language, a speaker engages in linguistic practices implicitly agreed on by all other members of that linguistic community. In fact, I said earlier that speakers of a linguistic community use more or less the same set of semantic postulates. This can be shown from the fact that the speakers within a particular linguistic community can successfully communicate with each other. And there is nothing wrong with this. What the indeterminacy thesis claims is that it is possible, in principle, to use other sets of semantic postulates while interpreting the same linguistic expressions giving rise to mutually incompatible meanings. All these different sets of semantic postulates agree with the totality of available evidence. The fact that we use one particular set of semantic postulates does not invalidate others' claims. Thus, indeterminacy thesis does not rob the language of its social character, emphasizes it.

NOTES

[1]Perhaps the most systematic account of the doctrine of indeterminacy of translation can be found in his *Word and Object,* Cambridge, Mass., The M. I. T. Press, 1960, pp. 26-79.

[2] Quine, W. V., "On the Reasons for Indeterminacy of Translation", *The Journal of Philosophy,* Vol. 67, 1970, p. 179.

[3]Davidson expressed his formulation of indeterminacy thesis in many of his essays like "Semantics for Natural Languages", "Belief and the Basis of Meaning", "Reality Without Reference", "The Inscrutability of Reference". All these essays can be found in his *Inquiries into Truth and Interpretation*, Oxford, Clarendon Press, 1986.

[4]Davidson, D. *Inquiries into Truth and Interpretation,* p.152

[5] Ibid., p. 225.

[6] Ibid., p. 154.

[7] Ibid., p. 239.

[8] Katz, Jerrold J., "The Refutation of Indeterminacy" in *The Journal of Philosophy*, Vol. 85, 1988, p. 232.

[9] Fodor, J. and E. Lepore, *Holism: A Shopper's Guide*, Oxford: Basil Blackwell, 1992, p. 73.

[10] Ibid., p. 75.

[11] Ibid., p. 80.

[12] Wallace, J., "Translation Theories and the Decipherment of Linear B" in *Truth and Interpretation*, ed. by E. Lepore, Oxford, Basil Blackwell, 1989, pp. 211-234.

[13] Vermazen, Bruce, "Testing Theories of Interpretation" in *Truth and Interpretation*, ed. by E. Lepore, p. 237.

[14] Searle, J., "Indeterminacy and The First Person" in *The Journal of Philosophy*, Vol. 84, 1987, p. 123.
[15] Van Cleve, James, "Semantic Supervenience and Referential Indeterminacy," *The Journal of Philosophy*, Vol. 89, 1992 pp. 344-61.
[16] Searle, J., "Indeterminacy and the First Person", p. 141.
[17] Alston, William, P., "Quine on Meaning" in *The Philosophy of W. V. Quine*, Ed. by L. E. Hahn and P. A. Schilpp, La Salle, Illinois, Open Court, 1986, p. 55.
[18] Ibid., p. 58.
[19] Ibid., p. 59.
[20] Ibid., p. 63.
[21] Dummett, Michael. "The Significance of Quine's Indeterminacy Thesis" in *Truth and Other Enigmas*, Cambridge, Mass., Harvard University Press, 1980, p. 391.
[22] Ibid., p. 398.
[23] Ibid., p 395.
[24] Ibid., p. 406.
[25] Van Cleve, James, "Semantic Supervene and Referential Indeterminacy", p. 349.
[26] Ibid., p. 349.
[27] Ibid., p. 351.
[28] Ibid., p. 353.
[29] Dummett, Michael, "The Significance of Quine's Indeterminacy Thesis", p. 406.
[30] Ibid., p. 407.
[31] Ibid., p. 410.
[32] Ibid,. 401

CONCLUSION

When I hear two speakers talking to one another in a language that I do not know, I have the feeling that the two speakers are just emitting certain sounds using their vocal organs. But 'emitting certain sounds' will not be a proper description of what they are doing. They are doing something more. They are communicating with each other. This means that they are exchanging information (in a broad sense) with each other. So the sounds they are making convey some information to each other. In other words, those sounds convey some meaning to each other.

But what is this 'meaning'? Is it something like an image that we conjure up in our mind when we utter a sentence? Is it some kind of information residing in our brain which is typically private and then we decode it in sentences in order to be able to communicate with other people? Or is it just the convention of using words in certain ways? Philosophers have come up with these and many other suggestions.

Notice that each of these views is an attempt to give an answer to the question 'What is meaning?' In the present work, following Davidson, I put the issue in a different perspective. For a while let us grant our pre-philosophical notion of meaning, however vague that might be. Given this, how can we develop a theory of meaning for a language? But before we set ourselves to this task, we have to know what is the aim of a theory of meaning? A theory of meaning will give the meaning of any given expression of a language. So a theory of meaning for a language L will give the meaning of any sentence s of L such that 's means p' (call this M-sentence). Since a language potentially consists of infinitely large number of sentences, a theory of meaning must show how to generate an infinitely large number of M-sentences out of a finite stock.

But this is not enough. Since our aim is to explain meaning, if our theory of meaning generates M-sentences like 's means p', it does not get us further in our understanding of meaning. For the problem still remains how to interpret 'means' in 's means p'. So we need some non-circular device for explaining 'means'. Davidson has proposed to use 'is true' in the place of 'means'. So what we get is 's is true if, and only if, p' (T-sentence). Even though p is a translation of s in meta-language, we do not require the notion of translation to arrive at a T-sentence. Nor do we need any previous knowledge of 'meaning'— whatever that means. The only knowledge that we need to arrive at a T-sentence is the knowledge of a speaker's holding a sentence true. And this much we can know without even knowing what meaning is.

But does 's is true if, and only if, p' encompass everything expressed by 's means p'? One way of settling this question is by looking at whether a theory that generates, T-sentences suffices for one's mastery of a language. In other words, is it enough to know a theory of T- sentences in order to know a language? Critics have responded in the negative. I agree with Dummett and other people in claiming that a theory of meaning must explain one's mastery of a language. The reason why I accept this claim is as follows. A theory of meaning (in the form Davidson has advocated) will generate T-sentences for any sentences of the language which we are interpreting. But what guarantee is there that the T-sentences are really interpretative of that language? How can we be sure that the bi-conditional really holds true? The answer lies in observing the native speaker's verbal behaviour. If our T-sentences match the native speaker's behaviour, our theory can claim to be interpretative in nature. Such a theory will, consequently, reflect the speaker's knowledge or mastery of the language.

While defending Davidson's truth conditional semantics, I have explained that the aim of a theory of meaning is to reconstruct the speaker's knowledge of a language. And a theory of truth—provided it works under formal and empirical constraints— gives us such a theory of meaning, i.e., if a speaker knew a theory of truth for the language L, then she could claim to know L in the sense that she could communicate in L with the speakers of L. So Dummett is wrong in thinking that Davidson's theory of meaning is a modest theory that does not explain the speaker's mastery of her language. Dummett's so called undecidable statements can be incorporated in a truth conditional semantics if by the knowledge of the truth condition we mean the ability to state the truth condition and not the ability to observe whether or not the sentence is true. I have also shown that the existence of predicates which are coextensive but possess different meaning do not pose any threat to truth conditional semantics.

Defending truth conditional semantics amounts to defending a version of extensional semantics. I have explained the reasons for what I call 'non-reductive extensionalism'. I have argued that extensional semantics does not deny Chomskyan 'creativity', nor does it reject 'innate ideas' in the sense of an innate ability or predilection to learn a language. Chomsky's criticism that Quine II has abandoned Quine I— signifying the rejection of extensionalism— is ill–grounded for it involves, misunderstanding of the Quinean methods of language learning on the part of Chomsky. Extensionalism denies that a theory of Fregean sense can generate a theory of meaning that will clarify our knowledge of what meaning is. But, at the same time, extensionalism claims that a theory of truth (which belongs to a theory of reference) can generate a theory of meaning which amounts to a theory of interpretation or understanding. I have also shown that how, on the basis of extensionalism, we can explain the meaning of the sentences expressing the speaker's aspirations, goals, etc.

Since language potentially consists of infinitely many sentences, our theory of meaning must have a device for generating the meaning of those large number of sentences out of a finite stock. In other words, a theory of meaning must possess a holistic structure. I have given arguments (from Quine and Davidson) for the semantic holism thesis. I have distinguished extreme holism from moderate holism and I have expressed my sympathy for moderate holism. I have shown that if we want to include a new sentence to the linguistic network of sentences, our theory of meaning for such a language must possess a holistic structure. Semantic holism does not make the two speakers' disagreement about a particular belief impossible. I have given a transcendental argument for the compositional structure of a language. I have also interpreted and defended the nomological nature of the T-sentences.

Extensional semantics along with semantic holism leads to the indeterminacy of meaning. I have explained Quine's picture of 'radical translation' and Davidson's picture of 'radical interpretation'. I have argued that even though 'actual translation' is more common than radical translation, the latter is not a logically incoherent notion. I have shown that radical interpretation is possible in the sense that a theory of truth for the language L will serve as a theory of interpretation for L. I have picked up the interpretation of Linear B as an example of radical translation/ interpretation and cautioned against conflating decipherment with interpretation. Truth conditional semantics is not opposed to the speaker's intentions, etc. as such, it only denies their foundational role in a theory of meaning. Here I introduce the notion of semantic supervenience and argue that the philosophers, who either advocate or oppose indeterminacy, do accept semantic supervenience, but they differ as to the range of the non-semantic facts. I have argued that indeterminacy cannot be eliminated by better understanding of the speaker's utterances. I bring in the "just more theory" objection to show that the attempts to make meaning determinate fail.

The theory of meaning, as I look at it (following Davidson), is a meta-linguistic theory. It is a theory about the semantics of a language. It is a theory in the sense that it is a philosophical description of what suffices one's mastery of a language. It tells us the story of what one could know (not what one really knows) if one wanted to be an interpreter (speaker) of a language. In this sense, a theory of meaning is an idealized theory. It is only in this perspective that we must understand the role of a radical interpreter (or a radical translator in Quine). It does not constitute a counter–argument to say that, in reality, we can never have the situation exactly like a radical interpreter or translator. This may very well be true. But it is not logically impossible to conceive of someone from a different planet coming to the earth and trying to interpret our language, for example, English. Of course, since we are dealing with a theory of meaning for a natural language, we must be careful as to whether the consequences of our theory correspond to the speaker's verbal behaviour. Our theory must be empirically verifiable, and, in the case of natural language, the ultimate court of appeal against which we can verify our theory is the native speaker's linguistic behaviour. And I hope to have shown earlier that a truth conditional semantics does justice to that requirement.

I view the present work as an attempt to justify the claim that there is a reasonable ground to be hopeful about having a theory of meaning on the basis of a theory of truth condition à la Davidson. I think that this project of truth conditional semantics consists of two parts. The first part should give us a theoretical foundation. It should justify why we need a truth conditional semantics and, also, it should give us some indication about the structure (formal and empirical) of such a semantics. This part should also make us aware of the consequences of adopting such a theory and show that why such consequences are not inimical to understanding meaning. Basically, I have tried to accomplish this first part in the present thesis.

Once this theoretical part is laid down, we can start applying truth conditional semantics to various parts of language. This is the practical application of the truth conditional semantics. In the following pages, I will briefly mention some of the attempts made by Davidson himself toward that aim in order to show that how this project of truth conditional semantics can be developed further. Of course, I shall not engage myself in a critical assessment of them.

First we can take that part of language which seems easily amenable to a theory of truth condition. Naturally, the indicative sentences fall into this category. Davidson's favourite example 'Snow is white' is an example of an indicative sentence. But not all sentences are so simple. We have indicative sentences containing demonstratives like 'This', 'That' etc. Davidson has argued that we can accommodate demonstratives within a theory of truth condition— if we take truth to be a property of utterances and relate the truth condition of the utterance to changing time and speaker. So a T-sentence of 'I am hungry' will have the form ' "I am hungry" is true spoken by p at t if, and only if, p is hungry at t.'

There are different philosophical views about how to explain the meaning of the sentences occurring within quotation. A theory of meaning must show how the meaning of a sentence is built of the meaning of the finite stock of parts by iteration of some formation rules. So our theory of quotation must also share the same structure. Accordingly, Davidson advocates what he calls "demonstrative theory of quotation".[1] On this demonstrative theory, what appears within quotation is only an inscription which does not refer to anything at all, nor is it a part of an expression that refers. Davidson analyzes a sentence like " 'Snow is white' is a sentence" as

Snow is white.

The expression of which this is a token is a sentence.

Now it is easy to construct T-sentences of these above mentioned two sentences.

Davidson requires that a theory of meaning show the logical form of the sentences. By 'logical form' he means an account that will show how the truth/falsity of a sentence is composed of a finite stock by the application of a finite number of devices. Keeping this in mind, Davidson analyzes the meaning of the sentences in indirect discourse. The problem with indirect discourse is that, if we take their surface structure to be the logical form, it would lead to problems. In 'Galileo said that the earth moves', if we take the whole expression containing the sentence 'the earth moves' where 'the earth' is the singular term and 'moves' is the predicate, then we should be able to replace the terms 'the earth' by a co-referential term without changing the truth/falsity of the whole expression. But this is not obviously true.

Davidson criticizes many theories that fail to show the logical form of those sentences. He gives his analysis of indirect discourse by introducing the relation of the same sayer.[2] He analyzes the sentence 'Galileo said that the earth moves' into two sentences:

The earth moves.

Galileo said that.

Here 'that' is a demonstrative term which refers to the utterance mentioned just before. So when I say that Galileo said that the earth moves, I represent myself and Galileo as same sayers. On this account the content sentence (the sentence after 'that') is not contained in the sentence whose truth counts, the sentence which ends with 'that'. The reason why extensional substitution failed is that we took the whole thing to be one sentence, where there are really two sentences. Since these two sentences are semantically independent, their truth-values as well are independent.

Davidson applies a similar method while explaining the meaning of non-indicative sentences. Davidson considers the sentences in imperative, optative mood and tries to accommodate them in his truth conditional semantics. Philosophers (Frege, Dummett) agree that there is something common in the following sentences uttered in different mood : 'The door is closed,' 'Close the door', 'Could you close the door'? etc. In English, we change the mood by changing the form of the verb or changing the word order. We can think of a non-indicative sentence as an indicative sentence plus an expression that represents the transformation in the non-indicative mood. Davidson calls this "mood-setter".[3] So now a non-indicative sentence can be analyzed into two independent semantic units— mood-setter, and the indicative case. We can give the meaning of non-indicative sentence by giving the truth condition of the mood-setter and the indicative case.

So far we have been dealing with what might be called the literal meaning of the sentences. Here we use the sentences according to their dictionary meaning. But there are occasions where, if we take sentences to convey their literal meaning, it would lead us to absurdity. Davidson discusses two such instances, one is metaphor and the other is malapropism. Davidson is opposed to the view that there is a metaphorical meaning over and above literal meaning.[4] He makes a distinction of what words mean and what words are used to do. The realm of metaphor belongs to the latter. In metaphor, we use words with their ordinary (literal) meanings, but use it in such an imaginative way that it brings out certain novel features. Davidson is not denying metaphorical truth. Metaphor helps us to take note of something that might otherwise go unnoticed. And a metaphor is able to do this only because sentences expressing a metaphor work in the same way sentences do in non-metaphorical cases. That is why metaphors are usually patently false. And they are false because of their ordinary meaning. Another limiting case of literal use of language is malapropism. Think of the sentence 'We are all cremated equal'. Even though the sentence, in its literal meaning, does not make any sense, we do not have any problem in understanding what the sentence means when uttered by a speaker. Here Davidson makes a distinction between 'prior' and 'passing' theories.[5] The interpreter's prior theory is the theory that she already possesses prior to interpreting an utterance of the speaker. And the passing theory is the one that the interpreter intends the speaker to use. In order to be able to successfully communicate with the speaker using malapropisms, we have to use the passing theory, for prior theory will not work there.

By raising the issue of malapropism, Davidson is arguing against the assumption that convention plays an important role in linguistic communication. According to this assumption, the mastery of a language consists in the mastery of a set of conventions. Davidson's point is that what is needed for successful communication is not the prior theory, rather the passing theory which is not learned before-hand. This means that the notion of language governed by conventions is not needed for successful communication. The essence of linguistic competence lies in the ability to continuously form and reform the passing theories aiming at interpreting the utterances on the whole true. Davidson is not denying that there are conventions involved in communication. He is denying their explanatory role in communication. Communication does not presuppose convention.

From this Davidson reaches the startling conclusion "that there is no such thing as a language."[6] If convention fails to explain communication, then the notion of language specifiable by conventions is not needed anymore. If so, then we can hardly give any content to the notion of language as having a clearly well-defined shared structure.

These are some of the consequences of applying truth conditional semantics in different areas of language. Evaluating these is not my aim in the present work. I mentioned them to show that there are many ways in which the project to develop a truth-conditional semantics could be carried on further. Whether this project will succeed is a matter of further discussion.

NOTES

[1] Davidson, D., *Inquiries into Truth and Interpretation*, Oxford, Clarendon Press, 1986, p. 90.
[2] Ibid., p. 104.
[3] Ibid., p. 119.
[4] Ibid., p. 246.
[5] Davidson, D., "A Nice Derangement of Epitaphs" in *Truth and Interpretation* ed. by E. Lepore, Oxford, Basil Blackwell, 1989, p. 442.
[6] Ibid., p. 446.

BIBLIOGRAPHY

Alston, William P., "Quine on Meaning" in Lewis Edwin Hahn and Paul Arthur Schilpp (eds.), *The Philosophy of W. V. Quine*, La Salle, Illinois, Open Court, 1986.

Asher, Nicholas, "The Trouble With Extensional Semantics", *Philosophical Studies*, 47, 1985, pp. 1-14.

Barret, Robert B. and Gibson, Roger F. (eds.), *Perspectives On Quine*, Oxford, Basil Blackwell, 1990.

Bilgrami, Akeel, "Meaning, Holism and Use" in Ernest Lepore (ed.), *Truth and Interpretation*, Oxford, Basil Blackwell, 1989, pp. 101-122.

Brandl, Johannes and Gombocz, Wolfgang L. (eds.), *The Mind of Donald Davidson*, Amsterdam, 1989.

Burdick, Howard, "On Davidson and Interpretation", *Synthese*, 80, 1989, pp. 321-345.

Callaway, Howard G., "Semantic Competence and Truth-Conditional Semantics", *Erkenntnis,* 28, 1988, pp. 3-27.

Chomsky, Noam, *Aspects of the Theory of Syntax*, Cambridge, Mass., M.I.T. Press, 1965.

_______ "Knowledge of Language", *The London Times Literary Supplement*, 1968, pp. 523-525.

_______ *Language and Mind*, New York, Harcourt Brace Jovanovich, Inc., 1968.

_______ "Quine's Empirical Assumptions" in Donald Davidson and Jaakko Hintikka (eds.), *Words and Objections: Essays on the Work of W. V. Quine*, Dordrecht, D. Reidel, 1969, pp. 53-68.

_______ *Reflections on Language*, New York, Pantheon Books, 1975.

Davidson, Donald and Harman, Gilbert (eds.), *Semantics of Natural Language*, Dordrecht, D. Reidel, 1972.

Davidson, Donald, *Inquiries into Truth and Interpretation*, Oxford, Clarendon Press, 1984.

_______ "A Coherence Theory of Truth and Knowledge" in Ernest Lepore (ed.), *Truth and_Interpretation*, Oxford, Basil Blackwell, 1989, pp. 307-319.

_______ "Empirical Content" in Ernest Lepore (ed.), *Truth and Interpretation*, Oxford: Basil Blackwell, 1989, pp. 320-332.

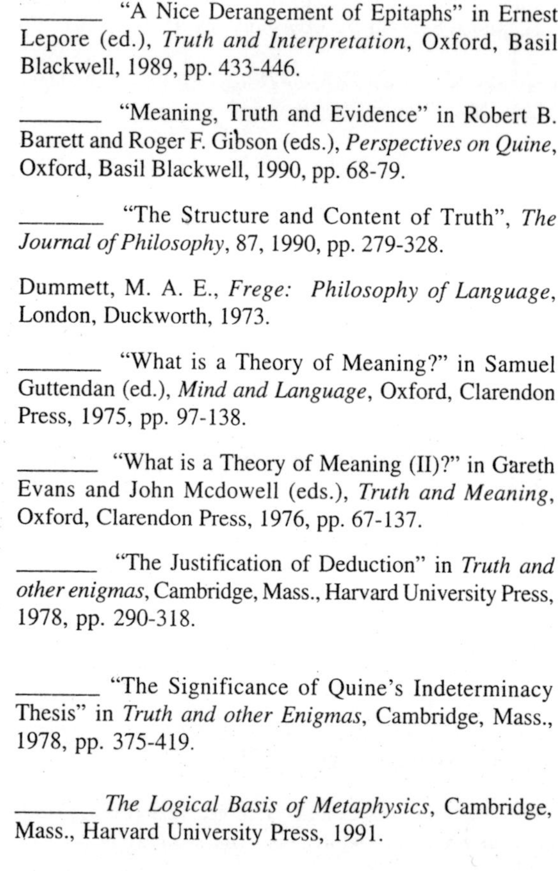

_______ "A Nice Derangement of Epitaphs" in Ernest Lepore (ed.), *Truth and Interpretation*, Oxford, Basil Blackwell, 1989, pp. 433-446.

_______ "Meaning, Truth and Evidence" in Robert B. Barrett and Roger F. Gibson (eds.), *Perspectives on Quine*, Oxford, Basil Blackwell, 1990, pp. 68-79.

_______ "The Structure and Content of Truth", *The Journal of Philosophy*, 87, 1990, pp. 279-328.

Dummett, M. A. E., *Frege: Philosophy of Language*, London, Duckworth, 1973.

_______ "What is a Theory of Meaning?" in Samuel Guttendan (ed.), *Mind and Language*, Oxford, Clarendon Press, 1975, pp. 97-138.

_______ "What is a Theory of Meaning (II)?" in Gareth Evans and John Mcdowell (eds.), *Truth and Meaning*, Oxford, Clarendon Press, 1976, pp. 67-137.

_______ "The Justification of Deduction" in *Truth and other enigmas*, Cambridge, Mass., Harvard University Press, 1978, pp. 290-318.

_______ "The Significance of Quine's Indeterminacy Thesis" in *Truth and other Enigmas*, Cambridge, Mass., 1978, pp. 375-419.

_______ *The Logical Basis of Metaphysics*, Cambridge, Mass., Harvard University Press, 1991.

Evans, Gareth and Mcdowell, John (eds.), *Truth and Meaning*, Oxford, Clarendon Press, 1976.

Evnine, Simon, *Donald Davidson*, Oxford, Polity in association with Basil Blackwell, 1991.

Fodor, Jerry, *Psychosemantics*, Cambridge, Mass., The M.I.T. Press, 1987.

Fodor, Jerry and Ernest Lepore, *Holism A Shopper's Guide*, Oxford, Basil Blackwell, 1992.

Foster, J. A., "Meaning and Truth Theory" in Gareth Evans and John Mcdowell (eds.) *Truth and Meaning*, Oxford, Clarendon Press, 1976, pp. 1-32.

Frege, G., "On Sense and Nominatum" in Herbert Feigl and Wilfrid Sellars (eds.) *Readings in Philosophical Analysis*, New York, Appleton-Century-Crofts, Inc., 1949, pp. 85-102.

_______ "The Thought : A Logical Inquiry" in P. F. Strawson (ed.), *Philosophical Logic*, Oxford, Oxford University Press, 1967, pp. 17-38.

Gibson, Roger, F. Jr., *The Philosophy of W. V. Quine: An Expository Essay*, Tampa, University of South Florida Press, 1982.

_______ *Enlightened Empiricism*, Tampa, University of South Florida Press, 1988.

Gunderson, Keith (ed.), *Language, Mind and Knowledge*, Minneapolis, University of Minnesota Press, 1975.

Guttenplan, Samuel, (ed.), *Mind and Language*, Oxford, Clarendon Press, 1975.

Hacking, Ian, *Why Does Language Matter to Philosophy*?, Cambridge, Cambridge University Press, 1975.

Hahn, Lewis Edwin and Paul Arthur Schilpp (eds.), *The Philosophy of W. V. Quine*, La Salle, Illinois, Open Court, 1986.

Harman, Gilbert, "An Introduction to 'Translation and Meaning'. Chapter Two of Word and Object" in Donald Davidson and Jaakko Hintikka (eds.), *Words and Objections: Essays on the Work of W. V. Quine*, Dordrecht: D. Reidel, 1969, pp. 14-26.

_______ "Meaning and Semantics" in Milton K. Munitz and Peter K. Unger (eds.), *Semantics and Philosophy*, New York, New York University Press, 1974, pp. 1-16.

_______ "Language, Thought and Communication" in Keith Gunderson (ed.), *Language, Mind and Knowledge*, Minneapolis, University of Minnesota Press, 1975, pp.270-298

_______ "Quine's Grammar" in Lewis Edwin Hahn and Paul Arthur Schilpp (eds.), *The Philosophy of W. V. Quine*, La Salle, Illinois, Open Court, 1986. pp. 165-180.

_______ "(Nonsolipsistic) Conceptual Role Semantics" in

Ernest Lepore (ed.), *New Directions in Semantics*, London, Academic Press, 1987, pp. 55-81.

_______ "Immanent and Transcendent Approaches to the Theory of Meaning" in Robert B. Barrett and Roger F. Gibson (eds.), *Perspectives on Quine*, Oxford, Basil Blackwell, 1990, pp. 144-157.

Heal, Jane, *Fact and Meaning*, Oxford, Basil Blackwell, 1989.

Hintikka, Jaakko, "Behavioral Criteria of Radical Translation" in Donald Davidson and Jaakko Hintikka (eds.), *Words and Objections: Essays on the Work of W. V. Quine*, Dordrecht, D. Reidel, 1969, pp. 69-81.

_______ "Game Theoretical Semantics as a Synthesis of Verificationist and Truth-Conditional Meaning Theories" in Ernest Lepore (ed.), *New Directions in Semantics*, London, Academic Press, 1987, pp. 235-258.

_______ "Quine as a member of the Tradition of the Universality of Language" in Robert B. Barrett and Roger F. Gibson (eds.), *Perspectives on Quine*, Oxford, Basil Blackwell, 1990, pp. 159-175.

Katz, Jerrold, "Logic and Language: An Examination of Recent Criticisms of Intensionalism" in Keith Gunderson (ed.), *Language, Mind and Knowledge*, Minneapolis, University of Minnesota Press, 1975, pp. 36-130.

_______ "Why Intensionalists ought not to be Fregeans"

in Ernest Lepore (ed.), *Truth and_Interpretation,* Oxford, Basil Blackwell, 1989, pp. 59-91.

_______ "The Refutation of Indeterminacy" in Robert B. Barrett and Roger F. Gibson (eds.), *Perspectives on Quine*, Oxford, Basil Blackwell, 1990, pp. 177-197.

_______ "The Domino Theory", *Philosophical Studies*, 58, 1990, pp. 3-39.

Kirk, R., *Translation Determined*, Oxford, Clarendon Press, 1986.

Larson, David, "Tarski, Davidson and Theories of Truth", *Dialectica*, 42, 1988, pp. 3-16.

Lepore, Ernest, "In Defense of Davidson", *Linguistics and Philosophy*, 5, 1982, pp. 277-294.

_______ "The Concept of Meaning and its Role in Understanding Language", *Dialectia*, 37, 1983, pp. 133-139.

Lepore, E. and Loewer, B. "Dual Aspect Semantics" in Ernest Lepore (ed), *New Directions in Semantics,* London, Academic Press, 1987, pp. 83-112.

_______ "What Davidson should have said" in Johannes Brandl and Wolfgang L. Gombocz (eds.), *The Mind of Donald Davidson*, Amsterdam, 1989, pp. 65-78.

Lewis, David, "Radical Interpretation", *Synthese*, 23, 1974, pp. 331-344.

______ "Languages and Language" in Keith Gunderson (ed.), *Language, Mind and Knowledge*, Minneapolis, University of Minnesota Press, 1975, pp. 3-35.

Loar, Brian, "Two Theories of Meaning" in Gareth Evans and John Mcdowell (eds.), *Truth and Meaning*, Oxford, Clarendon Press, 1976, pp. 138-161.

Lycan, William G., *Logical Form in Natural Language*, Cambridge, Mass., The M.I.T. Press, 1984.

Malpas, Jeff, "Holism and Indeterminacy", *Dialectica*, 45, 1991, pp. 47-58.

Mates, Benson, "Synonymity" in Leonard Linsky (ed.), *Semantics and the Philosophy of Language,* Urbanna, Illinois, University of Illinois Press, 1952, pp. 118-125.

Matthews, Robert, "Learnability of Semantic Theory" in Ernest Lepore (ed.), *Truth and Interpretation*, Oxford, Basil Blackwell, 1989, pp. 49-58.

Millar, Alan, "Where's the Use in Meaning?" *Dialectica*, 39, 1985, pp. 35-51.

Mulhall, Stephen, "Davidson on Interpretation and Understanding", *The Philosophical Quarterly*, 37, 1987, pp. 319-322.

Neale, Stephen, "Meaning, Grammar, and Indeterminacy", *Dialectica*, 41, 1987, pp. 301-319.

Nozick, Robert, "Experience, Theory and Language" in Lewis Edwin Hahn and Paul Arthur Schilpp (eds.), *The Philosophy of W. V. Quine*, La Salle, Illinois, Open Court, 1986, pp. 339-363.

Peacocke, Christopher, "Truth Definitions and Actual Languages" in Gareth Evans and John Mcdowell (eds.), *Truth and Meaning*, Oxford, Clarendon Press, 1976, pp. 162-188.

Putnam, Hilary, "The Meaning of 'Meaning'" in Keith Gunderson (ed.), *Language, Mind and_Knowledge*, Minneapolis, University of Minnesota Press, 1975, pp. 131-193.

_______ "Meaning Holism" in Lewis Edwin Hahn and Paul Arthur Schilpp (eds.), *The Philosophy of W. V. Quine*, La Salle, Illinois, Open Court, 1986, pp. 405-426.

Quine, W. V., *Word and Object*, Cambridge, Mass., The M.I.T. Press, 1960.

_______ *From a Logical Point of View*, Cambridge, Mass., Harvard University Press, 1961.

_______ *Ontological Relativity and Other Essays*, New York, Columbia University Press, 1969.

_______ *Philosophy of Logic*, Englewood Cliffs, N.J., Prentice Hall, 1970.

_______ *The Roots of Reference*, La Salle, Illinois, Open Court, 1974.

_______ *The Ways of Paradox and Other Essays*, Cambridge, Mass., Harvard University Press, 1976.

_______ *Theories and Things*, Cambridge, Mass., Harvard University Press, 1981.

_______ *Pursuit of Truth*, Cambridge, Mass., Harvard University Press, 1990.

_______ "Three Indeterminacies" in Robert B. Barrett and Roger F. Gibson (eds.), *Perspectives on Quine*, Oxford, Basil Blackwell, 1990, pp. 1-16.

Quinton, Anthony, "Doing Without Meaning" in Robert B. Barrett and Roger F. Gibson (eds.), *Perspectives on Quine*, Oxford, Basil Blackwell, 1990, pp. 294-308.

Ramberg, Bjorn, T., *Donald Davidson's Philosophy of Language*, Oxford, Basil Blackwell, 1989.

Rorty, Richard, *Philosophy and the Mirror of Nature*, Princeton, Princeton University Press, 1979.

_______ "Pragmatism, Davidson and Truth" in Ernest Lepore (ed.), *Truth and Interpretation,* Oxford, Basil Blackwell, 1989, pp. 333-355.

Roth, Paul, "Semantics without Foundations" in Lewis Edwin Hahn and Paul Arthur Schilpp (eds.), *The Philosophy of W. V. Quine,* La Salle, Illinois, Open Court, 1986, pp. 433-458.

Schuldenfrei, Richard, "Quine in Perspective", *The Journal of Philosophy*, 69, 1972, pp. 5-16.

Searle, John, "Indeterminacy, Empiricism and the First Person", *The Journal of Philosophy*, 84, 1987, pp. 123-146.

Shahan, Robert and Chris Swayer (eds.), *Essays on the Philosophy of W. V. Quine*, Norman, University of Oklahoma Press, 1979.

Shanks, Niall, "Indeterminacy and Verificationism", *Southern Journal of Philosophy*, 21, 1983, pp. 301-312.

Solomon, Miriam, "Quine's Point of View", *The Journal of Philosophy*, 86, 1989, pp. 113-136.

Tarski, Alfred, "The Semantic Conception of Truth" in Leonard Linsky (ed.), *Semantics and the Philosophy of Language*, Urbana, Illinois, University of Illinois Press, 1952, pp. 13-47.

Taylor, Charles, *Human Agency and Language*, Cambridge, Cambridge University Press, 1985.

Taylor, Kenneth, "Davidson's Theory of Meaning" *Philosophical Studies*, 48, 1985, pp. 91-105.

Van Cleve, James, "Semantic Supervenience and Referential Indeterminacy", *The Journal of Philosophy*, 89, 1992, pp. 344-361.

Vermazen, Bruce, "Testing Theories of Interpretation" in Ernest Lepore (ed.), *Truth and Interpretation,* Oxford, Basil Blackwell, 1989, pp. 235-244.

Wagner, Steven, "Quine's Holism", *Analysis*, 46, 1986, pp. 1-6.

Wallace, John, "Translation Theories and the Decipherment of Linear B" in Ernest Lepore (ed.), *Truth and Interpretation*, Oxford, Basil Blackwell, 1989, pp. 211-234.

Weir, Allan, "Against Holism", *The Philosophical Quarterly*, 35, 1985, pp. 225-244.

Wettstein, Howard, *Has Semantics Rested on a Mistake*?, Stanford, Stanford University Press, 1991.

INDEX

O

P

Q